The
Music of Canada

by
TIMOTHY J. McGEE
Associate Professor of Music, University of Toronto

W · W · NORTON & COMPANY · NEW YORK · LONDON

Permissions

p.3: *Le Prince d'Orange*. With acknowledgment to the Marius Barbeau Collection, Canadian Centre for Folk Culture Studies, National Museum of Man, National Museums of Canada, Ottawa. Published in *Romancero du Canada*. Montreal: Editions Beauchemins and Toronto: Macmillan, 1937.

pp.15-16: *Motet à la Ste. Vierge*. Archives du Monastère des Ursulines de Québec. Transcribed and edited by Erich Schwandt. © 1981 by Editions Jeu, Victoria, BC, Canada.

p.28: *Oxford*. Transcription from Richard Appel, *The Music of the Bay Psalm Book*, 9th Edition (Brooklyn: Institute for Studies in American Music, 1975), pp. 14-15. Reproduced by permission.

p.47: *Donkey Riding*. Collected by T. Wood. From the *Oxford Song Book*, Volume 2. By permission of Oxford University Press.

p.47: *The Shantyman's Life*. Text: © Copyright 1954 Waterloo Limited, Waterloo, Ontario, Canada. International Copyright Secured. Printed and Published in Canada. All rights reserved. Music: Copyright 1926 by Harvard University Press, © 1954 by Lillian Rickaby Dykstra.

p.76: Calixa Lavallée, *Le Papillon*. Canadian Musical Heritage Society/Société pour le patrimoine musical canadien (Ottawa).

pp.94-95: Claude Champagne, *Altitude*. Used by permission of Berandol Music, Ltd. Toronto.

p.117: Jean Papineau-Couture, *Le débat du coeur et du corps de Villon*. Kindly authorized by the composer.

p.120: Godfrey Ridout, *Fall Fair*. Copyright by Gordon V. Thompson Limited, Toronto, Canada. Used by permission.

p.121: Violet Archer, *Prelude and Allegro*. Used by permission of Berandol Music, Ltd., Toronto.

p.123: Oskar Morowetz, *From the Diary of Anne Frank*. Used by permission of the composer.

p.127: Barbara Pentland, *Symphony for Ten Parts*. Used by permission of Berandol Music, Ltd., Toronto.

pp. 128-29: John Beckwith, *The Shivaree*. Used by permission of the composer. This prologue was composed in the summer of 1982 as an addition to the original score for a production in Banff.

(*continued on p. x*)

Published simultaneously in Canada by Penguin Books Canada Ltd, 2801 John Street, Markham, Ontario L3R 1B4.

Printed in Canada

First Edition

The text of this book is composed in Times Roman, with display type set in Caslon. Typesetting by Vail-Ballou. Manufacturing by The Bryant Press Limited.
Library of Congress Cataloging in Publication Data
McGee, Timothy J. (Timothy James), 1936–
    The music of Canada.

    Includes bibliographies and discography.
    "Anthology" (music): p.
    1. Music—Canada—History and criticism.
I. Title.
ML205.M37   1985   781.771   84-27318

ISBN 0-393-95376-9 {PBK}
ISBN 0-393-02279-X

W.W. Norton & Company, Inc.
500 Fifth Avenue, New York, N.Y. 10110
W.W. Norton & Company, Ltd.
10 Coptic Street, London WC1A 1PU

4 5 6 7 8 9 0

Contents

List of Illustrations   ix
Preface   xi

CHAPTER I: *New France*   1

Folk Music   2
Voyageurs. Order of Good Cheer

Aristocratic Music and Theatre   9
Theatre of Neptune. Réceptions. Quebec Society and Cultural Activities

The Missionaries and Music   12
Music Education. Sacred Music Performance and Compositions

Summary   18

CHAPTER II: *The British Influence and Post-Conquest Quebec*   19

The British Influence   19

Folk Music   21

Dancing   23

Formal Musical Activities   24
Sacred Music. Military Bands. Concert Programmes. Theatre. Other Activities

Post-Conquest Quebec   31
Concerts. Frédéric-Henri Glackemeyer

Other Cities and Settlements   33

Composition   35
Joseph Quesnel

Summary   37

CHAPTER III: *Nineteenth Century to Confederation*   38

Music in Church   40
Protestant Congregations. Singing Schools. Catholic Church Music

Popular Music   43
French-Canadian Folk Songs. Anglo-Canadian Folk Songs. Ballads. Salon Music. Dancing

Formal Music Making   50
Niagara. Toronto. Opera. Touring Musicians

The Business of Music   53

Outstanding Personalities   53
Jonathan Sewell. Charles Sauvageau. Charles Sabatier. Theodore Molt. Antoine Dessane.
James Clarke

Children of Peace   58
Summary   59

CHAPTER IV: *Confederation to the End of the First World War,
1867–1920*   61

The West   62

Popular Music   63
Ballads and Parlor Songs

Church Music   65

Formal Music Making   66
Vocal Music. Instrumental Groups. Opera. Concert Repertory. Virtuosi

Outstanding Performers   70
Frantz Jehin-Prume. Luigi von Kunits. Emma Albani

The Business of Music   72
Publishing and Instrument Building. Music Instruction

Composers and Their Works   74
Calixa Lavallée. Guillaume Couture. Alexis Contant. Other Composers: French Canada. Other
Composers: English Canada

Summary   81

CHAPTER V: *To the End of World War II, 1920–1945*   82

Radio and Phonograph   83

Repertory   85
Popular Music

Instrumental Ensembles   87
Orchestras. Chamber Music

Vocal Music   88
Choral Music. Opera

Music Education   89

Outstanding Personalities   89
Edward Johnson. Harry Adaskin and Kathleen Parlow. Percy Faith. Wilfrid Pelletier

Composers 91
Claude Champagne. Rodolphe Mathieu. Healey Willan. Ernest MacMillan. Other Composers

Summary 103

CHAPTER VI: *Recent Developments, 1945–1984*   104

Multiculturalism 105
French- and English-Canadian Folk Song Today. Other Cultural Traditions. Integrated Cultures

Performing Groups 107
Orchestras. Choral Music. Opera. Chamber Music

Popular Musicians 110

Music Education 111

Support Organizations 112
Canadian Music Centre. John Adaskin Project. Canada Council. CBC

Centennial Celebration 113

Composition 114
Jean Papineau-Couture. Gilles Tremblay. Other French-Canadians. Godfrey Ridout. Violet Archer. Oskar Morawetz. Others

Modern Directions 124
John Weinzweig. Harry Freedman. Barbara Pentland. John Beckwith. István Anhalt. Harry Somers. R. Murray Schafer

Electronic (Electroacoustic) Music 138
Gustav Ciamaga. David Keane. Barry Truax. Other Electronic Composers

Summary 140

CHAPTER VII: *Music of the Original Canadians*   141

Canadian Indians 142
Eastern Woodlands, Nomadic (Algonkian). Eastern Woodlands, Sedentary (Iroquoian). Plains. Mackenzie River. Plateau. Pacific Coast. A Contemporary Powwow Ceremony

Inuit 156
Inuit Drum Dance

Summary 161

ANTHOLOGY:

1   Joseph Quesnel, "Rions chantons" from *Colas et Colinette* 163

2   James P. Clarke, "The Emigrants Home Dream" from *Lays of the Maple Leaf, or Songs of Canada* 166

3   Charles D'Albert, Waltz No. 2 from *Grand Trunk Waltzes* 168

4   Calixa Lavallée, *Mouvement à la Pavane*   169

5   Calixa Lavallée, "Single I Will Never Be" from *The Widow*   171

6   Claude Champagne, *Danse villageoise*   173

7   Healey Willan, *Introduction, Passacaglia and Fugue*   179

8   Healey Willan, *Rise Up, My Love, My Fair One*   199

9   Jean Papineau-Couture, Prelude from *Suite pour Piano*   202

10   Gilles Tremblay, "Phases" from *Pièces pour piano*   203

11   Godfrey Ridout, Etude II from *Two Etudes*   206

12   John Weinzweig, *Movement No. 1* from *Divertimento No. 1*   219

13   R. Murray Schafer, Part V from *Requiems for the Party Girl*   226

APPENDIX: *Readings, Recordings, and Films*   229

Index   247

List of Illustrations

Earliest settlement at Port Royal from Samuel de Champlain, *Oeuvres* (Thomas Fisher Rare Book Library, University of Toronto)   1

C. W. Jefferys, *Frontenac on the Way to Cataraqui* (C-70237 Public Archives Canada)   7

C. W. Jefferys, *The Order of Good Cheer* (C-13986 Public Archives Canada)   8

Jesuits among the Hurons (Thomas Fisher Rare Book Library, University of Toronto)   13

From the *Office for Ste. Famille* by Charles-Amador Martin (National Library of Canada)   17

Final Kyrie from *Livre d'orgue de Montreal* (Fondation Lionel-Groulx, Montreal)   17

F. F. Palmer, *The Home of Evangeline, "In Acadian Land"* (Royal Ontario Museum, Toronto)   19

Benjamin West, *Mort du Général Wolfe* (Royal Ontario Museum, Toronto)   22

J. C. Stadler, *Dance at the Chateau St. Louis* (National Library of Canada)   23

Oxford from the *Bay Psalm Book,* 1698   27

Canada in 1851 from Robert Montgomery Martin, *Tallis's Illustrated Atlas,* (Thomas Fisher Rare Book Library, University of Toronto)   39

View of Quebec from a drawing by Captain B. Beaufoy (Royal Ontario Museum, Toronto)   43

The Ottawa River at Bytown from a drawing by W. H. Bartlett (Royal Ontario Museum, Toronto)   46

Cover of *Grand Trunk Waltzes* by Charles D'Albert (National Library of Canada)   48

Beethoven's autograph sketch of *Freu Dich des Lebens* for Theodore Molt (Lawrence Lande Collection, National Library of Canada)   54

Title page: *Lays of the Maple Leaf* by James P. Clarke (Metropolitan Toronto Library Board)   57

Temple of the Children of Peace at Sharon, Ontario (Photo by Elaine Keillor)   58

Mother Britannia: "Cut her adrift, eh! How dare you?" from the *Canadian Illustrated News,* July 9, 1870 (Royal Ontario Museum, Toronto)   61

The Halifax Haydn Club, 1885 (Collection Elaine Keillor)   66

The Ottawa amateur Orchestra Society, 1898 (National Library of Canada)   67

Emma Albani, 1896 (National Library of Canada)   71

Cartoon, ca. 1893, depicting the competition for students between the Toronto College of Music and the Toronto Conservatory of Music (Collection Elaine Keillor)   73

Sheet music cover of *O Canada,* first edition (Séminaire de Québec)   75

Guillaume Couture (National Library of Canada)   78

Rural Ontario scene, ca. 1906 (Ontario Archives)   83

Ben Hokea's Orchestra (Ontario Archives)   86

Edward Johnson (National Library of Canada)   90

Topographical sketch from Claude Champagne's *Altitude* (Berandol Music, Ltd.)   93

Healey Willan (National Library of Canada)   98

Louis Riel, an opera by Harry Somers. (Photo: Alex Gray. Canadian Opera Company Archives)   109

Phil Nimmons (Photo: Bruce Litteljohn, Toronto, Ontario)   111

Man and Music Pavilion at Expo '67 (National Library of Canada)   113

Twentieth anniversary conference of the Canadian League of Composers, University of Victoria, 1971 (Photo by Helmut Kallmann)   115

Lawren S. Harris, *Lake and Mountains* (Art Gallery of Ontario, Toronto)   126

Sun God mask from *Ra* by R. Murray Schafer (Photo by Suzanne Sutcliffe)   137

Indian and Inuit tribes and languages of Canada (map)   143

Indian flute from the Eastern Woodlands area. (Royal Ontario Museum, Toronto)   145

The Great Defender, a false face mask from the Iroquois Indians (Royal Ontario Museum, Toronto)   146

A Blood (Blackfoot) drum (Royal Ontario Museum, Toronto)   149

Two Pacific Coast rattles and two Pacific Coast masks (Royal Ontario Museum, Toronto)   153

Paul Kane, *Medicine Pipe Stem Dance* (Royal Ontario Museum, Toronto)   155

Drum dancers Donald and Alice Suluk (Photo: R. Hummelen, Toronto)   158

Permissions (*continued from p. iv*)

p.130: Harry Somers, *North Country*. Used by permission of Berandol Music, Ltd., Toronto.

p.131: Harry Somers, *Voiceplay*. Courtesy of the composer.

pp.133-35: Harry Somers, *Louis Riel*. Courtesy of the composer.

pp.135-36: Harry Somers, *Kuyas*. Used by permission of Berandol Music, Ltd., Toronto.

p.146: *Don't Leave Me*. From Gertrude Kurath, *Songs and Dances of the Great Lakes Indians*, Folkways FE 4003.

pp.147-48: *Iroquoian Corn Dance*. From Gertrude Kurath, *Songs and Dances of the Great Lakes Indians*, Folkways FE 4003.

p.148: *Drum Dance Song*. From Gertrude Kurath, *Dances and Song Rituals of Six Nations Reserve, Ontario*. Ottawa: National Museum of Canada, Bulletin 220, 1968, 87.

p.150: *Blackfoot Indian Song*. From Bruno Nettl, "Studies in Blackfoot Indian Musical Culture; Notes on Composition, Text Settings, and Performance," *Ethnomusicology*, 19 (1975), 251. Used by permission.

p.152-54: *Potlatch song: He is lying*. Reproduced by permission of the American Ethnological Society (a division of the AAA) from "The Tsimshian: Their Arts and Music," Publication of the AES #18.

p.157: *Song for healing sickness*. From Helen H. Roberts and D. Jenness, *Eskimo Songs of the Copper Eskimos. Report of the Canadian Arctic Expedition 1918*, Vol. 14, Ottawa: F. A. Ackland, 1925.

p.160: *Drum Dance Song*. Reproduced from paper #82 of the Canadian Ethnology Service. National Museum of Man Mercury Series entitled *Music of the Netsilik Eskimo: A Study of Stability and Change* by Beverly Cavanagh (1982).

Preface

This book is addressed to all those interested in the history of music in Canada. I have tried to achieve maximum flexibility by writing a general narrative that can be understood by the layman, while at the same time including some technical details for those who are interested in that kind of information. To assist the reader I have separated the technical sections from the more general discussion by enclosing them within boxes. Those reading for narrative only can skip over the boxed-in sections and follow the story line without interruption.

The analyses are intentionally incomplete. What I have done is suggest the way in which the reader (or teacher) might approach a close analysis of the music if one is desired, but I have left most of the work undone. These sections should be considered analytical hints rather than attempts at comprehensiveness.

Although the history of Canada begins with the earliest inhabitants, the Indians and Inuit who have inhabited the country for thousands of years, their music is considered in the last chapter as a completely separate entity. I have done this because the discussion of Indian and Inuit music must deal with the entire culture in order to be understood by an audience that by and large knows little or nothing of native customs.

The name ''Canada,'' derived from the Huron word ''Kanata'' meaning village or community, first appears in Jacques Cartier's 1534 narrative in reference to the Indian community of Stadacona. Canada is called ''New France'' from its earliest settlement until the British Conquest in 1763. In our discussion of events after that date, the geographic areas are designated individually as ''the Maritimes,'' ''Lower Canada'' (Quebec), and ''Upper Canada'' (Ontario and the West). After Confederation (1867), the provinces are identified by name and geographical area, as, for example, ''the Maritimes'' for Nova Scotia, New Brunswick, and Prince Edward Island. Newfoundland is included in the discussion of the eastern provinces as early as the nineteenth century, although it remained politically independent until 1949. The assignment of names to the various areas is, in fact, far more complex, but this system has been adopted to avoid confusion.

In addition to a list of the works referred to in the text, the Appendix includes additional readings, recordings, and films relative to each chapter to assist the reader and classroom teacher. The Anthology appended here provides a basic overview of the field, although space limitations and the availability of material cause it to be a bit uneven. Fortunately, however, the publications of the recently formed Canadian Musical Heritage Society will fill in many of the gaps prior to 1940 (see Appendix for details), and the Canadian Music Centre can provide music in quantity from that date forward.

Acknowledgements

It is with great pleasure that I acknowledge those who have assisted me. My heartfelt thanks go to the several anonymous readers of the early drafts of the book who offered advice and encouragement. Most expressly I would also like to thank John Beckwith, Beverley Cavanagh, John Mayo, John Moir, and especially Elaine Keillor, who also provided me with a large amount of material. I am grateful for various kinds of assistance to David Boe, Paula Conlon, Doreith Cooper, Elizabeth Crysler, Ivan Harris, Catherine McClelland, Lynn McIntyre, Mabel Laine, Barclay McMillan, Carl Morey, Timothy Rice, Robert Witmer, Henry Mutsaers of the Canadian Music Centre, PRO Canada, Helmut Kallmann, Maria Calderisi Bryce, and Florence Hayes of the music division of the National Library, the staffs of the Vincent Bladen Library at Scarborough College and the Edward Johnson Library at the Faculty of Music of the University of Toronto, and the Royal Ontario Museum. I am indebted to my wife Bonnie for typing the first several drafts; to Lise Boutin-Visentin and Leonard Doucette for translations of French material; to the University of Toronto for providing research travel funds; and to Claire Brook and Susan Zurn of W.W. Norton for advice and skillful editing.

The footnotes do not adequately acknowledge my dependence on Helmut Kallmann's *A History of Music in Canada, 1534–1914,* nor on the *Encyclopedia of Music in Canada,* edited by Kallmann, Gilles Potvin, and Kenneth Winters. While I was writing this book, those two publications were my constant companions not only as prime sources of information but also for confirmation of the overall picture.

TIMOTHY J. McGEE

1

New France

Our survey of the music of Canada begins with the establishment of permanent colonies in the early years of the seventeenth century. The northeastern area of North America had been discovered much earlier; it was first officially documented in 1497 by John Cabot, who was in the service of the king of England. In July of 1534 Jacques Cartier explored the great gulf of the St. Lawrence River and claimed the surrounding territory in the name of King Francis I of France. In 1599 the entire area was named "New France," but it was not until Samuel de Champlain established a colony on the Bay of Fundy at Port Royal, Nova Scotia, in 1604, and another at Quebec in 1608, that there was a continuous settlement of Europeans in Canada.

Earliest settlement at Port Royal.

A Logemens des artifans.
B Plate forme où eftoit le canon.
C Le magafin.
D Logement du fieur de Pontgraué & Champlain.
E La forge.

F Paliffade de pieux.
G Le four.
H La cuifine.
O Petite maifonnette où l'on retiroit les vtanfiles de nos barques; que depuis le fieur de Poitrincourt fit

rebaftir, & y logea le fieur Boulay quand le fieur du Pont s'en reuint en France.
P (1) La porte de l'abitation.
Q (2) Le cemetiere.
R (3) La riuiere.

The earliest settlers came from France to farm, trade furs, and look for minerals. Accounts of the colonists' early years describe many hardships. They had to build homes, clear the land for farming, lay away sufficient food for the harsh winters, and contend with Indians who were often hostile. Not all of their time was spent on work, however—they found time to relax and enjoy one another's company, and music figured prominently in their lives at such times.

As early as 1607, in the accounts of Marc Lescarbot, a lawyer and amateur musician from Paris who accompanied the explorers, one finds the observation: "I recall that on a Sunday, the 14th of the month [January], after mid day, we entertained ourselves singing music on the Equille river."[1]

The accounts of musical life in New France are spotty and incomplete. Our information comes mainly from private correspondence, from travellers' reports, and especially from the *Jesuit Relations,* communications sent by the missionaries to their superiors in France (1625–70), and from the *Jesuit Journal,* a diary kept by the Quebec superior, begun in 1645.[2] Enough information survives to give us a general picture of the part music played in the daily lives of the colonists, and from the details we have, it would appear that a great variety of music making went on.

Folk Music

By far the largest quantity of secular music performed in Canada from its founding until the mid-nineteenth century was folk music. From the early days of the country, immigrants of all origins brought their traditional music with them, but the contribution of the French was especially rich in this regard. During the seventeenth and eighteenth centuries most of the French colonists were farmers and labourers who sang and played the music they had learned in their homeland—folk songs and dance tunes that could be performed by amateurs without elaborate planning, rehearsal, or special facilities. Their extensive repertory was passed on orally from one generation to another; it was not to be written down until the nineteenth century.

Of the approximately nine thousand French-Canadian folk songs collected over the last 150 years, over 90 percent have been traced to northern France. The majority of them were brought over during the years 1664–72, a period when the active recruitment of immigrants by Jean Talon, the king's representative, doubled the population of French Canada to nearly seven thousand.[3] This music was sung in the homes, in the fields, and at social gatherings; it reverberated on the rivers and lakes as the Voyageurs paddled along.

1. Marc Lescarbot, *The History of New France,* ed. and trans. W. L. Grant, 3 vols. (Toronto, 1907; reprint, New York: Greenwood Press, 1968), 1:346.

2. *The Jesuit Relations and Allied Documents, 1610–1791,* ed. Ruben Gold Thwaites, 73 vols. (Cleveland: Burrows Brothers, 1896–1901). *Le Journal des Jésuites,* 2nd ed., ed. Laverdière and Casgrain (Montreal: Valois, 1892).

3. Helmut Kallmann, *A History of Music in Canada, 1534–1914* (Toronto: University of Toronto Press, 1960), 25.

French-Canadian folk songs are a continuation of the tradition of unaccompanied song that dates back to the troubadours of the Middle Ages. They resemble their medieval forebears in subject matter, in the formal design of both text and musical phrases, and in the scales used in the melodies. Some of the songs can even be dated. *Le Prince d'Orange,* for example, is a satire on the virtue of Jean de Chalon, who died in 1507,[4] although it is not likely that the colonists who sang it knew to whom it referred. To them it was probably just an attractive melody with a wry text.

Example I–1: *Le Prince d'Orange*

C'é - tait   le prin - ce d'O - ran - ge, Là, _   C'é - tait   le prin - ce d'O - ran - ge.   C'é -

tait   le prin - ce d'O - ran - ge, Là, _ C'é - tait   le prin - ce d'O - ran - ge.   Grand ma - tin _ s'est le -

vé, _   Ma - don - dai - ne,   Grand ma - tin _ s'est le - vé, _   Ma - don - dé. _____

C'était le prince d'Orange, Là,	It was the Prince of Orange, La,
C'était le prince d'Orange.	It was the Prince of Orange.
Grand matin s'est levé,	Rose early in the morning,
Madondaine,	Madondaine,
Grand matin s'est levé,	Rose early in the morning,
Madondé.	Madondé.
Il appela son page, Là,	He called his page, La,
Mon âne est-il bridé?	''Is my donkey bridled?''
Madondaine,	Madondaine,
Ah, oui, vraiment, beau prince, Là	''Oh yes indeed, fine prince, La,
Il est bridé, sellé,	it is bridled, saddled!''
Madondaine,	Madondaine,

etc.

English translation by
Leonard Doucette

Other texts express such ageless emotions as love, jealousy, loneliness, or joy. The sentiment in *A la claire fontaine* (example I–2)—a contrast of placid waters and the joyful song of a nightingale with the pain of lost love—is as fresh and poignant today as it was for the early settlers and their ancestors in France.

This tune is reported to have been sung by Champlain's men in 1608 and has

4. Marius Barbeau, *Romancero du Canada* (Ottawa: Beauchemin, 1937), 13–18.

Example I–2: *A la claire fontaine*

A   la clai - re fon-tai - ne   M'en al -lant pro-me-ner,   J'ai   trou-vé l'eau si bel - le

Refrain

Que   je m'y suis bai-gné.   Lui   ya long-temps que je t'ai - me   Ja - mais je ne t'ou-blie-rai.

A la claire fontaine	By the clear fountain
M'en allant promener,	Out strolling one day
J'ai trouvé l'eau si belle	I found the water so lovely
Que je m'y suis baigné.	I bathed in it.
Lui ya longtemps que je t'aime	I have long loved you
Jamais je ne t'oublierai.	Never will I forget you.
J'ai trouvé l'eau si belle	I found the water so lovely
Que je m'y suis baigné;	I bathed in it;
Sous les feuilles d'un chêne	Under the leaves of an oak
Lui ya . . .	I dried myself off.
Sous les feuilles d'un chêne	Under the leaves of an oak
Je me suis fait sécher;	I dried myself off;
Su la plus haute branche	On its highest bough
Le rossignol chantait.	The nightingale was singing.
Lui ya . . .	
Sur la plus haute branche	On its highest bough
Le rossignol chantait.	The nightingale was singing;
Chante, rossignol, chante,	Sing, nightingale, sing,
Toi qui as le coeur gai.	You who are gay at heart.
Lui ya . . .	
Chante, rossignol, chante,	Sing, nightingale, sing,
Toi qui as le coeur gai;	You who are gay at heart;
Tu as le coeur à rire,	You have a heart for laughing:
Moi je l'ai-t-à pleurer.	Mine I have for weeping.
Lui ya . . .	

etc.

English translation by
Leonard Doucette

remained popular through the centuries. It has been closely associated with French-Canadian nationalism since its adoption in 1834 as the anthem of the St.-Jean-Baptiste Societies.[5]

   The folk song tradition allows for many variations: multiple texts for any one melody, or many melodies for any one text. There is not one "correct" version of most folk songs, therefore, but several, some with a few words or notes changed,

   5. The St.-Jean-Baptiste Society was founded in Montreal in 1834 as the national society of French-Canadians. Since that time special ceremonies have been conducted on June 24, the feast of St. John the Baptist. See *Encyclopedia of Music in Canada* (hereafter *EMC*), ed. Helmut Kallmann, Gilles Potvin, and Kenneth Winters (Toronto: University of Toronto Press, 1981), 836b–37a.

others with entirely new verses or melodies. The French-Canadians adopted some texts with little change, such as *Le Prince d'Orange* and *A la claire fontaine*. (*A la claire fontaine* does have several different melodies.) Others, however, were given completely new texts: *Par derrièr' chez mon père* eventually became *Vive la canadienne* (example I–3).

Example I–3: *Par derrièr' chez mon père / Vive la canadienne*

| Par derr-ièr'chez mon pè - re | Vo - le mon coeur,vo - le. Par derr-ièr'chez mon pè - re, Lui |
| Vive la ca - na - di - en - ne, | Vo - le mon coeur,vo - le Vive la ca - na - di - en - ne Et |

| ya-t-un pom-mier doux. | Lui ya-t-un pom-mier doux,doux,doux,Lui ya-t-un pom - mier doux. |
| ses jo - lis yeux doux. | Et ses jo - lis yeux doux,doux,doux,Et ses jo - lis yeux doux. |

Par derrièr' chez mon père.
Vole, mon coeur, vole,
Par derrièr' chez mon père
Lui ya-t-un pommier doux.
Lui ya-t-un pommier doux, doux, doux
Lui ya-t-un pommier doux.

Behind my father's house,
Fly, my heart, fly,
Behind my father's house
There's an apple-tree sweet.
There's an apple-tree sweet, sweet, sweet
There's an apple-tree sweet.

Les feuilles en sont vertes,
Vole, mon coeur, vole,
Les feuilles en sont vertes
Et le fruit en est doux.
Et le fruit en est doux, doux, doux,
Et le fruit en est doux.

Its leaves are green,
Fly, my heart, fly,
Its leaves are green,
And its fruit is sweet . . .

Trois filles d'un prince,
Vole, mon coeur, vole,
Trois filles d'un prince
Sont endormies dessous.
Sont endormies dessous, doux, doux,
Sont endormies dessous.

Three daughters of a prince,
Fly, my heart, fly,
Three daughters of a prince,
Are sleeping beneath it . . .

etc.
*   *   *

Vive la canadienne,
Vole, mon coeur, vole,
Vive la canadienne
Et ses jolis yeux doux.
Et ses jolis yeux doux, doux, doux,
Et ses jolis yeux doux.

Long live the Canadian girl,

And her pretty eyes sweet . . .

Nous la menons aux noces,
Vole, mon coeur, vole,
Nous la menons aux noces
Dans tous ses beaux atours.
Dans tous . . .

We take her to the wedding,

In all her pretty finery . . .

Là, nous jasons sans gêne,	There we chat freely,
Vole, mon coeur, vole,	
Là, nous jasons sans gêne;	
Nous nous amusons tous,	We all amuse ourselves . . .
Nous nous . . .	

etc.

English translations by
Leonard Doucette

The three songs demonstrate some of the different kinds of formal designs found in the texts and their musical settings. The text of *Le Prince d'Orange* consists of couplets that all end with the syllable "é." In the musical setting, the lines are separated, and the first line is repeated four times, the second line twice. Vocables (nonsense words or sounds) "La," "Madondaine," and "Madondé" are inserted into each of the couplets.

A la claire fontaine is separated into stanzas of four lines with a two-line refrain repeated at the end of each verse. The second pair of lines from each verse is then repeated with two new lines, forming the next verse. In performance, a soloist would sing the verses and the entire group (chorus) would sing the refrain. In *Le Prince d'Orange,* however, since there is no separate refrain, there could be no exchange between soloist and chorus.

Each six-line stanza of *Par derrièr' chez mon père / Vive la canadienne* contains only two new lines—1 and 4—a refrain made up of two repeats of line 4, with the addition of the vocables "doux, doux," and the line "vole, mon coeur, vole" which appears in each stanza. ("Vole, mon coeur, vole" is the only line of text that is the same in both the French and the Canadian versions of the song.)

Many of the songs have refrains, allowing the entire group to participate in the singing. In performance a soloist sings the four lines of verse and then the chorus repeats them; the refrain is sung in the same manner. During the informal social evenings that were the main form of entertainment in the early centuries of the country, each person in turn would select a favourite song to lead, and all would join in the refrains.

Voyageurs

The most colourful accounts of folk singing are included in stories of the Voyageurs—the French-Canadians, often of Indian ancestry, who paddled canoes on the lakes and rivers of Canada and the United States. Their chief occupation was the transportation of goods and passengers for large fur-trading companies, a field they monopolized from its beginning in the seventeenth century until the mid-nineteenth century, when steamboats and the railway replaced them.

Tales of the Voyageurs conjure up romantic visions of the rugged frontier life. They travelled far into the interior, hunted and fished for their food, and slept under their canoes. Their distinctive dress included a red woolen cap, an Indian breech cloth, deer-skin leggings reaching from ankle to above the knee leaving the thigh bare, a baggy shirt, a gaudy sash with a beaded bag suspended from it,

Voyageurs in action. **Frontenac on the Way to Cataraqui,** *an engraving by C. W. Jefferys.*

and a pipe—used as much for measurement as for relaxation (in the time it took to smoke a pipe they could paddle approximately four miles. A distance of twelve miles, therefore, was usually called "three pipes").[6]

Song was evidently a constant companion of the Voyageurs:

> They strike off singing a song peculiar to themselves called the Voyageur song. . . . It is extremely pleasing to see people who are toiling hard, display such marks of good humor . . . although they know that for a space of more than 2,000 miles their exertions must be unremitting. . . . The song is of great use: they keep time with their paddles to its measured cadence.[7]

> They sang their gay French songs, the other canoe joining in the chorus. This peculiar singing has often been described; it is very animated on the water and in the open air, but not very harmonious. They all sing in unison, raising their voices and marking the time with their paddles. One always led, but in these there was a diversity of taste and skill. If I wished to hear "En roulant ma boule, roulant" I applied to Le Duc. Jacques excelled in "La belle rose blanche," and Louis was great in "Trois canards s'en vont baignant."[8]

Order of Good Cheer

The social tradition brought from the old country called for songs and dance music to enliven feasts. Fiddles, woodwinds, and other portable instruments are known to have been brought with the early settlers, and were undoubtedly played

6. Grace Lee Nute, *The Voyageur* (New York: D. Appleton, 1931), 50, 58.

7. Hugh Gray, *Letters from Canada, Written During a Residence There in the Years 1806, 1807, and 1808* (London, 1809), 155. Cited in Barclay McMillan, "Music in Canada 1791–1867: A Travellers Perspective," M.A. thesis, Carleton University, 1983.

8. Anna Jameson, *Winter Studies and Summer Rambles in Canada* (New York, 1839; reprint, Toronto: McClelland & Stewart, 1923), 260. In this quotation she describes an 1837 trip on Lake Huron.

The Order of Good Cheer *by C. W. Jefferys (1869–1951).*

on these occasions. The most famous celebrations were sponsored by the Order of Good Cheer *(Ordre de bon temps)*. Champlain established this social order of chivalry during the winter of 1606–07 to distract the colonists from cold and loneliness. In Champlain's words, it was something that

> everybody found beneficial to his health, and more profitable than all sorts of medicine we might have used. This Order consisted of a chain which we used to place with certain little ceremonies about the neck of one of our people, commissioning him for that day to go hunting. The next day it was conferred upon another, and so on in order.[9]

Lescarbot provides details of the ceremony at the evening meal:

> for that was our chief banquet, at which the ruler of the feast or chief butler . . . having had everything prepared by the cook, marched in, napkin on shoulder, wand of office in hand, and around his neck the collar of the Order, which was worth more than four crowns; after him all the members of the Order each carrying a dish. The same was repeated at dessert, though not always with so much pomp. And at night, before giving thanks to God, he handed over to his successor in charge the collar of the Order, with a cup of wine, and they drank to each other.[10]

9. Samuel de Champlain, *Works,* trans. and ed. H. P. Biggar (Toronto: The Champlain Society, 1922–36), 1:447–48.
10. Lescarbot, *New France,* quoted in Champlain, *Works,* 448, note 1.

Aristocratic Music and Theatre

Among the earliest settlers were a few merchants and military leaders who had travelled in aristocratic circles in France. There they were exposed to the more sophisticated forms of entertainment—for example, the *ballets de cour* (theatrical spectacles with dancing) and the elegant vocal and instrumental music cultivated at the French court. While there was little prospect of reproducing those elaborate activities in the New World, the theatrical spectacle described below testifies to the colonists' ability to improvise and their desire to maintain the cultural traditions of the Old World.

Theatre of Neptune

The first theatre spectacle in the New World was produced in 1606 as a welcoming celebration for Baron de Poutrincourt, lieutenant governor of Port Royal, who had been away exploring the coast with Champlain. The *Théâtre de Neptune* was written by Marc Lescarbot and presented by a cast of Port Royal settlers and local Indians:

> After many difficulties . . . M. de Poutrincourt reached Port Royal on November 14th [1606] where we happily received him with a ceremony absolutely new on that side of the ocean. . . . I decided to meet him with a pleasant spectacle, and so we did. Since it was written hastily in French rhymes I have placed it among my *Muses of New France* under the title of "Théâtre de Neptune."[11]

Lescarbot's offering is the type of presentation known as the *entrée royale* or *réception* that became very stylized in France in the sixteenth and seventeenth centuries. Before the establishment of a permanent residence at Versailles in the mid-seventeenth century, the king moved from manor to manor every few months. Upon his arrival at each location a royal reception was presented to welcome him. This generally involved *tableaux* (mimed scenes), some verse, and music. Lescarbot was fully acquainted with the tradition, having participated in the writing and performance of a *réception* in 1598.[12] His presentation in Port Royal follows one of the standard outlines: an appropriate god is called upon to bid welcome to the distinguished guest. In this case, Neptune arrives in a barque surrounded by a court of Tritons and Indians who recite verse in French and in the Indian language of Souriquois. At the end everyone sings "Vray Neptune": ←

Vray Neptune donne nous	(True Neptune, grant us
Contre tes flots asseurance,	Protection against thy billows
Et fay que nous poissions tous	And grant us that we may all
Un jour nous revoir en France.[13]	Meet again some day in France.)

---

11. Lescarbot, *New France*, 2:340–41.
12. The occasion was the visit of the papal legate to Vervins, Lescarbot's hometown in Picardy. Lescarbot wrote at least part of the *réception*, and delivered a *Harangue d'action de grâces*, the formal welcoming address. See Roméo Arbour, "Le Théâtre de Neptune de Marc Lescarbot," in *Archives des lettres canadiennes* 5 (1976): 23.
13. Marc Lescarbot, *Les Muses de la Nouvelle-France*, ed. Tross (Paris, 1886), 28, cited in Willy Amtmann, *Music in Canada, 1600–1800* (Montreal: Habitex, 1975), 48.

The text of the play contains only two cues for music—a trumpet call and the song "Vray Neptune." After his return to France Lescarbot published the text but not the music, leaving us in the dark about the song and any other music that may have been interpolated into the script.

Given what is known of the facilities and performers available at that time in Port Royal, the *Théâtre de Neptune* was an ambitious undertaking. The tradition of theatre in France was strong in the seventeenth and eighteenth centuries, however, and we should not be surprised that theatrical events were mounted in New France as soon as there was a sufficient number of aristocrats to appreciate them.

Réceptions

Following the tradition established by Lescarbot, *réceptions* were held on other occasions in the seventeenth and eighteenth centuries to mark a special occasion. Two are known to have been performed in Quebec by the Jesuits: *La Réception de Monseigneur le Vicomte d'Argenson*, presented in 1658 to welcome the new governor of New France, and an untitled *réception* presented in 1727 in honour of Bishop Saint-Vallier.[14] The performance in 1658 calls for a cast of school-children, ages ten to sixteen. It is written in French, Huron, and Algonquin, symbolizing the purpose of the *réception* as stated in the full title: *La Réception de Monseigneur le Vicomte d'Argenson par toutes les Nations du païs de Canada à son entrée au Gouvernement de la Nouvelle France.* (The Reception of the Lord Viscount of Argenson by all the peaceful nations of Canada upon his entrance into the Government of New France). The script does not mention music, but several of the speeches are in verse and could have been set to music.

The *réception* of 1727 is totally in French verse. The various characters extoll the virtues of the bishop, ending with:

Un prélat sur la fin d'une illustre carrière
Des indigens plus que jamais le père,
Cherchant deux successeurs de ses pieux travaux,
Les trouve, et, plein d'ardeur, leur adresse ces mots:
'vous que je vous orné du brillant assemblage
'de cent exlatantes vertus;
'Vous qui vous trouvez revêtus
'Du pouvoir d'une monarque à qui tous rendent hommage,
'acceptez aujourd'huy mon plus cher héritage.'

(A prelate at the end of an illustrious career, but more than ever the father of the poor seeks them out and addresses them with these words of warmth: "You whom I see clothed in the brilliance of a hundred shining virtues; you who find yourselves invested with the power of a monarch to whom all render homage, accept from me today my dearest legacy.")[15]

An epilogue also refers to verses and music.

---

14. Text (defective) published in *Monseigneur de Saint-Vallier et l'Hôpital Général de Québec* (Quebec, 1882). I am indebted for the corrected text and for much of the information about the *réceptions* to Professor Leonard Doucette of the University of Toronto.

15. Translation by Leonard Doucette.

Quebec Society and Cultural Activities

The social life of the political and military leaders in Quebec improved as a result of the 1663 reorganization of the government. King Louis XIV designated the colonies a royal province, and his personal representative, an intendant, was appointed as the principal administrator. This replaced the previous government, the unwieldy "Company of One Hundred" which since 1629 had been made up of frequently feuding representatives of the king, business leaders, and clergy. The new arrangement was similar to the governing bodies of the provinces in France.

In 1665, soon after the arrival of the first intendant, Jean Talon, a concerted effort was made to imitate the social as well as the political life of France. Comte Louis de Frontenac, governor in 1672–82 and 1689–98, furthered efforts along this line, using Versailles as his model. Parties and dances were held frequently at the governor's palace, the Chateau St. Louis (the earliest recorded ball took place in 1667), and there were *soirées musicales* at the homes of the cultured citizens. Participation in these activities was limited to the government officials, military officers, and the wealthy citizens of Quebec.

Since instruction in singing and playing an instrument was considered part of the education of any well-bred young lady in France, we can suppose that the tradition was pursued among the elite of Quebec. Instrumentalists are implicit in the many references to balls, and there were always instrumentalists in the military. It is reported that in the nineteenth century, ten long-forgotten viols were found in a vault of the Hôpital-Général in Quebec City. They were built in Paris in the late seventeenth century by one Nicolas Bertrand, and may well have been in use in Quebec in the early 1700s (their present location is not known).[16]

Amateur theatrical performances were presented frequently, with casts chosen from the military officers and the well-born ladies. Frontenac had a small theatre built in the Chateau St. Louis, where Corneille's *Nicomède* and Racine's *Mithridate* were presented in 1693–94. A performance of Molière's *Tartuffe,* proposed by Frontenac, brought a swift condemnation from the local clergy who considered the comedy immoral, and the officer scheduled to play the title role was placed under interdict (forbidden the sacraments) by the bishop. The performance was cancelled.

The opposition of the clergy to some cultural and social activities was a tradition of long standing in New France. There are several unfavourable references in the *Jesuit Relations* to folk songs with unacceptable texts, and on the occasion of the 1667 ball, the superior of the Jesuits recorded in the *Journal,* "May God grant that nothing further come of [this kind of event]."[17] These incidents underline the continuing tension between civil and clerical authorities, a problem Louis XIV had hoped to minimize with the political reorganization of 1663. The clerics were not opposed to all cultural activities, as witness the two *réceptions* described

---

16. Nazaire le Vasseur, "Musique et musiciens à Québec," *La Musique,* 1919–22. Cited in Kallmann, *A History,* 20–21.

17. *Journal,* 353 for February 1667. Quoted in Amtmann, *Music in Canada,* 146–47.

above, but they considered that some plays were not in the best spiritual interests of the people. The positive contribution of the clergy to music education was a large one, however, as we shall see below.

The Missionaries and Music

French Roman Catholic missionaries played an important role in the settlement of New France. Their primary aim was to bring the word of God to the Indians and to tend to the spiritual needs of the colonists. In doing so they built schools, exercised a strong influence on the government of each community, and in general served as some of the strongest pillars of society. (There were Huguenots—French protestants—among the earliest settlers, but they were expelled in 1629 when Cardinal Richelieu, chief minister to Louis XIII, established the Company of One Hundred. After that date residence in New France was forbidden to anyone but French Catholics.)

The first missionaries to arrive were members of the Recollect order, who came to Quebec with Champlain on his voyage of 1615. The Jesuits arrived in 1625, and in 1639 four nuns of the Ursuline order disembarked there "to the sound of cannons, fifes and drums . . . to take possession of the post that God had assigned them on the shores of the St. Lawrence."[18]

Missionaries travelled from their administrative centre in Quebec to the small colonies in Trois Rivière and Montreal, and into the Huron country where a mission was established at Ste. Marie (near Midland, Ontario). Gradually they moved to the western areas of Canada, and south into the middle of the United States. Life was difficult for these first missionaries in the unsettled land. The Indians were unpredictable, and there was always the threat of violence and death. The Jesuit martyrs Isaac Jogues, Jean de Brébeuf, and Gabriel Lalemant all worked in Canada among the Hurons; Brébeuf and Lalemant were tortured to death in 1649 when the Iroquois overran the village of Ste. Marie.

From the *Jesuit Relations* we learn that it was through music that the missionaries first established a basis for teaching religion to the Indians. Rev. Gabriel Sagard-Théodat reported ca. 1618:

> It is necessary to be good-natured and show a happy and satisfied face, and to sing from time to time, hymns and spiritual songs, as much for one's own contentment as for the happiness and edification of the savages, who take a singular pleasure in hearing sung the praises of Our Lord rather than the profane songs, against which I have seen them show distaste.[19]

18. C. Dorveau, *Les Ursulines de Québec*, 2 vols. (Quebec, 1878), 1:24. Quoted in Amtmann, *Music in Canada*, 73.

19. Gabriel Sagard-Théodat, *Historie du Canada et Voyages que les frères mineurs Recollects y ont faicts pour la conversion des infidèles*, new ed. (Paris, 1866), 173–74. Quoted in Kallmann, *A History*, 11.

Jesuits among the Hurons. *A 17th-century depiction of the martyrdom of (left to right) Isaac Jogues, Jean de Brébeuf, and Gabriel Lalemant.*

Within a month of their arrival, a chapel was built for the Recollects and they began daily celebration of the Mass, including the singing of chants and hymns. The Indian converts were encouraged to join with the colonists in singing during the services, and the missionaries translated many of the sacred texts into the Indian languages and wrote new texts for them.

The Huron carol *Jesous Ahatonhia* (example I–4a) is a work preserved to this day which was probably written in 1642 for the Hurons at Ste. Marie by the Jesuit missionary Jean de Brébeuf. The melody is an adaptation of a sixteenth-century folk song *Une jeune pucelle* (example I–4b).[20]

Example I–4a: *Jesous Ahatonhia.*

20. *EMC,* 474b,c. This version of *Une jeune pucelle* is taken from Jean-Denis Daulé, *Nouveau Recueil de Cantiques à l'usage du diocèse de Québec* (Quebec, 1819), 99–100.

You are human beings
take heart, Jesus is born;
The spirit who enslaved us has
departed. Do not listen to him
for he corrupts our minds
Jesus, he is born.

English translation by
John Steckley

Example I–4b: *Une jeune pucelle*

Irony

Jesous Ahatonhia was a great favourite with the Hurons and was passed down through the generations as part of the tribal tradition. It was finally written down at the end of the eighteenth century.

Music Education

The arrival in 1632 of Father Paul le Jeune as superior of the Jesuit mission in Quebec marks the beginning of formal music education in Canada. He opened the first school where, among other subjects, he taught both French and Indian boys to sing sacred music:

> I carefully pronounced the Pater or the Credo which I had arranged in verse for them to sing; they followed me word by word learning very nicely by heart.[21]

of what

> It is a sweet (consolation) to hear them [the Indians] sing in our chapel the symbols of the Apostles in their own language. Now, in order to animate them even more, our Frenchmen sing one strophe in our language and then the [Indian boys] another in Huron, and then all together sing a third verse, each one in his own language and in nice harmony.[22]

A school for girls was opened in 1640 by the Ursuline nun Mother Marie de St. Joseph, a gifted singer and viol player from Tours. Singing was taught to all the girls, and the more talented were also given lessons on the viol. One of the

---

21. Paul le Jeune, *Jesuit Relations* (1637), 223. Quoted in Amtmann, *Music in Canada,* 68.
22. *Jesuit Relations,* 66. Cited in Amtmann, *Music in Canada,* 68–69.

Indian students, Agnes, was singled out for praise by Marie de l'Incarnation, the superior of the convent:

> She has made great progress amongst us in the knowledge of the mysteries of the faith as in good manners, and morals, in handicraft and reading, as in playing the viol.[23]

Sacred Music Performance and Compositions

Music is mentioned frequently in the *Jesuit Relations* from 1640 until the records cease in 1673. We learn from them that in the Quebec church, music for church services was provided not only by the clergy, but on various occasions by school boys, by some of the adult males of the community, and even occasionally by soldiers. In 1646 the choir sang in four-part harmony, and shortly afterward in improvised harmony *(fauxbourdon)*. In November of 1645 two violins were used at a wedding ceremony, and at the Christmas service that same year both a violin and flute were played, and the congregation sang the carol *Chantons noe* and the hymn *Venez mon Dieu*. By the end of the decade it is reported that viols were played during Mass at the elevation.[24]

The Ursulines in Quebec assembled a large collection of music during the seventeenth and eighteenth centuries, both at their convent and at the hospital run by the order of Hospitalières, the Hôtel-Dieu. The collection of manuscripts and prints used for Mass, the sacred Offices, at Benediction, and for procession, includes books of plainchant (some printed in Quebec in the nineteenth century), polyphonic Masses, Magnificats, motets, devotional songs, and instrumental music. While much of the music is anonymous, there are compositions by André Campra, Marc-Antoine Charpentier, Henri Dumont, Jean-Baptiste Morin, and other respected French composers of the time.[25] It is possible that some of the anonymous works in the collection were composed by members of the clergy living in Quebec. There is no record of the date of acquisition of this material, but from what is known about the activities and background of Mother Marie de St. Joseph, we can assume that some of the music was assembled for performance during her years as music teacher (1639–52).[26]

Example I–5a: *Motet à la Sainte Vierge,* opening measures

23. Letter from Marie de l'Incarnation, 1640, cited in Amtmann, *Music in Canada,* 74.
24. *Jesuit Relations,* 27:113, 101; 36:173–75. Quoted in Kallmann, *A History,* 17–18.
25. Erich Schwandt, *The Motet in New France* (Victoria: Jeu Editions, 1981), 1–2, 26–27.
26. The music is presently located in the archives of the Monastère des Augustines de la miséricorde de Jésus and the archives of the Monastère des Ursulines de Québec.

Example I–5b: *Motet à la Sainte Vierge,* florid passage

(de-)vo - to_ fe - mi - ne - o__ se - xu, pro de-vo - - - - - - to

Example I–5 is from one anonymous work in the Ursuline collection, an unaccompanied motet to the Virgin. The piece begins in a rather simple song style
(example I–5a), but later sections include more florid passages (example I–5b).
The motet bears a close resemblance to the *air de cour,* the French art song of
the baroque period, a style that was adopted frequently for devotional songs.

Fr. Charles-Amador Martin (1648–1711) is usually credited with the first
Canadian composition. The young priest studied in Quebec at the Jesuit College
and seminary where he was known as a capable singer. It is thought that he
wrote the Prose sections for the Office of the Holy Family, although the date of
composition is not known. The music—chant, written in square notation—survives in several manuscript copies and was first printed in *Le graduel romain* of
1800 in Quebec. It was sung at the Quebec cathedral on the feast of the Holy
Family until the 1950s.[27]

A church organ is first mentioned in Quebec in 1661,[28] and we know that in
1663 Bishop Laval brought an even larger organ back with him from France.
The new instrument was quickly installed in Parish Church, and in 1664 Laval
wrote to the pope giving details of music in the Quebec cathedral:

> There is here a cathedral made of stone; it is large and splendid. The divine service is
> celebrated in it according to the ceremony of bishops; our priests, our seminarists, as
> well as ten or twelve choir-boys, are regularly present there. On the greater feasts, the
> Mass, Vespers, and the late Salve are sung in music of various hexachords and modes
> [lit. numbers], and organ sweetly mixed with voices wonderfully adorn this musical
> harmony.[29]

The famous explorer of the Mississippi, Louis Jolliet, may have been among
the first organists at Parish Church. He took minor orders in 1662, and was a
classmate of Charles-Amador Martin at the Jesuit College.[30]

By 1705 the Church of Notre Dame in Montreal had also acquired an organ;
a recently discovered book of organ music provides an idea of the kind of compositions performed there. The *Livre d'orgue de Montreal,* as it is presently
called, contains 398 anonymous compositions including Masses, Magnificats,

---

27. *EMC,* 600b,c. I am indebted to Maria Calderisi Bryce for the date of first publication.

28. This is the earliest known organ in North America.

29. A. Leblond de Brumath, *Bishop Laval* (Toronto: Morang, 1906), 84–85. Translation amended
from Kallmann, *A History,* 20.

30. Amtmann, *Music in Canada,* 120. Amtmann reports that Jolliet studied harpsichord in Europe
before returning to North America. That Jolliet was a musician is recorded in the *Jesuit Relations,*
but details of his performance are not well documented. See *EMC,* 484b,c.

From the Office for Ste. Famille *by*
Charles-Amador Martin.

Te Deums, and some incidental pieces. The only composer identified to date is
Nicholas Lebègue (1630–1702), organist for the king of France. In all probabil-
ity the book originated in France and was transported to Canada by Lebègue's

Final Kyrie from Livre d'orgue de Montreal.

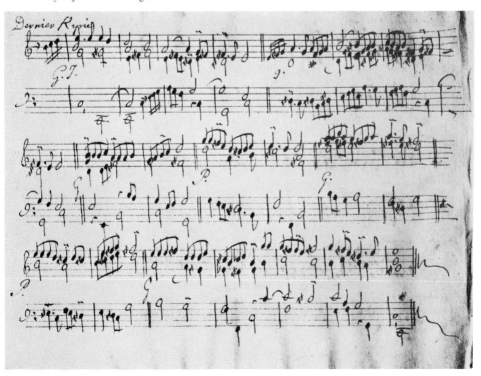

student, Jean Girard.[31] Girard (1696–1765), a cleric in the Sulpician order, emigrated in 1724 from Bourges to Montreal where he taught at the Sulpician school and played the organ at Notre Dame Church.

The compositions in the *Livre d'orgue,* like most French organ works of the period, are relatively short and have clearly marked sections. The Masses and Magnificats are actually only sections of those compositional types (see illustration on page 17), indicating that they were intended to alternate with passages of chant sung by the choir.

Summary

We can see that music was firmly rooted in New France from the earliest days. A vast collection of folk songs was brought over from France, and was the constant companion of most of the settlers. Portable instruments such as violins, viols, lutes, and flutes were played at simple dances, fancy balls, and theatre presentations, and even at church services where they substituted for or joined with the organ. Both Indian and French children learned to sing and read sacred music, and adult choirs sang part-music in church.

The French-Canadians brought with them the musical traditions of France—their heritage. From the beginning they adapted it to their needs and the situations of the New World. To be sure, the music heard in New France was all founded on European models, but as we have seen with the songs of the Voyageurs and the hymns sung in Indian languages, it quickly took on a distinctly Canadian flavour. Most of the music of Canada comes—as do the people—originally from other places. Our story will show how, as with the music of the early French settlers, it was changed to form a repertory uniquely Canadian.

31. See Elisabeth Gallat-Morin, "Le livre d'orgue de Montreal aperçu d'un manuscrit inédit," *Canadian University Music Review / Revue de musique des universités canadiennes,* 1(1981):1–38. Facsimile of book published as: *Le Livre d'orgue de Montreal* (Montreal: Fondation Lionel-Groulx, 1981).

2

The British Influence and Post-Conquest Quebec

The British Influence

Great Britain, as well as France, has been a major influence on Canada. Although settlers from other European countries made significant contributions, the strong national identities of France and Britain have remained the two primary sources from which Canadian culture has evolved.

There had been rivalry between France and England for control of the northeastern coastal lands from the time of their discovery; the two European powers fought constantly for New World territory. From their stronghold in Quebec, the French launched attacks as far south as New York, and the British assaulted Quebec and Acadia (Nova Scotia) with troops and ships stationed along the New England coast.[1] For various periods of time in the seventeenth century, the Brit-

The Home of Evangeline "In Acadian Land", *a colour lithograph by F. F. Palmer.*

1. There were other battlefronts in this contest, including Louisiana, a French possession. Our discussion is limited to those events that directly affected Canada.

19

ish established footholds in Acadia, and between 1629 and 1632 they gained control of Quebec. With the Treaty of Utrecht in 1713, France ceded to Britain all of Nova Scotia except Cape Breton Island. In 1755, as another war loomed between the two powers, approximately six thousand Acadians (French settlers who had remained in Nova Scotia after the 1713 treaty) were forceably removed from their homes to various communities on the southern Atlantic coast. The tragic expulsion is described in Longfellow's poem *Evangeline.*

> This is the forest primeval; but where
> are the hearts that beneath it
> Leaped like the roe, when he hears in
> the woodland the voice of the huntsman?
> Where is the thatch-roofed village, the
> home of Acadian farmers,—
> Men whose lives glided on like rivers
> that water the woodlands,
> Darkened by shadows of earth, but
> reflecting an image of heaven?
> Waste are those pleasant farms, and the
> farmers for ever departed!
> Scattered like dust and leaves, when the
> mighty blasts of October
> Seize them, and whirl them aloft, and
> sprinkle them far o'er the ocean.
> Nought but tradition remains of the
> beautiful village of Grand-Pré.[2]

In 1758 British forces captured the fort of Louisbourg on Cape Breton, and in 1759 they won a decisive battle on the Plains of Abraham at Quebec. The Treaty of Paris in 1763, marking the end of the Seven Years' War, gave Britain complete control of Canada.[3]

Soon after the Conquest, settlers from New England and Britain flocked into the Maritimes, and henceforth French influence was centred mainly in the province of Quebec. British culture, now dominant, spread westward to the Pacific from the Maritimes and Ontario.

The roots of the British influence were more broadly based than the French.

2. Henry Wadsworth Longfellow, *Evangeline: A Tale of Acadie* (reprint, New York: D. McKay, 1963).

3. Two of the musical compositions written in London to celebrate the British victory are especially noteworthy: James Nares, a composer in the Royal Chapel, wrote *A Thanksgiving Anthem for the taking Montreal and making us Masters of all Canada.* An even more ambitious work was undertaken by Franz Kotzwara (or Kočzwara), a Czech who worked in London during the second half of the eighteenth century. He began *The Siege of Quebec,* dedicated to "The Officers &c Engag'd in the Glorious Service, Sept. 10, 1759," for harpsichord or piano, accompanied by violin, cello, and timpani ad lib. Kotzwara died in 1791 before finishing the work, and *The Siege of Quebec* was completed by W. B. de Krifft. The composition describes the major events of the siege in music. It begins with a favourite song of General Wolfe, followed by a slow march, the attack with sounds of artillery and hand-to-hand combat, a lament for the death of Wolfe, and finally a march of victory. It was performed in Quebec in 1806—no doubt before an English audience! See Kallmann, *A History,* 28–29.

The French settlers had come from the same general area of northern France, and shared a common heritage. The English-speaking settlers, however, came from different countries—Scotland, Ireland, and England, and from New England where their several backgrounds had already been mixed together,[4] and they brought with them a variety of political, social, and religious experiences.

Their music included many of the same types as that of the French, although of a different flavour, and with a more extensive regional variety. There was the rich heritage of Scottish, Irish, and English folk songs and dances, ballads of various kinds, and instrument playing, much of which survives today in the small villages of most of the provinces. Common musical traits help to identify all of that music as from the British Isles, but Scottish reels, Irish jigs, and English folk songs each present individual regional characteristics. And the several different traditions of sacred music—Anglican, Presbyterian, Methodist, and Roman Catholic—each with its own sacred repertory and practices, added further variety to the Canadian musical culture.[5]

Folk Music

Folk music from the early years of the English-speaking areas of Canada is not as well documented as that from New France. Serious collecting of folk songs in the Atlantic provinces, Ontario, and the West did not begin until the early twentieth century, although many of the songs in the famous collection of Francis Child, *The English and Scottish Popular Ballads* (1882–98), were also popular in Canada.[6] But it was not until the publication of the collections of W. Roy MacKenzie in 1928, and the work of Kenneth Peacock, Helen Creighton, Edith Fowke, and others, that the extent of the English-language folk repertory became known. Partly because the collecting was left until so late, little is known about which songs were sung in the earliest years.

One song that was probably popular during the second half of the eighteenth century is *Bold Wolfe* (example II–1), a romantic tale about General James Wolfe, who died while leading the British forces in the siege of Quebec in 1759.

Example II–1: *Bold Wolfe*

Come all   ye young men_ all,   Let_ this de - light you;_   Cheer up, you young men

4. The separation of the American colonies from Britain in 1783 resulted in the immigration of about forty thousand United Empire Loyalists who settled in the Maritimes and in Upper Canada—the later British name for the Canadian territory west of Quebec.

5. Cultural life in British Canada was quite similar to that in Boston, New York, Philadelphia, and a number of other cities in the United States. See Charles Hamm, *Music in the New World* (New York: W.W. Norton, 1983), chs. 2–4; Gilbert Chase, *America's Music*, 2nd ed. (New York: McGraw Hill, 1966), chs. 1–3, 5–7; and H. Wiley Hitchcock, *Music in the United States* (Englewood Cliffs, N.J.: Prentice-Hall, 1974), chs. 1–2.

6. Francis James Child, *The English and Scottish Popular Ballads,* 5 vols. (New York: Houghton, Mifflin, 1882–98; reprint, New York: Dover, 1965).

Mort du Général Wolfe. A la Bataille de Quebeck dans l'Amerique Septentrionale le 13 7bre 1759. *Engraving after Benjamin West by A. Zassonato.*

Bold Wolfe is a strophic song without a refrain or any repeated text. The melody is hauntingly beautiful and sets the mood of eventual sadness even though the words of most of the stanzas are full of hope and optimism. There are only two phrases in the melody: the first, from the beginning to bar 4, is repeated exactly from bars 5 to 8, and again from 13 to 16, setting off the contrasting phrase in bars 9–12. The melodic shape of this basically sad song suggests a relationship with medieval folk music (as do the early French folk songs discussed in chapter 1).

The subject of *Bold Wolfe* would seem to indicate that the song comes from Canada, and yet its music bears a close resemblance to English folk music. Many other early songs were taken over from the English folk repertory, for example, *Ye Maidens of Ontario,* which was known in England as *Ye Gentlemen of England.*[7] Some folk songs from the eastern provinces bear close resemblance to songs

7. Edith Fowke, *Folk Songs of Canada* (Waterloo: Waterloo Music, 1954), 76–77.

from Ireland and Scotland, such as *The Banks of Newfoundland*[8] and *The Squid-Jiggin' Ground*,[9] both of which have the melodic character of traditional Scottish and Irish sea chanteys. When first collected in the Maritimes in the nineteenth century, they were already part of a tradition of long standing.

Dancing

Numerous accounts—mostly in diaries—leave no doubt that dancing was as popular a pastime among the English-speaking settlers as it was among the French-speaking. Elizabeth Simcoe, wife of the lieutenant governor of Upper Canada, described many dances and balls in her diary, and in a letter of February 13, 1792, she reported on the social life in Quebec:

> You cannot think what a gay place this is in winter, we do not go to half the amusements we are invited to, & yet are few days alone; a week without a Ball is an extraordinary thing & sometimes two or three in that time.[10]

We can assume that both country dances and minuets were performed on these occasions.

Dance at the Chateau St. Louis, *1801, by J. C. Stadler.*

8. In Kenneth Peacock, *Songs of the Newfoundland Outports,* 3 vols., National Museum of Canada Bulletin no. 197, Anthropological Series no. 65 (Ottawa, 1965), 1:108; Edith Fowke, ed., with Keith MacMillan, *The Penguin Book of Canadian Folk Songs* (n.p., Penguin Books, n.d.), 40; and Fowke, *Folk Songs of Canada,* 36.
  9. In Fowke, *Folk Songs of Canada,* 51.
  10. Mary Quayle Innis, *Mrs. Simcoe's Diary* (Toronto: Macmillan, 1965), 48.

During the eighteenth and nineteenth centuries "country dances" were enormously popular in English-speaking Canada at all levels of society. These folk dances, originating in the Middle Ages, had been adopted by the upper classes of England in the seventeenth century and were brought to Canada by the settlers.[11] The more formal minuet was the other prevalent dance in eighteenth-century British Canada and was all the rage at balls in the cities.

Music for the dancing was provided by amateurs as well as professional military bandsmen who played a variety of string and wind instruments, harpsichords, and the recently invented piano.

In the rural areas of Canada, as in Britain, folk dances were accompanied by fiddlers:

> At their dances [in a Scottish settlement in Canada] . . . they, however, generally prefer the old Highland fiddler . . . [the fiddle] is at all times played with the spirit and rapidity of which the Scotch reels and strathspeys are so eminently susceptible.[12]

Formal Musical Activities

The formal musical activities of the British settlements differed slightly from those of the French. In both cases, the church and the military played important roles. However, in the French communities art music was the exclusive province of the aristocrats, while in the British communities it was available to the middle classes as well. They enjoyed a unique tradition that did not exist in France—that of the coffee house, which they quickly established in their New World settlements. In these coffee houses both amateurs and professionals gave performances of ballads, opera songs, and instrumental music. These concerts, together with the eventual expansion of the church-based ensembles, became the basis of the performance tradition throughout Canada.

The various kinds of formal music in early British communities can be illustrated by examining the extant records of a typical city; for these purposes we have chosen Halifax, founded in 1749 as a naval base.

Sacred Music

The records of St. Paul's Anglican Church, written shortly after the founding of Halifax, mention its hymnal and choir, and in 1766, an organ. The hymnal, supplied by the Society for the Propagation of the Gospel in England, was probably *Hymns and Spiritual Songs* by Isaac Watts (first published in 1707). Watts'

---

11. John Playford's book *The English Dancing Master: or Plaine and easie Rules for the Dancing of Country Dances,* first published in England in 1651, gave both the music (over one hundred tunes) and the choreography for these dances. They still exist in the twentieth century as "square dances." Modern ed.: Margaret Dean-Smith, *Playford's English Dancing Master, 1651* (London: Schott, 1957). For an extended description of the eighteenth- and nineteenth-century tradition in the American colonies, see Hamm, *Music in the New World,* ch. 3.

12. John M'Gregor, *British America,* 2nd ed. (London, 1833), 2:451, quoted in Kallmann, *A History,* 37–38.

texts were set in verse form. Some were taken from various books of the Bible while others were newly written texts of a pious nature. No music was included in this collection; the verses were meant to be sung to tunes from other sources.

The psalms were also sung in Protestant churches, the texts undoubtedly from the "Sternhold and Hopkins" metrical translation.[13] Music for the psalms would have come from either of two sources: Thomas Ravenscroft's *The Whole Book of Psalms* (first published in 1621), in four-part harmony; or John Playford's *The Whole Book of Psalms* (1667), in three-part harmony. *Oxford* (examples II–2a and 2b), a favourite tune in Britain, dating back as far as 1564, is an example of a psalm tune included in both collections.[14]

Example II–2a: *Oxford,* Ravenscroft's setting

O God that art my righteousnesse,
Lord heare me when I call:
Thou hast set me at libertie
when I was bound and thrall.

13. In fact, the metrical versions of the psalms written in the sixteenth century by Thomas Sternhold and John Hopkins were added to by several different authors, but always were referred to as the "Sternhold and Hopkins" psalms. The 1562 version of the complete English psalter with all 150 psalms, printed in England by John Day, became the standard psalter, and was usually bound with the Book of Common Prayer. Hamm, *Music in the New World,* 27.

14. Richard G. Appel, *The Music of the Bay Psalm Book,* 9th ed. (1698) (New York: Institute for Studies in American Music), 5.

Example II–2b: *Oxford,* Playford's setting

O God that art my right'ousness,
Lord, hear me when I call:
Thou hast set me at liberty
When I was bound in thrall.

The two settings shown here have essentially the same melody with small variants (in example II–2a the melody is in the tenor part; in II–2b it is in the top voice), but pitched a whole step apart. Although the same version of the psalm text is used in both settings, the rhythms are quite different. Ravenscroft (II–2a) has used a rather free rhythm, reminiscent of earlier Renaissance practices—that is, the rhythms do not form regular groups—while Playford's long-short rhythm (II–2b) suggests the dance rhythms frequently used in the seventeenth century. They both contain a change in the rhythmic pace in the last four notes.

This psalm tune is in Common Metre, meaning that its four musical phrases will accommodate lines alternating between eight and six syllables, expressed as 8.6.8.6. (Other popular metres were Short Metre, 6.6.8.6., and Long Metre, 8.8.8.8.; see example II–4.)[15] Any psalm text with the same metre could be sung to this tune. Conversely, Psalm IV could be sung to any Common Metre melody; tradition allowed this kind of interchange between text and tune.

An organ was purchased from London for St. Paul's Church, and installed in 1766. Four years later the organist and choir director came under severe censure by the church "worthies" (elders). The choir director, Mr. Godfrey, was criticised for his choice of anthems, and the organist, Viere Warner, both for his choice of instrumental selections (voluntaries), and for his improvisations while playing the psalm tunes.[16]

15. See Hamm, *Music in the New World,* 28. For a more detailed explanation of metre in psalms, see *ibid.,* 26–30.

16. Voted that whereas the Anthems Sung by the Clerk [Godfrey] and the others in the Gallery

Oxford *from the* Bay Psalm Book, *1698.*

The organist apparently improvised around the melodies of the anthems and psalm tunes in a way that distracted and confused the congregation who were trying to sing. (The same reason was given for Johann Sebastian Bach's dismissal from his position at Arnstadt in 1707.) The voluntaries Warner played were short, free compositions that were commonly performed in church in Britain, but evidently some of them were not serious enough for the congregation at St. Paul's.

The other major church in Halifax, the Presbyterian "dissenters" church of St. Matthew, was founded in part as a protest against the Anglican adoption of the Catholic practice of using an organ. St. Matthew's congregation followed the Scottish custom of a "kirk fiddle" (in this case, a cello) for accompaniment of the singing during service. Their hymnal was Watts' *Hymns and Spiritual Songs,* used until 1853. Since the ministers at St. Matthew's were supplied from

---

during Divine Serivce have not Answered the intention of raising the Devotion of the congregation to the Honour and Glory of [God], in as much as the Major Part of the Congregation do not understand either the Words or the Musick and cannot join therin,

Therefore for the future the clerk have express orders not to Sing any such Anthems, or leave his usual Seat without directions have first [been] Obtained from the Reverend Mr. Breynton.

Voted that whereas: also the Organist discovers a light mind in the several tunes he plays, called Voluntaries to the great offence of the Congregation, and tending to disturb, rather than promote true Devotion.

Therefore he be directed for the Future to make a choice of such his Voluntaries, and that he also for the future be directed to play the Psalm Tunes in a plain Familiar Manner without unnecessary Graces.

St. Paul's Church Records, vol. 1. For additional information about the records of these early years see Timothy J. McGee, "Music in Halifax, 1749–1799," *The Dalhousie Review* 49 (1969):377–87; Reginald V. Harris, *The Church of Saint Paul in Halifax, Nova Scotia: 1749–1949* (Toronto: Ryerson, 1949); and Frederick A. Hall, "Musical Life in Eighteenth-Century Halifax," *Canadian University Music Reveiw* 4 (1983):278–307.

Boston until 1787, the version of psalm texts (and probably tunes) they used was undoubtedly *The Whole Booke of Psalmes Faithfully Translated into English Metre*, the first book printed in British North America.

The "Bay Psalm Book," as *The Whole Booke* was known, represented the combined efforts of a number of Puritan clergymen in Boston (the Bay Colony). It was published in 1640 and was widely used not only in North America but also in Britain. By 1773 there had been seventy North American editions, and numerous editions in England and Scotland. The early editions of the Bay Psalm Book contained texts only; the psalms were to be sung to the tunes in Ravenscroft's book. The ninth edition of 1698, however, contained a supplement of psalm tunes, borrowed from John Playford's *A Brief Introduction to the Skill of Musick;* see also example II–3.[17]

Example II–3: *Oxford,* "Bay Psalm Book" setting

God of my justice, when I call,
O hear me: when distrest
Thou hast inlarg'd me shew me grace,
and hear thou my request.

The "Oxford" melody used in the Bay Psalm Book is similar to that found in both of the examples cited earlier (example II–2a, tenor part, example II–2b, top part), as is the bass line. But the rhythms of the Bay Psalm Book version are much more regular, and the translation of the psalm text is different from that used in the earlier settings. The bass line would have been played on the "kirk fiddle," while the congregation sang the melody.

In this collection, too, the same tune was intended to be sung with different psalm texts. According to the prefatory notes, *Oxford* and two other tunes were to be sung "to psalms consolatory" as opposed to others designated "to psalms of prayer, confession, and funerals," or "to psalms of praise and thanksgiving."[18] The congregation could memorize the few tunes that were commonly used so that it was not difficult to sing the psalm texts to whichever tune was assigned.

A number of other hymn and psalm collections were in use in both the American colonies and Canada, although none were as popular as those already mentioned. One collection used in Baptist congregations of New Brunswick and Nova Scotia was *Hymns and Spiritual Songs* (Boston, 1786) by Henry Alline,

17. See Appel, *Music of the Bay Psalm Book*, 1–5.
18. From the final page of the Bay Psalm Book, reproduced *ibid.*, 2.

an Evangelical preacher who travelled widely in the Maritime provinces and New England.[19]

Another collection was *Urania, or a choice collection of psalm-tunes, anthems and hymns* . . . (Philadelphia, 1761), collected by James Lyon. Lyon was a missionary from Princeton, New Jersey, who served as a minister in various parts of Nova Scotia from 1765 to 1771. It is probable that his congregation in Pictou sang from his collection, and perhaps it was used when he preached from time to time at St. Matthew's in Halifax.[20]

Military Bands

Military bandsmen have played an important role in music making in Halifax and elsewhere in Canada from the eighteenth century until very recently. Stationed at all major military garrisons, they were well trained in Britain. They constituted a steady source of music teachers and participated in civilian ensembles. Their high standards of performance have served as models for Canadians for generations.

The regimental bands stationed in Halifax during the last half of the eighteenth century typically not only supplied music for military activities but also often played at various civic ceremonies. The Nova Scotia *Chronicle* reported in 1770 that "two bands of music" travelled to St. Paul's church for the celebration of the feast of St. John the Baptist (June 24).[21] In 1789 "the Final Chorus of the Messiah and the Coronation Anthem by Handel" were performed at a church service by "several gentlemen and the music Bands of the Regiments who played with the organ."[22] And after the arrival at Halifax in 1794 of Prince Edward Augustus, later the duke of Kent, his regimental band played promenade concerts each Saturday morning.

Concert Programmes

Members of the bands frequently joined with citizens of the city in presenting concerts. The programme for one such concert, advertised in the *Royal Gazette* in 1790, indicates the type of music heard in Halifax forty years after its founding:

Act 1

Overture, composed by Toeschi
Quartetto, ditto Davaux
A Song of Dibdin—*Was I a Shepherd's Main to keep*, [sung by] Mrs. Mechtler
Overture, composed by Bach

end of the 1st act

19. See George A. Rawlyk, ed., *New Light Letters and Spiritual Songs, 1778–1793* (Hantsport, Nova Scotia: Lancelot Press, 1983).

20. Oscar Sonneck, *Francis Hopkinson, the first American poet-composer (1737–1791), and James Lyon, Patriot, Preacher, Psalmodist (1735–1794: Two Studies in Early American Music* (Washington, D.C., 1905; reprint, New York: Da Capo, 1967).

21. Nova Scotia *Chronicle,* August 7, 1770.

22. *Royal Gazette,* May 26, 1789.

Act 2nd

Overture composed by Mebes
Giordani's *Ronda of Heart Beating*—by Mrs. Mechtler
Quartetto, of Avisons

end of Act 2d

A concerto on the Harpsichord—by the Master of the 20th Band

Act 3d

Overture by Abel
A song, by Mrs. Mechtler
Quartetto, by Vanhall
A favourite Song out of *Rosina*—by Mrs. Mechtler
The Concert to conclude with an Overture of Bach's[23]

Most concerts comprised similar mixtures of arias, ballads, and instrumental works. Typical programmes from the last decade of the eighteenth century include works by J. C. Bach, Stamitz, Abel, Pleyel, Pichl, and Kotzwara, some of the most popular composers in Europe at that time. Concerts were held at "the Coffee-House," the usual place for any large social gathering, including balls and theatre productions.[24]

Theatre

The presentation of dramatic works began in the 1780s, and from newspaper advertisements, we know they included songs and dancing. This practice followed the popular British tradition of the time, in which instrumental and vocal music was performed before, during, and after dramatic productions. Musical works known as ballad operas (operas made up of relatively simple songs, tied together with spoken dialogue), such as *Rosina* by William Shield, and *No Song, No Supper* by Stephen Storace (both British composers), were performed in Halifax shortly after 1791, and in 1798 André Grétry's opéra comique *Richard Coeur-de-Lion* was performed. It was the custom to hold "a Ball for the Ladies and Gentlemen" immediately after concerts and dramatic productions.

Other Activities

Evidence of other musical activities in Halifax can be found in newspaper advertisements beginning as early as three years after the founding of the city. Dancing lessons were already available in 1752, and in 1761 Jacob Althus advertised in the *Halifax Gazette* that he taught "German flute, violin, French horn, Hautboy [oboe], Basson [sic], or any other instrument of the like kind."[25] Dur-

23. *Royal Gazette,* September 28, 1790. A similar programme was presented in Boston in 1771; see Hamm, *Music in the New World,* 84–85.

24. The advertisements frequently give the location of events as simply "the Coffee House," probably referring to a specific establishment. But coffee houses were popular in Halifax from as early as 1751, and many of them offered entertainment. See Hall, "Eighteenth-Century Halifax," 287–97.

25. May 21, 1761.

ing those same decades there were also advertisements for the sale of musical instruments and books containing various kinds of music, such as "Scots tunes" and sonatas by Haydn, Boccherini, and Stamitz. Among the notices of voice lessons was one placed by Reuben M'Farlen in 1791, offering to teach the rules of psalmody.

Post-Conquest Quebec

After 1763 the city of Quebec was for all intents and purposes two distinct social entities: one French, one British. The French, far larger in population, kept to themselves but continued to present concerts, plays, and dances as they had before the Conquest. The British quickly established a society of their own similar to that in Halifax, and distinct from that of the French. Thus, concerts and theatre were separately developed by the two main groups in Quebec City (the settlers from elsewhere—Germany, for example—mixed with both major groups). Mrs. Simcoe, however, mentions attending a performance of Molière's *Le Médecin malgré lui* in 1792, performed by "some Canadian Gentlemen,"[26] so evidently the English-speaking population occasionally attended French theatre productions.

Concerts

Although scattered bits of information indicate that the French continued to have an active musical life, most of what is known of formal music making in Quebec after the Conquest is from British accounts. These generally indicate a heavy reliance on the musicians of the military bands. One function of the bands was to perform concerts in the open air, as described in the accounts of a visitor in 1785:

> We went at 7 o'clock to the Parade, a spacious opening made for Place d'Armes. Here we saw the 53rd Regiment and the 65th, which are in garrison here. . . . [The 65th] have an elegant band of music. The 53rd have one also, but not equal to the other. (11 August)

> In the evening we took a walk upon the ramparts and parade. . . . The music of the two bands and the company of so many officers must be a very great inducement for preferring this place to any other. (13 August)[27]

In 1791 Prince Edward Augustus arrived in Quebec with his band of the Royal Fusiliers, and he encouraged his musicians to perform there, as he did later in Halifax. One of his more enterprising musicians, Sieur Jouve, immediately set about selling music, promoting concerts, and offering lessons in voice, harp, cello, and French guitar. The programme for one of the concerts he organized was announced in the Quebec *Gazette* for 21 February, 1792:

26. Innis, *Mrs. Simcoe's Dairy*, 51.
27. Joseph A. Hadfield, *An Englishman in America, 1785*, ed. Douglas S. Robertson (Toronto: Hunter-Rose, 1933).

Premier Acte

Ouverture d'*Iphigenie*, Musique de Gluck
Second Quatuor, de Jouve
Ariettes Boufonnes d'Opéras Comique, avec
    accompagnement de Guitare Française
Pièce d'Harmonie, pour Clarinet et Basson oblige
Duo de Blaise et Babet, par Glackmeyer [sic] et Jouve
Carillon des Cloches de France, à grande
    orchestra, Musique de Jouve

Second Acte

Ouverture de *Panurge*, Musique de Grétry
Ariette du Soldat lassé des alarmes de la Guerre,
    qui a été redemandée, chanté par Jouve
Concerto de Cor de Chasse par Rhen
Une Scéne et Ariette d'Atis, avec accompagnement de Harpe
Le Sommeil d'Atis avec Harpe, chanté par
    Messieurs Bently, Glackmeyer et Jouve
Le Concert sera terminé par la Grande Chacoune de
    Cephale et Procris, musique de Grétry[28]

Like the Halifax programme of 1790, this ambitious amalgam clearly demonstrates that it was the custom in Quebec to mix vocal and instrumental music. And although this concert was performed by the British band, the compositions and the language of the programme are French, suggesting cooperation between the French- and English-speaking communities in public presentations.

In addition to being the organizer and promoter of the concert, Jouve is represented on the programme as composer, singer, and instrumentalist. Versatility was obviously a requirement for anyone wishing to make a career in music during those years.

Frédéric-Henri Glackemeyer

The career of Frédéric Glackemeyer (Hanover, 1751–Quebec City, 1836) is a good example of the life of an eighteenth-century musician in Canada. Arriving in Quebec in 1776 from Hanover as bandmaster in one of the Brunswick mercenary regiments, he stayed on to perform, teach, and repair instruments, and eventually to sell instruments and music. Glackemeyer played viol, violin, and keyboard instruments (see concert programme above), and he is known to have written several compositions, including the march *Châteauguay*, inspired by the Canadian repulsion of an American invasion at Châteauguay in 1813.

To earn a living as a professional musician he served as organist at the Quebec Basilica, and taught violin and piano to girls and ladies during the day and violin and viol three nights a week to men. He organized concerts and played in the theatre orchestra. In 1820 he founded the Quebec Harmonic Society, a group

28. Kallmann, *A History*, 59–60.

dedicated to presenting concerts, that functioned intermittently throughout most of the nineteenth century.

Glackemeyer imported music from Europe for performance by Quebec musicians. We can gain some idea of his taste and the contemporary level of performance ability from a collection of music that exists today in the Laval University Library. Glackemeyer's imports formed the basis of the approximately two hundred sets of performance parts that include string quartets by Haydn, Mozart, Abel, and Gossec, and symphonies by Abel, J. C. Bach, and Stamitz.

Other Cities and Settlements

Smaller cities and settlements were even more dependent upon the musicians of the military garrison. In Montreal and Niagara the military band played "on parade" (in the evening on the village green) regularly during the summer months. The military officers sponsored many of the balls throughout the year with music provided by the bandsmen. The redoubtable Mrs. Simcoe provides a description of daily life in Niagara in her 1793 diary entry:

> Immediately after I have dined I rise from table one of the Officers attends me home & the Band plays on the parade before the House till 6 o'clock. The Music adds cheerfulness to this retired spot.[29]

In the last decade of the eighteenth century, Niagara-on-the-Lake (then called Newark) became the political centre of Upper Canada. It was in fact only a small village, but the presence of the military brought to the settlement a high degree of social sophistication. In addition to the description above by the wife of the lieutenant governor, we have the words of another of the settlers, Hannah Jarvis, who tells of one of the fortnightly balls:

> At six o'clock we assembled at the Place appointed—when I was called to open the Ball—Mrs. Hamilton not choosing to dance a minuet—this is the first assembly that I have been at in this country that was opened with a Minuet—not one in the room followed my example—of course Country Dances commenced—and continued until Eleven when supper was announced . . . supper being ended the Company returned to the Ball Room when two Dances finished the night's entertainment with the sober Part of the Company. The rest stayed until Daylight and would have stayed longer if their Servants had not drank less than their Masters.[30]

Newspaper advertisements in Saint John, New Brunswick, offering musical instruments and lessons indicate the presence of a fairly high level of musical activity in that city. Stephen Humbert, a loyalist from New Jersey, arrived there in 1783, and eventually opened a singing school. In 1801 he published a collec-

29. John Simcoe, lieutenant governor of Upper Canada, and his wife first arrived in Canada in Quebec where they spent seven months—November 1791 to June 1792. They then moved to Niagara-on-the-Lake (Newark), the temporary capital of the new province, and later to Toronto (York).

30. Quoted in Elizabeth Crysler, "Musical Life in Present Day Niagara-on-the-Lake in the late Eighteenth and Nineteenth Centuries," M.A. thesis, Carleton University, 1981, 5.

tion of sacred music: *Union Harmony, or British America's Sacred Vocal Musick;* music by the "most approved English and American Composers, with some original Musick on special occasions." No copies of the first edition have survived, but later editions contained three- and four-part settings, including some by Humbert himself.[31]

Some of the works in Humbert's collection were "fuging tunes," a type of sacred setting that includes a section in which the voice parts enter one at a time. Fuging tunes were popular in the United States at the time; some of the best examples of the style were written by the New England composer William Billings.[32]

Example II–4: Daniel Read, *Greenwich*

31. Kallmann, *A History*, 43–44.
32. See Hamm, *Music in the New World*, ch. 6.

Example II–4 illustrates the two typical kinds of settings in Humbert's *Union Harmony;* the first fifteen bars are written in the usual style with the voices moving along more or less simultaneously. In bar 16 the "fuging" section begins, in which the voice parts enter one at a time, each starting with the melody, in the style of a baroque fugue. Like the Ravenscroft and Bay Psalm Book examples seen above (examples II–2a and II–3), the melody is in the tenor part throughout. The text is in Long Metre (L.M.).

The *Union Harmony* was widely used in Canada, and editions appeared in 1816, 1831, and 1840. It served as the standard hymnal for many of the Canadian Methodist congregations until the second half of the nineteenth century.

Composition

Musical composition in Canada during those years was totally an amateur endeavour, that is, it was an avocation rather than a vocation. Talented individuals regularly wrote songs and song texts to entertain their friends, although few ever attempted it seriously.

Joseph Quesnel

One of the most talented amateur composers at the end of the eighteenth century was Joseph Quesnel (St.-Malo, France, ca. 1746–Montreal, 1809). His immigration to Canada resulted from the capture of his ship in 1779 off the coast of Nova Scotia, while it was delivering munitions from Bordeaux to New York. He settled in Boucherville (near Montreal), where he established himself as an exporter of furs and importer of wine.

Quesnel was a cultured gentleman who played the violin and wrote poetry, songs, motets, quartets, symphonies, and ballad operas. It is unfortunate that most of his music has been lost with the exception of the vocal parts of his two ballad operas, *Colas et Colinette,* and *Lucas et Cécile.*

Quesnel's *Colas et Colinette* was probably the first opera composed in North America. Written in 1788, it was premiered in Montreal in 1790 by the Théâtre de Société, a theatrical production group formed by Quesnel and several others. The composer called it a "comedy in prose intermixed with ariettes," an accurate description of a play with songs—much like the comic operas popular in France at that time (for example, works by Le Sage and Duni). In the tradition of *opéra comique,* the plot of *Colas et Colinette* is delivered in spoken dialogue—there is no recitative—and there are fourteen musical numbers: short ariettes (songs), duos, and a final four-part chorus sung by the complete cast of five (the lowest part is doubled—see Anthology #1).

The individual songs of *Colas et Colinette* are simply constructed in phrases of regular lengths, as in "Cher protecteur," example II–5, where the phrase lengths of the first section are eight + eight + four bars. The settings are all syllabic, and there are no virtuoso demands made on the singers.

Example II–5: Joseph Quesnel, "Cher protecteur" from *Colas et Colinette*

(Dearest protector of my childhood, for you alone I offer with thanks posies my hands have lovingly made to be a token of gratitude.)

Other than the vocal score and libretto, only the second violin part of the ballad opera survives, but that is enough to give us a good idea of Quesnel's compositional style. The melodies themselves suggest that his harmonies are uncomplicated. This is confirmed in the four-part finale of *Colas* and in the three- and four-part vocal numbers that are extant from his other opera, *Lucas et Cécile* (written sometime after *Colas*).

In "Rions chantons," Anthology #1, we can see again the straightforward musical construction that we find in "Cher protecteur." The harmonies of "Rions chantons" remain completely within the bounds of the key of F major, changing to the dominant, C major, from bars 31 to 49, and returning to the original key for the ending. Even without seeing a complete set of the orchestra parts we can be certain that Quesnel did not venture to any distant harmonies.

The objective of *Colas* was that of all ballad operas—simple entertainment. A contemporary newspaper review records the success of the work: "The piece pleases at first, then it charms, and then delights."[33]

Quesnel's operas exemplify the spirit of musical theatre entertainments established in 1607 by Marc Lescarbot's *Théâtre de Neptune* and continued throughout the seventeenth and eighteenth centuries in the *réceptions* and theatrical entertainments produced in Upper and Lower Canada in both the French- and English-speaking communities.[34]

Summary

By the end of the eighteenth century a rather diverse cultural life was available to the middle- and upper-class inhabitants of the larger Canadian cities: promenade concerts by the military bands, coffee-house concerts combining the talents of the local citizens and the military instrumentalists, formal balls, and theatrical productions of various types. In the smaller towns, villages, and outposts the secular music was more limited, consisting mainly of folk songs and dances. And everywhere there was music in churches.

The vast majority of musical activity during those years was re-creative rather ⌐ than creative. The compositions of Joseph Quesnel in Montreal were unusual in North America for such a small town. (There were composers writing similarly large works in the major cities of the United States such as Boston and New York.) The more prevalent amateur compositional effort was the simple song— a product that more closely answered the needs and tastes of the citizens.

At the close of the second century of settlement we can see that the Canadians were determined to enjoy a rich cultural life. A handful of gifted and ambitious amateurs and professionals, such as Jouve, Glackemeyer, and Quesnel, provided original works and the finest in European imports; the military bandsmen who cooperated with the citizens supplied the highly professional performances; and the spirit of the early Canadians who found time for music, dance, and theatre in the midst of building a country in the wilderness persisted and thrived.

33. *EMC*, 205c–6b. In 1963 the opera was reconstructed by Godfrey Ridout, English translation by Ridout and S. Lecavalier, published by Gordon V. Thompson in 1974. An abridged recording was made in 1968: RCI 234/Select CC.15.001 and SSC-24-160.

34. It should be noted, however, that *Colas et Colinette* differs from the earlier mentioned productions in that it was meant solely as entertainment rather than to mark a specific event.

3

Nineteenth Century to Confederation

During the nineteenth century the continuous westward expansion resulted in the broadening of Canada's commercial base and a shift in its enlarging population centres. These developments were accompanied by a growing interest in independence.

British exploration of the territory west of Upper Canada (Ontario) had gone forward at an accelerated pace in the last decades of the eighteenth century. British Columbia was discovered by Captain James Cook, who arrived by ship via Cape Horn in 1778; in 1793 Alexander Mackenzie reached the west coast by an overland route. As the nineteenth century progressed, outposts were established along the routes west from Ontario, and Montreal and Toronto became increasingly important as centres of trade, rivalling the ocean port cities on the east coast.

Canals were built along the St. Lawrence River in the early decades of the century when merchants began to realize their ambitions for a commercial empire around the Great Lakes, centred in Montreal. In 1796 Toronto (then the military settlement of York) became the permanent seat of government, and by the mid-nineteenth century it challenged Montreal in size. The economy was now based on exports of lumber and grain, replacing fur trading as the major source of commerce. The new products came from the northern and western areas, and were directed through the ports of Montreal and Toronto to Saint John and Halifax for shipment to Britain.

Violent threats to Canada's status occurred from both within and without. The 1812 war between the United States and Britain endangered Upper and Lower Canada. The presence of the British navy kept the Atlantic provinces safe, but the interior areas were vulnerable to American attack. Newark (Niagara-on-the-Lake) and York (Toronto) were captured by the Americans and partially destroyed, but the bravery of General Isaac Brock in the face of a much larger American army inspired the Upper Canadians to unite, and eventually the Americans abandoned their attempt to capture Canada.

Internal threats came in the form of rebellions. In Lower Canada (Quebec), French-English conflicts led to political polarization, and the French-Canadians formed L'Association des Fils de la Liberté under the leadership of Louis Joseph Papineau. Radicals agitated for insurrection in response to political moves made by the British-appointed governor, and in 1837 the government ordered their arrest for sedition. After a few skirmishes with the British troops, Papineau and his followers escaped to the United States in defeat.

Canada in 1851 according to Tallis's Illustrated Atlas.

In Upper Canada (Ontario) the political unrest was based on a number of explosive issues. William Lyon Mackenzie, mayor of the newly chartered city of Toronto, led a small group of radicals demanding the end of colonial status, and when news of Papineau's rebellion reached Toronto, Mackenzie's group attempted to capture the government. This uprising ended, as had the other, in the exile of the rebels to the United States. It would seem that both rebellions ended in victory for the British rulers, but the warning was clear: the Canadian colonists were developing political strength. Supported by a growing economy based upon rich natural resources, Canada was rapidly changing from a collection of small colonial settlements into a country with an increasing interest in self-determination.[1]

Musical life during the first two-thirds of the nineteenth century was slow to change from that described in the first two chapters. It continued to revolve around the local church, the coffee house, and, in the larger centres, the military band. The musicians in each locale joined together to perform, and as their numbers grew, they formed larger ensembles. What we shall note in this chapter, therefore, is not so much a change in the activities themselves as in their size, number, and quality. There was still very little exchange between Canadian cities. Culture was entirely local so that the quantity and quality of the music in any area depended almost entirely upon the individual abilities and ambitions of the musicians living there.

1. Material for the above paragraphs taken from John S. Moir and Robert E. Saunders, *Northern Destiny* (n.p., 1970), chs. 10–15.

Music in Church

Protestant Congregations

During this time there were gradual changes in the music sung by many of the congregations. The basic repertory in Protestant churches during the first sixty years of the nineteenth century consisted of the psalms and hymns described earlier, although by mid-century psalm singing had lost much of its popularity. The hymn collections in use initially included both British and American publications, but as the century progressed, more and more Canadian hymn books appeared; there were at least fifteen different collections published in Canada between 1801 (Humbert's *Union Harmony*) and Confederation.[2] Canadian hymnals soon gained wide circulation and eventually replaced the imported ones.

Hymnals published in Canada followed either the American or the British model. Those based on the United States books placed the melody in the tenor voice and included fuging tunes; Humbert's book was the most popular publication of this type (see example II–4). It contains compositions by some of the most famous "Yankee tunesmiths," such as Timothy Swan, Daniel Read, and William Billings. These and other United States composers were well known in Canada throughout the first half of the century, for their works appeared in numerous collections. Of special interest is *Sacred Harmony: Consisting of a Variety of Tunes, Adapted to the Different Metres in the Wesleyan-Methodist Hymn-Book and a few anthems and Favourite Pieces; Selected from the most Approved Authors, Ancient and Modern, under the direction of the conference of the Wesleyan Methodist Church in Canada by Alexander Davidson,* first published in 1838 with several later editions. This was the only Canadian hymn collection to adopt the United States shape-note format, a visual aid to sight-singing, in which the notes are given separate shapes to signify their place in the scale. An octave scale was divided into two groups of three notes each, having corresponding signs, plus a seventh note with a sign of its own:

ascending scale	1	2	3	4	5	6	7	8
sol-fa syllables	fa	sol	la	fa	sol	la	mi	fa . . .

(see example III–1).[3] The shape-note idea did not catch on in Canada, and was not included in other Canadian publications.

Hymnals based on the British model with the melody in the top voice were less popular in the first half of the century. George Jenkins' *A Selection from the Psalms of David*, published in Montreal in 1821, is of this type, and is based on Miller and Drummond's *The Psalms of David*.[4] Canadians also copied the Brit-

---

2. See Barclay McMillan, "Tune-book Imprints in Canada to 1867: A Descriptive Bibliography," *Papers of the Bibliographical Society of Canada* 16 (1977).

3. For more on shape-note hymns, see Hamm, *Music in the New World,* 264–78. Information for this section is taken from the *EMC* articles "Hymnbooks, Protestant" and "Hymn Singing," and from "Protestant Hymnbooks of 19th-Century Canada," an unpublished paper by John Beckwith.

4. First published in 1790.

ish customs of adapting works by composers such as Mozart, Handel, and Bee- thoven. An excerpt from Mozart's *The Marriage of Figaro*, for example, would be given a sacred text.

In Canadian hymnals, both original and adapted melodies often had local names such as the following found in Davidson's *Sacred Harmony: Belleville, Port Hope*, and *Niagara*.[5]

Example III–1: *Niagara*

1. My heart and voice I raise, To spread Mes - si - ah's praise; Mes - si - ah's praise let all re - peat; The u - ni - versal

Lord, By whose al - mighty word Cre - a - tion rose in form complete.

Niagara bears the marking "P.M.," indicating that it is in "Particular Metre," that is, a metrical scheme that is not usual. The setting of the melody in the tenor voice is evidence of United States influence, but the simplicity of the part writing (i.e., the absence of fuging style), with simultaneous movement in all voices and short phrases, reflects the prevailing British style.

After mid-century, Canadian hymnals contained some of the new "gospel songs," hymns with more sentimental texts and more chromatic music (for example, *What a Friend We Have in Jesus*), reflecting the current taste in pop- ular ballads.

Singing Schools

Singing, especially of psalms, was cultivated in many locations by the estab- lishment of singing schools. This was a familiar tradition in New England in the eighteenth century that gradually took hold in Canada, principally in the Mari- times. The first known singing master was Amasa Braman from Connecticut,

5. Crysler, "Niagara-on-the-Lake," 91–92.

who taught psalm singing in Liverpool, Nova Scotia, from 1776 to 1778. Stephen Humbert opened a Sacred Vocal Music School in Saint John in 1796, and numerous schools—most of them short-lived—were opened in Canadian cities throughout the nineteenth century. They taught the rudiments of music, using texts issued as separate publications or appended to hymn and psalm collections. For example, the "Introduction to the Science of Music," a section at the beginning of Davidson's *Sacred Harmony,* contained instructions on pitch, rhythm, the staff, clefs, scales, modulation, elementary rules of harmony, and a glossary of musical terms—all in fifteen pages!

Catholic Church Music

Music in the Roman Catholic church consisted of both chant and hymns. In 1800 *Le Graduel romain* was published in Quebec, followed by *Le Processional romain* in 1801, and *Le Vespéral romain* in 1802. All were books of chant for the liturgical services, and included square notation (see illustration on page 27). Modelled on the traditional French service, they included chants composed or adapted for the diocese of Quebec, such as that by Charles-Amador Martin for *La Fête de la Ste. Famille.*

Many of the hymns sung in the Roman Catholic churches were adaptations of secular songs; others were newly composed. A collection of texts only was published in 1795 (Jean-Baptiste Boucher-Belleville's *Recueil de cantiques des missions, des retraites et des catéchismes*); in 1819 Rev. Jean-Denis Daulé published another set of texts, *Nouveau Recueil de cantiques à l'usage du diocèse de Québec,* with a separate compilation of over two hundred tunes.[6]

Along with each text is the name of one or more tunes that may be used in the service. These tunes are a mixture of folk songs, classical airs, and some newly composed music in both styles. Example III–2 is one of the sacred texts that is to be sung to the air *Ah! vous dirai-je, maman,* better known today as *Twinkle, twinkle, little star,* a favourite French folk tune.

Example III–2: *O digne objet de mes chants*

O digne ob-jet de__ mes_ chants, daigne é - cou - ter mes_ ac - cens: C'est par
Rè-gne à ja-mais sur__ mon coeur. T'ai-mer c'est tout mon_ bon - heur.

toi que je__ res - pi - re: C'est pour toi que je__ sou - pi - re:

> O worthy object of my songs,
> Deign to listen to my pleas:
> It is for you that I long;
> It is for you that I sigh;

6. Kallmann, *A History,* 42–43.

View of Quebec, *a drawing by Captain B. Beaufoy.*

> Reign forever in my heart.
> To love you is all my joy.
> *etc.*

Another text, a dialogue between an angel and a shepherd, is to be sung to *Une jeune pucelle,* the folk tune used as the model for the Huron carol *Jesous Ahatonhia* (see chapter 1, pp. 13–14).

Popular Music

Throughout the nineteenth and into the twentieth century the music most often heard in Canada consisted of folk songs and ballads. Folk songs were sung, as before, in informal settings, and many were adopted into the repertory of the British military bands.[7] Ballads were sung at home, in the theatre, and in concerts. The term "ballad" can be somewhat confusing since it has several meanings and is used for a rather broad range of songs—including some folk songs. For simplicity's sake, I shall use "ballad" to refer to popular songs that were composed and written down as distinct from the folk repertory that was circulated orally and not originally notated.[8]

French-Canadian Folk Songs

It was during the mid-nineteenth century that the French-Canadian folk song repertory was first gathered. After a few small collections appeared in the first

7. McMillan, "Music in Canada 1791–1867," 39.
8. For a discussion of the various kinds of ballads, see *EMC*, 49c–50b.

half of the century, Ernest Gagnon published the first scholarly compilation of Quebec folk songs, *Chansons populaires du Canada,* in 1865. There were 104 songs in this collection, and several editions of it were widely circulated both in Canada and in France. Gagnon was unusual for his time in that he notated the songs as he heard them, rather than adding harmonic settings or "correcting" their modal scales and rhythmic irregularities, as many other nineteenth-century collectors had done.

Most of the folk repertory, as we have seen, originated in France as early as the Middle Ages, but there were some significant nineteenth-century Canadian additions. It was especially common to provide a new Canadian text; for example, the words for *Un Canadien errant* were written to replace the original Provençal *Si tu te mets anguille* (also known in Canada as *Par derrièr' chez ma tante*).[9]

Example III–3: *Un Canadien errant*

Par derrièr' chez ma tante   Il lui ya-t-un étang. — Un Ca - na - dien er - rant ban - ni de ses foy - ers

Je me met - trai an - guille, an - guil - le dans l'é - tang — Par - cour - ait en pleur - ant des pays é - tran - gers

Par derrièr' chez ma tante	Behind my aunt's house
Il lui ya-t-un étang.	There is a pond.
Je me mettrai anguille,	I shall become an eel,
Anguille dans l'étang.	An eel in the pond.
Si tu te mets anguille,	If you become an eel,
Anguille dans l'étang,	An eel in the pond,
Je me mettrai pêcheur:	I will become a fisherman:
Je t'aurai en pêchant.	I will catch you, fishing.
Si tu te mets pêcheur	If you become a fisherman,
Pour m'avoir en pêchant,	to catch me, fishing,
Je me mettrai allouette,	I shall become a meadowlark,
Allouette dans les champs.	Meadowlark in the fields.

etc.

Un Canadien errant,	A wandering Canadian
Banni de ses foyers,	Banished from his home
Parcourait en pleurant	Travelled, weeping,
Des pays étrangers,	Through foreign lands.

9. Ernest Gagnon, *Chansons populaires du Canada* (Montreal: Beauchemin, 1865), 81–82.

Un jour, triste et pensif,	One day, sad and thoughtful,
Assis au bord des flots,	Sitting at the water's edge,
Au courant fugitif	To the fleeting stream
Il adressa ces mots:	He addressed these words:

"Si tu vois mon pays,	"If you should see my homeland,
Mon pays malheureux,	My unhappy homeland,
Va, dis à mes amis	Go, tell my friends
Que je me souviens d'eux.	I do remember them.

English translations by
Leonard Doucette

Un Canadien errant concerns the plight of soldiers who were exiled for taking part in the 1837 political uprisings led by Mackenzie in Upper Canada and Papineau in Lower Canada. The words were written by Antoine Gérin-Lajoie:

> I wrote it in 1842 when I was taking my classical exams at Nicolet. I did it one night in bed at the request of my friend Cyp Pinard, who wanted a song to the tune of "Par derrière chez ma tante."[10]

The new words were first published in 1844, and later by Gagnon, who reported that the song was known in the far reaches of the Northwest. A short time later, the descendants of the expelled Acadians adopted Gérin-Lajoie's text with its reference to a far-away homeland, and set them to the Gregorian hymn tune *Ave Maris Stella,* thus creating a curious circle in which a medieval melody *Si tu te mets anguille* received nineteenth-century words *(Un Canadien errant),* which were then extracted and set to a different medieval melody *(Ave Maris Stella)!*

The words for *Vive la canadienne* (example I–3) were substituted for the original French *Par derrièr' chez mon père* early in the century, and in 1840 a piano arrangement of the song was published as *The Canadian / a French Air.*[11] The song became a favourite theme for variations, beginning with *Les Bords du St. Lawrence [sic] Brilliant variations on the Canadian national melody "Vive la canadienne".* by Charles Grobe, in 1859. The melody was also frequently used for salon music in arrangements for various instruments, and it served as a national song in Quebec until the composition of *O Canada* in 1880. It is still the regimental march of the 22 ème Régiment.

Other songs, such as *C'est dans la vill' de Bailtonne* (example III–4), have only a single Canadian text (Bailtonne or Bytown was the original name for Ottawa). We can be sure that the text is Canadian, but the melody has a modal flavour similar to the older folk tunes; Gagnon did not know if the melody was also by a Canadian, or if an old French tune had been borrowed.[12] In either case, *Vive la canadienne* and *C'est dans la vill' de Bailtonne* are examples of how the French folk song tradition was transformed in Canada.

10. *EMC,* 155b,c.
11. In *Literary Garland.* See *EMC,* 980b.
12. Gagnon, *Chansons populaires,* 66–67.

The Ottawa River at Bytown *from a drawing by W. H. Bartlett*

Example III–4: *C'est dans la vill' de Bailtonne*

It's in the town of Bytown
Where I once paid a visit;
Where there are pretty girls
Who are perfect and kind;
But there's one of them above all
That they say I make love to.

English translation by Leonard Doucette

Anglo-Canadian Folk Songs

Many of the Anglo-Canadian folk songs also come from the nineteenth century, either as original creations, or as new texts for old tunes. *Donkey Riding* (example III–5) is a sailor's song from the ships that transported lumber from Quebec to Glasgow and Liverpool, and refers to the "donkey" engine that winched the timber on board. It was adapted in the early nineteenth century from the Scottish *Highland Laddie*.[13]

Example III–5: *Donkey Riding*

The *Shantyman's Life* (example III–6) is of the same period, probably from New Brunswick. Although the words were very likely written in Canada, the melody suggests derivation from an Irish folk song.[14]

Example III–6: *The Shantyman's Life*

Many Anglo-Canadian songs have themes reflecting the particular activities of a locality. Songs from the Maritimes are often about the sea and fishing, for example, *Bury Me Not in the Deep Deep Sea*;[15] those from the inland areas concern subjects like lumbering, as in *The Shantyman's Life*. Songs about leav-

---

13. Fowke, *Folk Songs of Canada*, 38–39.
14. *Ibid.*, 67.
15. Peacock, *Songs of Newfoundland Outports*, 1:153–54.

ing home and loved ones were, of course, universal, as were those about the disasters of fires, war, and other hardships.

Ballads

Ballads resemble folk songs in length, in their short, clear phrases, and in the simplicity of their vocal line. Unlike folk songs, however, ballads usually have accompaniments, and are almost always quite sentimental. Their melodies and harmonies are related to the modern major-minor scale system rather than to the medieval modal scale patterns usually found in folk songs.

"The Emigrants Home Dream" (Anthology #2) is a good example of the mid-nineteenth-century ballad. The text is sentimental, the melody is not difficult in either range or rhythm, the harmonies are simple—that is, not complicated by chromatics—and the accompaniment could be performed by most amateurs.

Salon Music

Instrumental salon music published for the amateur market could be described in terms similar to those used above for the music of the ballad (i.e., phrase length, melodies, harmonies, and relative performance difficulty). Along with ballads, easy piano pieces (in the form of marches, waltzes, quadrilles, and galops) intended for the vast amateur market were published in Europe and the United States, and were imported by the thousands. In Canada they were first published in literary journals, but after 1840 a number of music publishing houses

Cover of **Grand Trunk Waltzes** *by Charles D'Albert.*

were founded in Halifax, Quebec City, Montreal, and Toronto that did a thriving business in "sheet music," as these individual publications were called.

A typical instrumental composition is Charles D'Albert's *Grand Trunk Waltzes* (Anthology #3).[16] The title refers to the Grand Trunk Railway, completed in 1861, linking Sarnia and Montreal, with extensions to Quebec City and Portland, Maine. Compositions of this type often bore local or nationalistic titles such as *Les Bords du St. Laurent*, or *Original Canadian Quadrilles*.

The *Grand Trunk Waltzes* (or *Grand Trunk Celebration Waltzes*) consist of five short waltzes with an introduction. The individual works are related by keys (F, B♭, F, c, F), and have related melodies.

The melodies of salon pieces are generally quite graceful and simply constructed. As in Waltz No. 2, (Anthology #3), phrases are usually eight bars long, and made up of two four-bar subphrases, reflecting their use as dance music. At the end of each eight-bar phrase in example III–7, the opening four bars are repeated (sometimes in a different octave—compare bars 17 and 25 of Anthology #3), followed by a new four-bar subphrase. Since these are waltzes, there is only one harmony and one rhythmic accent per bar.

Example III–7: Charles D'Albert, theme of Waltz No. 2 from *Grand Trunk Waltzes*

Dancing

Dancing continued to be a popular pastime for Canadians during the nineteenth century. Jigs, reels, and other traditional dances formed the repertory of the working classes, while the waltz and quadrille supplanted the minuet and English country dances for the well-to-do. Visitors were struck by the popularity of dancing and by the enthusiasm with which the Canadians entered into the activity:

Dancing is one of those relaxations which is carried out with great spirit. . . . On the most trivial occasions a dance is proposed, and if only two or three friends step in to tea in the evening, gossip and small talk generally resolve themselves into a hop. (ca. 1860, place unknown)[17]

At one end of the ball-room was the regimental band, whence the lungs of some dozen or so strong-built soldiers, assisted by the noisiest possible musical contrivances, thundered forth the quadrilles and waltzes. . . . There is a waltz! nearly everyone joins. At what a pace they go! (Quebec, 1846)[18]

---

16. Little is known of the composer apart from this and a few other works published in the 1850s and 1860s, and the fact that he performed on the piano in Bytown (Ottawa) in 1854. I am indebted to Clifford Ford and Helmut Kallmann for the example and the information.

17. Quoted in Ernest MacMillan, *Music in Canada* (Toronto: University of Toronto Press, 1955), 66.

18. *Ibid.*, 66–67.

Formal Music Making

In each community the focus for music making was the local church, where music had always been part of the regular service. Ambitious church choirs first expanded their sacred repertory beyond simple hymns and psalm tunes to include more ambitious part-songs. Soon they performed outside the confines of the church service, becoming the nucleus of concert ensembles. In Halifax, for example, the choir of St. Paul's church provided the basic membership of the St. Paul's Singing Society (founded in 1819); activities of the Parochial Choral Society in St. John's, Newfoundland, were first reported by the bishop in 1848;[19] and in 1834 Stephen Codman, music director of the Anglican Cathedral of the Holy Trinity in Quebec City, assembled 111 singers and 60 instrumentalists for a three-hour performance of sacred music that included compositions by Haydn, Mozart, Handel, Cherubini, and Rossini.[20]

The immigration of talented and ambitious musicians to the cities resulted almost immediately in the founding of glee clubs, singing societies, and groups dedicated to the performance of vocal and instrumental music. The talented family of John St. Luke moved to Halifax in 1842 and presented several recitals. (St. Luke had been a music and ballet director in Bristol and New York; his son and daughter performed as violinist and singer.) That year a group of citizens formed the Halifax Harmonic Society with John St. Luke as director, and began to perform oratorios (for example, Haydn's *The Creation* in 1843).[21] Frédéric Glackemeyer organized the Quebec Harmonic Society in 1820 to give concerts of instrumental ensemble music. And in 1849 Antoine Dessane, a talented organist, pianist, and cellist, immigrated to Quebec City from France with his wife Irma, a soprano. He gave numerous solo recitals, performed with various ensembles, and conducted the Quebec Harmonic Society in a number of concerts.

The musical activities in Niagara and Toronto, two of the newer communities, illustrate the quantity and variety of formal music making during this period.

Niagara

In 1792, the year Niagara (then Newark) became the administrative centre of Upper Canada, it was described as "a poor wretched straggling village."[22] But by the first decades of the nineteenth century it had grown both in size and quality. Its social life was enlivened by the presence of the military garrison at Fort George: the officers presented numerous theatrical productions and sponsored formal dinners with dancing. In 1819 a dinner at the fort was followed by a ball and "the charming music of the 70th regiment was heard."[23] In 1821 it

---

19. *EMC*, 838a.

20. Kallmann, *A History*, 82–83.

21. *Ibid.*, 86.

22. Crysler, "Niagara-on-the-Lake," 1.

23. Janet Carnochan, *History of Niagara (in Parts)*, (Toronto, 1914), 256. Quoted in Crysler, "Niagara-on-the-Lake," 30.

was reported that "during the winter season, public dancing assemblies are held once a fortnight in one of the hotels."[24]

Musical activities outside the garrison consisted of concerts and lessons by such individuals as Thomas Watts, who taught music, conducted his Quadrille Band, and performed solos on the flute.[25] Following its formation in 1841, the Niagara Temperance Society sponsored concerts and meetings which included music, treating the townspeople to performances by military bands, local soloists, ensembles, and touring musicians. In 1847 a visiting artist, "Mr. Wall, the blind harpist," played folk songs *(The Minstrel Boy)*, ballads *(The Last Rose of Summer)*, and instrumental music *(A French Quadrille)*.[26]

Toronto

Fort York grew quickly from a military outpost at the end of the eighteenth century to a city of approximately nine thousand inhabitants by 1834, when it was incorporated as the city of Toronto. The increase in population was echoed by larger musical organizations. In October of 1845 the Toronto Philharmonic Society was established and gave its first concert, which included Mendelssohn's Overture from *St. Paul,* Beethoven's *Prometheus Overture,* and choral selections by Haydn, Rossini, Handel, and Mehul. The orchestra was made up of amateur string players and the band of the 82nd Regiment, conducted by James P. Clarke, an energetic conductor, keyboard player, and composer (see below). Earlier that same year, on another programme made up of choral music by Handel, Haydn, and others, Clarke conducted "two symphonies by Mozart and Beethoven." (Customarily, only a movement or two of each work was performed.) The Toronto Philharmonic Society presented thirteen concerts in all before internal squabbles brought it to an untimely end in 1847. A newspaper review of the final concert was critical of the performance of a Mozart symphony because of "a decided deficiency in the number of amateur instrumentalists," and the choral numbers lost "the full effect of parts . . . by the weakness of the choir."[27]

In 1857 the Sacred Harmonic Choir presented Handel's *Messiah,* the first complete performance of an oratorio given in Toronto. This inspired the rival Metropolitan Choral Society to present Handel's *Judas Maccabaeus* the next year with an orchestra of 40 and a chorus of 150. From the middle of the nineteenth century forward, large choral works became regular features of the various singing societies.

Opera

Ballad operas were frequently sung in all large centres, and grand operas were also given in whole or in part. It has been estimated that by 1810 approximately

24. John Howison, *Sketches of Upper Canada* (London, 1821), 59–60. Quoted in Crysler, "Niagara-on-the-Lake," 30.

25. Crysler, "Niagara-on-the-Lake," chs. 2–4.

26. *Ibid.,* ch. 4.

27. *The Globe,* April 24, 1847. Quoted in David Sale, "Toronto's Pre-Confederation Music Societies, 1845–1867," M.A. thesis, University of Toronto, 1968. Information for this and the following paragraph taken from this source.

one hundred opera performances had taken place in the cities of Halifax, Quebec, and Montreal.[28] In St. John's, Newfoundland, Thomas Linley's ballad opera *The Duenna* was presented in 1820. The first opera produced in Newfoundland, it played for nearly two weeks with the proceeds going to the victims of the great fire of 1817.[29]

Performances of grand opera were less frequent, but by mid-century these works, too, could be heard in the larger cities. In the summer of 1841, for example, the citizens of Montreal could have attended Bellini's *La Sonnambula,* Auber's *Fra Diavolo,* Rossini's *La Cenerentola,* and Donizetti's *L'Elisir d'Amore,* presented by a touring company. In 1859 there were thirty-seven performances of operas in Toronto, including Verdi's *Il Trovatore* just six years after its premiere in Rome. Both Montreal and Toronto had resident companies that produced light opera, grand opera, and individual scenes and acts. To attract a large audience, the lead roles were usually played by well-known touring soloists, although occasionally local artists were used. The usual accompaniment for operas was piano, or piano and violin, while some of the touring companies brought larger instrumental groups; the resident companies in Montreal and Toronto occasionally worked with an orchestra.[30]

Touring Musicians

Touring musicians played frequently in Canadian communities. One colourful account was written by a traveller at the tiny settlement of Murray-Bay:

> During the day of coffee-coloured fog . . . I was reading in a little bed-closet . . . when I suddenly heard, within the house, two or three short delicious strokes of a fiddle-bow, succeeded immediately by a masterly execution, on one of Amati's best violins, of "Nel Silenzio" that mysterious and mournful air in [Meyerbeer's] "Il Crociato [in Egitto]", which again instantly ran off into one of the gay galloping melodies of Rossini. . . . Rushing in to see whence it came . . . I need not say that the violin did not cease; but that the musician received a reward. . . . He was a thoughtless, and possibly a dissipated, London artist, named Nokes, on a free ramble through the Western world, and subsisting on his violin.[31]

One entertainer toured the United States and Canada in 1859 as a part of a wager that he could support himself as an actor: Horton Rhys (stage name, "Morton Price"), a British army captain who sang tenor and had a flair for drama. He stopped in Quebec City and Montreal, where he incorporated the bands of the military garrisons into the musical portions of his show. The Quebec programme lists arias from *La Traviata,* ballads, and "an original duet for tenor and soprano"

28. *EMC,* 695c.

29. *Ibid.,* 838a,b.

30. Information for this section taken from *EMC,* 695–96b; Kallmann, *A History,* 104–7; and Dorith Cooper, "Opera in Montreal and Toronto: A Study of Performance Traditions and Repertoire 1783–1980," Ph. D. thesis, University of Toronto, 1984.

31. John J. Bigsby, *The Shoe and Canoe, or Pictures of Travel in the Canadas,* 2 vols. (London, 1850; reprint, New York: 1969), 1:232–33. Quoted in McMillan, "Music in Canada 1791–1867," 42–43.

(sung by Rhys and his travelling companion). The band performed the Overture to *William Tell,* an unnamed opera excerpt, and closed with *God Save the Queen.*[32]

Internationally famous virtuosi arrived regularly: pianist Sigismond Thalberg played in Quebec City and Toronto in 1857; soprano Jenny Lind, on her two-year tour of North America sponsored by P. T. Barnum, gave two recitals in Toronto in 1851; violinist Ole Bull played in Toronto in 1853 and again in 1857; and Henri Vieuxtemps, another well-known violinist, was there in 1858. The Germanians, a virtuoso orchestra from Berlin, performed in Montreal, Quebec City, Kingston, and Toronto in 1850 and 1852. Louis Moreau Gottschalk, the American piano virtuoso, appeared in Quebec City in 1862, and in 1865 when his programme included improvised variations on *A la claire fontaine.* (See example I–2.)

The Business of Music

An important indication of the growth of musical activity in Canada during the nineteenth century was the increasing number of people making a living in music. Aside from performers, this included vocal and instrumental teachers, as well as merchants selling instruments and books of music. Music publishing houses opened in Halifax, Saint John, Quebec City, Montreal, Toronto, and Hamilton, and by Confederation they had published over six hundred works by Canadian and foreign composers.[33]

Piano and organ building began at this time. The earliest known piano builder was Frederick Hund who worked in Quebec City in 1816. By 1851 there were seventeen piano makers in Upper and Lower Canada, including ten in Montreal.[34] The first resident organ builder, Richard Coates, emigrated from England and built barrel organs as early as 1817. The arrival of Samuel Warren from New England in 1836 resulted in a high calibre of pipe organ building, and in 1840 Joseph Casavant, the founder of the most famous Canadian organ-making company, delivered his first instrument to St.-Martin-de-Laval Church.[35]

Outstanding Personalities

Jonathan Sewell

Jonathan Sewell (1766–1839), chief justice of Lower Canada from 1808 to 1838, played the violin and led a small amateur orchestra for the duke of Kent in 1791–93; in the early decades of the nineteenth century he formed a quartet that included Edouard Glackemeyer (son of Frédéric).

32. McMillan, "Music in Canada 1791–1867," 48–51.
33. *EMC,* 782a.
34. *Ibid.,* 752c–53a.
35. *Ibid.,* 711a.

Charles Sauvageau

Charles Sauvageau (1804–49) founded the Orchestre quadrille in 1833 and the Musique canadienne, a twelve-member band, in 1836, and conducted the band of the Petit Séminaire from 1841 to 1844. He edited a book of music theory, *Notions élémentaires de musique, tirée des meilleurs auteurs et mises en ordre par Charles Sauvageau,* published at Quebec in 1844, and composed several salon pieces with titles such as *Gallopade* and *Valse du Ménestrel.*

Charles Sabatier

Charles Sabatier (1819–62) was a composer and piano virtuoso who taught music in Quebec City and Montreal, where one of his students was Calixa Lavallée, composer of *O Canada.* Sabatier wrote more than thirty compositions, mostly salon music such as *Le Bouton de rose* (a polka), and *Mazurka caprice.* His largest work was the *Cantata in Honour of the Prince of Wales,* consisting of an overture and nine vocal numbers, written for the visit of the prince to Montreal in 1860.

Theodore Molt

Theodore Molt (1795–1856) was born in Germany and learned music from his father and elder brother. After a brief time in Napoleon's army he moved to Quebec City in 1823, where he married the daughter of Frédéric Glackemeyer and established himself as a music teacher. In 1825 he spent a year in Europe where he claimed to have studied with Beethoven, Czerny, and Moscheles. He

Beethoven's autograph sketch for Theodore Molt.

actually did write in Beethoven's conversation book: "I am a music teacher in Quebec in North America. Your works have delighted me so often that I consider it my duty to pay you my personal gratitude." The page on which Beethoven replied is missing from the notebook. Shortly afterward Molt wrote to Beethoven, enclosing a sheet of music paper and requesting a musical souvenir. Beethoven's reply was the canon *Freu Dich des Lebens* (WoO 195).[36]

Molt taught piano, organ, violin, voice, and thorough-bass in Quebec, Montreal, and Burlington, Vermont. He was also a church organist and gave concerts with his thirty-six-voice choir at the Quebec Cathedral. He wrote piano tutors, theory books, a two-volume set of harmonized sacred songs (*Lyre sainte,* published in Quebec in 1844–45), and other compositions, including a Mass. In 1859 he published one of the earliest Canadian patriotic songs to the poem by Isidore Bédard, *Sol canadien, terre chérie* (example III–8). It was intended as a national song, but because the text describes the plight of the French under British rule, it was popular only in Quebec.

Example III–8: Theodore F. Molt, *Sol canadien, terre chérie*

36. *Ibid.,* 630a,b.

en-fants de leur vail-lan - ce n'ont ja-mais fié-tre les lau-riers.   Et leurs en-fants de leur vail-

lan - ce n'ont ja-mais fié - tre les_ lau-riers.

Sol Canadien, terre chérie,	Land of Canada, dear land,
Par des braves tu fus peuplé,	You have been inhabited by the brave.
Ils cherchaient loin de leur patrie,	Far from their homeland, they were searching
Une terre de liberté.	For a land of liberty.
Nos pères sortis de la France	Our fathers who left France
Etaient l'élite des guerrier	Were the elite of the warriors
Et leurs enfants de leur vaillance	And the children born of their valor
n'ont jamais fiétre les lauriers.	Have never dishonored their glory.

English translation by Lise Boutin-Visentin

Antoine Dessane

Antoine Dessane (France, 1826–Quebec City, 1873) moved to Quebec in 1849 and became organist at Notre Dame Basilica, succeeding Theodore Molt. He performed frequently as a cellist and pianist, and was conductor of a number of groups, including the Harmonic Society. He composed more than fifty works, including songs, instrumental works, and Masses. He often used Canadian subjects: *Quadrille sur cinq airs canadiens* is based on folk songs he heard while on a fishing trip on the St. Charles River, and *La Québécoise* is a tribute to the women of Quebec. His largest composition, *Suite* for orchestra, was never published, nor were most of his larger choral works and a manual on orchestration.

James P. Clarke

In 1835 James P. Clarke (1807–77), an organist and choir director in Scotland, came to live near Toronto where he became the organist at various churches and worked as an organ and piano tuner. He was the first music instructor at the University of Toronto, and the first person to earn its bachelor of music degree, in that order (one wonders if he examined himself!).

He also composed vocal music, taught voice and keyboard, performed as pianist, and conducted a number of large musical organizations including the Toronto Philharmonic Society. Much of his vocal music was published, as was the sacred collection he edited: *The Canadian Church Psalmody* (Toronto, 1845). Among his more popular works were *The Wild Stream Leaps, The Maple Leaf,* and *Lays of the Maple Leaf, or Songs of Canada.*

Lays of the Maple Leaf are seven nationalistic songs, which, when published by the A. and S. Nordheimer Company in 1853, constituted up to that time the largest single Canadian publication of sheet music. The songs cannot be considered a "cycle" in the sense of a Schubert or Schumann song cycle, in which there is an internal unity to the music and poetry. Their texts are by at least three different poets, and show no signs that their authors expected them to be assembled together. (The lyrics of songs 3, 5, and 6 are credited respectively to S. Thompson, Esq., Rev. R. I. MacGeorge, and A. D. Ferries, Esq. The other texts are unsigned and may be by Clarke.) The musical settings, too, suggest that the seven songs were not originally intended as a set: number 1 is called a glee, and number 5 is a ballad; some are for solo voice with piano, one for duet with piano, one for various combinations of chorus and soloists with piano, while the last song is for unaccompanied six-part chorus:

Lays of the Maple Leaf

I. "The Emblem of Canada"	—solo tenor, solo bass, ATTB chorus, with piano
II. "The Emigrants Home Dream"	—solo voice and piano
III. "Come to the Woods"	—solo voice and piano
IV. "Home Flowers"	—soprano and tenor solo with piano
V. "The Emigrants Bride"	—solo voice and piano
VI. "The Chopper's Song"	—solo voice and piano
VII. "Chorus of Hunters"	—double ATB chorus

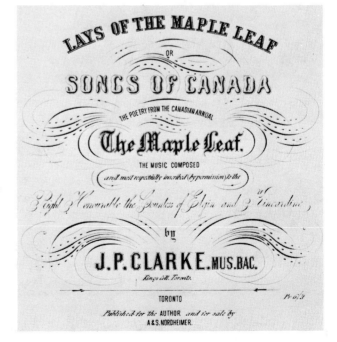

Title page of **Lays of the Maple Leaf** *by James P. Clarke.*

The printed format, with Clarke's name at the beginning of each song, suggests that they were intended at one time to be sold separately.

"The Emigrants Home Dream" (Anthology #2) is a typical example of the music that was sung in parlors and concert halls all over North America during the nineteenth century.

Children of Peace

Music was also found in special religious communities. One of these, perhaps the most successful at the time, was the Children of Peace in Sharon (originally Hope), Ontario. Its founder, David Willson (1778–1866), broke away from the Quaker community in 1814 over issues that included his interpretation of the Bible and some of the austere practices of the Quakers. In 1819 he established his own community, in which music had an important part.

Four buildings were constructed for the Children of Peace. The most interesting was the Temple, which has three stories to symbolize the Trinity, each one a square to express square dealing. The upper two stories are supported by twelve pillars, a symbol of the twelve apostles.

Vocal and instrumental music played an important part in the lives of the Children of Peace. Willson instituted singing classes for his followers, and whenever he preached he was accompanied by his "chorus of virgins," a select group of young women dressed in white.

Three organs (two barrel organs and one keyboard organ) were constructed for the group by the earliest known resident Canadian organ builder, Richard

Temple of the Children of Peace at Sharon, Ontario.

Coates. (Coates, also a painter, supplied paintings for the Temple. He later became leader of the instrumental ensemble.) The extant barrels and the community records show that the repertory of the Children of Peace consisted primarily of hymn tunes from British collections, with at least one by a New England composer (Timothy Swan's *China*). There was also a barrel containing some secular tunes, such as *Blue Bells of Scotland*.[37]

Willson used instrumentalists in the services both to accompany singing and as an independent performance group. The instrumental ensemble was originally composed of winds, strings, and keyboards, but after the middle of the century, following the purchase of a set of silver instruments, it was known as the "Sharon Silver Band." In addition to performing during the religious services of the community, it also provided general entertainment. Two reports from William Lyon Mackenzie (later the first mayor of Toronto) give us a description of the ensemble:

> 1828: Early in the morning after I arrived, I found some of the singers in the chapel practising their hymns and tunes. A number of young females sang a hymn, composed, as is all of their poetry, by members of the society. Two young men had bass-viols, and the full-toned organ aided the music which, I will venture to say, is unequalled in any part of the Upper, and scarcely surpassed even by the Catholics in the Lower province.[38]

> 1831: The meeting in East Gwillimbury, to petition the king for a redress of grievances, was followed in the evening by many demonstrations of joy; and the spirited young men of the volunteer amateur musicians, composing the powerful band of the militia regiment, marched up and down the streets of Hope, playing cheerful and enlivening airs. I had the curiosity to count their instruments and there were three or four clarionets, two french horns, two bassoons, besides German and octave flutes, flageolets, & they have also violins and violoncellos, and are masters of their delightful art.[39]

In its later years the band apparently functioned primarily in a nonreligious capacity, playing mostly American secular pieces such as *Yankee Doodle, Dixie,* and *Old Folks at Home*. It is reported that a few years before the final dissolution of the Children of Peace in 1886, the band entered a competition in Philadelphia held in conjunction with the United States Centennial celebration of 1876 and won first prize as the best band in North America.[40]

Summary

During the first two-thirds of the nineteenth century music in Canada expanded in quantity and variety. An increase in the demand for instruments, music les-

---

37. *Ibid.,* 187c–88c.
38. W. L. Mackenzie, *Sketches of Canada and the United States* (London, 1833), 122–23. Quoted in Kallmann, *A History,* 75.
39. *Ibid.,* 74.
40. *EMC,* 188b,c.

sons, printed music, and performances led to the development of music as a profession. The music itself took on a Canadian complexion as songs, instrumental pieces, and hymns were written by Canadians using local subject matter. Bands and other instrumental groups were organized to play for civic celebrations, parades, and festivities. Repertory ranged from ballads and salon music to oratorios and operas. The church choirs and military bands both grew beyond their original purposes and were the antecedents of the amateur and professional groups that have flourished into the present century.

4

Confederation to the End of the First World War, 1867–1920

Canada developed rapidly during the nineteenth century. The cities grew larger, the West was settled, and communications improved greatly. Dramatically increasing trade and growing industrialization produced a thriving economy. A general feeling prevailed that the country was ready to stand on its own in matters of government.

The result was the 1867 Confederation which created one central federal government over the provinces of Nova Scotia, New Brunswick, Quebec, and Ontario. The British North America Act, the legal document by which the confederation was created, provided for a House of Commons elected on the principle of representation according to population. To the more than three million citizens of the new nation, confederation affirmed its unity and independence. It gave Canada a new and separate identity apart from its existence as a British colony, and recognized its unique character. By the First World War five additional provinces had joined the Confederation: Manitoba in 1870; British Columbia in 1871; Prince

Mother Britania: "Cut her adrift, eh! How dare you?" *from the* Canadian Illustrated News, *July 9, 1870.*

Edward Island in 1873; Alberta and Saskatchewan in 1905 (Newfoundland did not join until 1949.)

The introduction of the telegraph in 1847 connected Canadian cities with cities in the United States; steamships sped goods and passengers across the Atlantic from the major port of Halifax; and the railway linked centres all across the country with one another and with the United States. Within a few decades Canada was transformed from a series of small isolated cities and outposts to a thriving industrial nation.[1]

In spite of this remarkable expansion in communications, the development of music during this period remained on a regional level. There are some similarities in the musical activities of the various centres, but these can be attributed more to the general political, economic, and cultural growth of Canada as a part of the Western world than to any organized effort. There is little evidence of any attempt to coordinate the arts of the various areas.

The West

The western provinces were finally settled during the second half of the century. Although coastal British Columbia had been inhabited since 1778 because it was accessible by sea, the interior of Canada, from Ontario to the Pacific Ocean, had only minor frontier outposts. The transcontinental Canadian Pacific Railway, completed in 1885, was a major factor in opening the West, while the gold rushes of 1858 and 1869 had already lured enormous numbers of people to the Rockies.

The new western centres attracted a wide variety of Europeans and Asians, many of whom had originally settled in the United States. The Chinese, who were the mainstay of the railway work crew, remained on the west coast. Slovaks came to Alberta, Ukrainians to several of the prairie provinces, and Germans, Italians, and Japanese as well as other nationals to various villages and cities throughout western and central Canada. Many national and religious groups, such as the Mennonites and Doukhobors, established their own communities. The new settlers brought with them cultural backgrounds far more diverse than those of the primarily French and British colonists in the first 250 years of Canada's history.

Music making in the western settlements developed in approximately the same sequence as that in the early years of the eastern areas, except that, as Kallmann noted, it was "telescoped into the short space of a few decades."[2] When in 1858 the discovery of gold in British Columbia caused the population of Victoria to grow from five hundred to over twenty thousand in just four months, the cultural life took a similar jump forward. Casual musical entertainment by a few singers, fiddlers, and pianists was augmented by the establishment of the Victoria Philharmonic Society in 1859, and the Germania Singverein and Les Enfants de Paris

---

1. Historical information taken from Moir and Saunders, *Northern Destiny;* chs. 16–19.
2. Kallmann, *A History,* 158.

in 1861. The Victoria Theatre was built in 1861, and in 1864 a concert was presented there by the Philharmonic Society, the Germania Singverein, and other local professional musicians. Victoria was soon visited by touring Italian and English opera troupes, and the citizens themselves produced many performances of vocal and instrumental music. One of the most active groups in Victoria was the choir of St. Andrew's Presbyterian Church, which presented frequent concerts of choral music, often in conjunction with other church choirs. By 1878 there was a small amateur orchestra in the community, and in 1887 an orchestra of twenty-two players, together with a chorus of eighty-four, presented a full performance of Handel's *Messiah*.[3]

Vancouver, Winnipeg, and the other western centres developed along the same lines as Victoria, although at a somewhat slower pace. By the year 1900 most of the western cities had made the transition from frontier outpost to cultivated city with musical activities similar to those in eastern Canada.

Popular Music

By the last decades of the nineteenth century Canadian taste in popular music had undergone some changes. The folk songs that had previously dominated the field were heard less frequently. The colourful age of the Voyageur had passed with the coming of the railway, and in many other ways the majority of Canadians had become distanced from a culture best expressed in that kind of music. Although folk songs were still sung—mostly in the rural areas—the growing taste for ballads almost totally eclipsed them. When they were sung in urban areas they were nostalgic reminders of earlier years and of a European heritage rather than an expression of contemporary life.

Ballads and Parlor Songs

The ballads and parlor songs popular during this period are similar in many ways to those described in chapter 3: they have simple and rather sentimental texts; the phrases are short and of regular length; the melodies have a relatively narrow range and are easily remembered; and the piano accompaniment parts are easy enough for amateurs to play.

The difference between these songs and those written in the earlier decades of the century is a matter of chromaticism; whereas the earlier ballads were mostly diatonic (scale-wise) in their melodies and accompaniments, the later ones included accidentals (sharps and flats), as in example IV–1, one of a set of patriotic songs composed by E. Cadwallader (identified on the title page as "Instructor of Music, Normal School, Fredericton, N.B.").

3. For additional information on musical activities in Victoria, see Robert D. McIntosh, *A Documentary History of Music in Victoria, British Columbia,* vol. 1, *1850–1899* (Victoria: University of Victoria, 1981).

Example IV–1: E. Cadwallader, *I Know a Land*

A comparison of *I Know a Land* with "The Emigrants Home Dream," Anthology #2, will demonstrate the differences. In example IV–1, the accompaniment has a number of chromatic alterations between bars 4 and 8 which do not function to change the key but instead are introduced to add colour to the diatonic melody. The chromatics in the vocal trio in bars 10 and 12 serve the same purpose.

Parlor songs, ballads, and patriotic songs, similar to example IV–1, and their instrumental counterparts—salon pieces such as dances, marches, etc.—were written by both amateurs and professionals and aimed at the amateur market. They were performed more often than any other kind of music. Titles such as *A Handful of Maple Leaves* (about a Canadian soldier killed in a foreign country) and *Red Roses* (first lines: "Alone in my bower I am dreaming, All careless of time in its flight, Dreaming of blushing red roses, Red roses you sent me tonight") indicate the kinds of subjects that were popular.

Many amateur composers chose Canadian topics for their works. For example, Alexander Muir, a Toronto school principal, wrote *Canada Forever, Young Canada Was Here,* and a song that has remained popular in English-speaking Canada, *The Maple Leaf For Ever,* written in the year of Confederation. Muir originally wrote the poem for a patriotic poetry contest in Montreal, winning second prize. He then looked for an existing melody that would fit—a very common practice. (It was not unusual for a poem printed in a journal to bear the statement "May be sung to the tune of . . .") When he failed to find a suitable tune, Muir wrote the music himself.

One of the most popular songs in North America throughout the first half of the twentieth century was *The World Is Waiting for the Sunrise,* written in 1918 by Ernest Seitz (Hamilton, 1892–Toronto, 1978). The optimistic tone of the text was just what the public needed at the end of the First World War. (Over the decades it has been recorded over one hundred times; a 1949 recording by Les Paul and Mary Ford sold over a million copies.)[4] Neither composers nor performers drew a line between this kind of composition and the more "serious" vocal and instrumental works; *Red Roses* was written by W. O. Forsyth while he was director of the Metropolitan School of Music in Toronto. Until after the Second World War, the two repertories—popular music and art music—were frequently performed together.

Church Music

In the period between Confederation and the end of the First World War, sacred music flourished as the churches continued to play a large role in the musical life of the communities—they spawned many choral groups and constituted a source of employment for performers and composers. In addition to the traditional hymns, the sacred repertory now included a large number of new works written by professional Canadian composers. The new pieces were not necessarily in the traditional style, and not all of them were intended for church performance. New hymns and hymn books were published, and a change in style is apparent in those written after the mid-nineteenth century: the texts were more sentimental than earlier ones, and the music more chromatic; both elements reflected the same musical characteristics of the last decades of the nineteenth century that we noted in the ballads described above.

With the exception of these stylistic changes, however, traditional church music has remained much the same up to the present day. Because the new developments in sacred music originated with professional composers, we will consider sacred music within that context from now on.

4. *EMC,* 1014a.

Formal Music Making

Vocal Music

The formation of large choral and instrumental groups begun earlier in the century continued—a trend also found in Europe and the United States. Almost all cities had singing groups: in Halifax, the Orpheus Club; in Saint John, the Saint John Oratorio Society; in both Montreal and Toronto, Mendelssohn choirs; in Quebec, the Union musicale; and in both Victoria and Kitchener (formerly Berlin)-Waterloo, several German singing societies. Their repertory, which was much the same as that found in the United States and Europe, favoured the Masses, oratorios, and cantatas of Palestrina, Bach, Handel, Haydn, Beethoven, and Dvořák, and included folk songs, ballads, and art songs.

Instrumental Groups

Instrumental music making on a small scale had always been present in Canadian communities, but toward the end of the century efforts were made to form large orchestras, a move also discernible in the United States and modelled on nineteenth-century trends in Europe. Few of these large orchestras lasted for more than a dozen years, and many had only months or a single year of life. The usual problem was money. Regardless of how long the ensembles lasted, they added to the artistic life of their communities, and enthusiasm was such that whenever one group failed, another quickly took its place. One of the most successful ensembles began as the Septuor Haydn, founded in 1871 in Quebec by Arthur Lavigne. It soon became the core of various orchestras, and by 1903

The Halifax Haydn Club in 1885.

The Ottawa amateur Orchestra Society, 1898.

the original Septuor had disbanded in order to concentrate totally on orchestral repertory. It became known as the Société symphonique de Québec until 1941, when it merged with the Cercle philharmonique de Québec to form the Orchestre symphonique de Québec. In Montreal numerous attempts were made to form permanent orchestras; the most successful were the Philharmonic Society under the direction of the composer Guillaume Couture, and the Goulet Orchestra, organized by Joseph Goulet, and later named the Montreal Symphony Orchestra (1898–1919). In Toronto F. H. Torrington, an indefatigable music enthusiast and organizer, conducted a number of large ensembles including the Philharmonic Society, but none succeeded in becoming permanent in spite of the fact that Torrington's benefit performances in the 1880s helped generate enough money to build Massey Music Hall (later Massey Hall), with a sizable contribution from manufacturer and art patron Hart Massey.

Notable performances of large works were undertaken during those years; in 1880 a Quebec rendition of a Beethoven Mass required the services of the Union musicale, church choirs, the Société Sainte-Cécile, and an instrumental ensemble that included the members of the Septuor Haydn, all conducted by Joseph Vézina.[5] In 1886 Torrington amassed one thousand choristers, twelve hundred children, and one hundred instrumentalists in Toronto for three evening performances and a matinee. (The programme included arias from well-known operas sung by Lilli Lehmann and Max Heinrich.)[6]

Opera

Throughout the nineteenth century opera continued to be a favourite form of entertainment. Comic operas, ballad operas, grand operas, and a mixture of acts and scenes from several different works were presented in the larger centres by

5. Exactly which Beethoven Mass is not recorded, but the Mass in C was one of the works in the repertory of the Union musicale. See *ibid.*, 944b.

6. Lehmann was not favourably impressed by the event, and in her memoirs noted that she had called Torrington "a veritable ass" in the presence of the concert committee. See Lilli Lehmann, *My Path Through Life* (New York and London, 1914), 357, quoted in Kallmann, *A History*, 145.

touring companies and performed with increasing frequency by local groups.

The first resident opera ensemble was established in Canada in 1867 when the Holman English Opera Troupe moved from the United States to Toronto. (It settled in London, Ontario, in 1873.) The troupe toured the United States and eastern Canada along the route of the Grand Trunk Railway and until the end of the 1880s was the best-known Canadian company. The group consisted of George Holman, his wife Harriet, and their children Sallie, Julia, and Alfred, augmented by local citizens when necessary. The most acclaimed member was Sallie— many people came just to see and hear her. After a performance of Offenbach's *The Grand Duchess of Gérolstein* in 1869, the *Montreal Gazette* reported:

> The Holman English Opera Troupe have come and conquered, and Miss Sallie Holman may safely be said to have taken the hearts of the Montreal public by storm. This she has done by her charming and lady-like appearance, artistic singing and spirit with which she played the difficult role of the Grand Duchess.[7]

The troupe's repertory included at least thirty-five different productions of ballad opera, comic opera, *opera seria* (tragic opera) and *Singspiel* (the German form similar to ballad opera). Its 1870 production of Weber's *Der Freischütz* brought praise from a reviewer for the singing, the orchestra, and the stage effects. Other presentations included Balfe's *The Bohemian Girl*, Auber's *Fra Diavolo*, Verdi's *Il Trovatore*, and in 1879 the second Canadian production of *H.M.S. Pinafore*, a year after it was written. (It had been performed in Montreal a month earlier by the Martinez English Opera Company, a touring group from the United States.)

In the three decades before the First World War, local opera companies were established in Montreal, Toronto, and Quebec as the rage for opera and vaudeville (which they also produced) swept across North America. The relative popularity of this type of musical stage entertainment can be gauged by the fact that in the final decades of the nineteenth century there were as many as a dozen performances a month in Montreal and Toronto (the only cities for which that kind of data is currently available).[8]

Concert Repertory

Audiences in the major Canadian cities during this period enjoyed a fairly rich diet of music. Surviving programmes show that chamber ensembles, touring orchestras, and opera groups presented the most current repertory of European composers, while the local oratorio and philharmonic societies performed Handel, Mozart, Haydn, and Beethoven as well as lesser eighteenth- and nineteenth-century composers. There is some indication that "contemporary" music was played by resident groups—such as the Toronto performances of works by Dvořák and Max Bruch, under the leadership of F. H. Torrington—but generally, the music performed by Canadian ensembles tended to be retrospective, partly

---

7. June 23, 1869, quoted in Cooper, "Opera in Montreal and Toronto," 236.
8. For additional details see *EMC*, 434a,b, 695b–96b; Carl Morey, "Canada's First Opera Ensemble," *Opera Canada* II (1970): 15, 75; and Cooper, "Opera in Montreal and Canada," chs. 2 and 3.

because of the developing tastes of the audience and partly because the newer music was relatively difficult for the predominantly amateur performers who had limited opportunity for rehearsal.

From time to time Canadian orchestras and other ensembles did play the works of composers living in their cities, e.g., Couture and Contant in Montreal and Forsyth and Ham in Toronto, but it is doubtful that the music of Toronto composers was performed frequently in Montreal, or vice versa. There was neither that kind of national spirit nor exchange of cultural ideas among the cities of the young country. The exceptions to this rule were events such as the 1878 band festival in Montreal that attracted nineteen military and civilian bands from Quebec and Ontario. (One of the judges for the occasion was Calixa Lavallée, composer of *O Canada*.)

Two programmes of the Toronto Mendelssohn Choir under its founding director, A. S. Vogt, show the spectrum of vocal music offered to the public by one of the more capable ensembles:

January 28, 1897

Chimes of Oberwesel	Baumer
Humpty Dumpty	Caldicott
By Babylon's Wave (Ps. 137)	Gounod
Trisagion & Sanctus	Hawley
Scots Wha Hae	Leslie (arr.)
Come with Music	Macy
Hear My Prayer	Mendelssohn
The Legend of Briar Rose	Vierling
Bold Turpin	Bridge

February 1914 (a combination of offerings on programmes for February 2, 3, 4, and 5)

Cherubim Song	Tschaikovsky
How Sweet the Moonlight Sleeps	Faning
On Himalay	Bantock
Manzoni Requiem (excerpts)	Verdi
Nottingham Hunt	Bullard
The New Life	Wolf-Ferrari
The Goslings	Bridge
Tale of Old Japan	Coleridge-Taylor
The Music Makers	Elgar
The Viking Song	Harrison
Prince Eugene	Kremser
Joshua	Moussorgsky
Slavic Folk-Scene	Nowowiejski
Meine Schätzlein	Reger
The Broken Melody	Sibelius
Sleep Little Baby Sleep	Taylor
Stabat Mater Dolorosa	Verdi
The Sorrow of Werther	Wolstenholme[9]

9. I am indebted to Lynn McIntyre for the lists of programmes.

These typical concerts freely mixed opera excerpts, ballads, folk songs, and art compositions reflecting contemporary practice in Europe and the United States.

The Toronto Mendelssohn Choir also gave extremely ambitious programmes with the visiting Pittsburgh, Philadelphia, and Chicago orchestras. In 1902 for example, with Victor Herbert leading the Pittsburgh Orchestra, they performed excerpts from Bizet's *Carmen,* and in 1908 with Frederick Stock and the Theodore Thomas Orchestra (Chicago) they sang Brahms' *A German Requiem.*

Virtuosi

The nineteenth century is often called the age of the virtuoso—a time when gifted soloists astounded the public with dazzling technical displays. Musicians from Europe frequently docked at Halifax and started their North American tours there. The major cities of eastern Canada were on the same circuit as Boston, New York, Chicago, Philadelphia, and other large cities in the United States. Between 1870 and 1900 the performers of international stature who toured in Canada included Henri Wieniawski, Anton Rubinstein, Hans von Bülow, Eduard Remenyi, Ignaz Paderewski, Lilli Lehmann, and Eugène Ysaÿe. Two distinguished foreign-trained soloists, violinists Frantz Jehin-Prume and Luigi von Kunits, not only toured in Canada, but chose to make Canada their home. In addition, for the first time, Canada produced its own native virtuosi.

Outstanding Performers

 ### Frantz Jehin-Prume

Frantz Jehin-Prume, born in Belgium in 1839, studied violin with both Wieniawski and Vieuxtemps, and played in North and Central America as well as Europe. He married Montreal singer Rosita del Vecchio in 1866. They toured together and later settled in Montreal to give recitals and teach, and Jehin-Prume became concertmaster of the Montreal Philharmonic Society. Like many celebrated soloists of the late nineteenth century, Jehin-Prume composed several virtuoso works in the current salon-music style, such as *Romance sans paroles* and *Souvenir d'Amérique* for violin and piano.

Luigi von Kunits

Born in Vienna in 1870, Luigi von Kunits had a similarly successful career as a touring violinist. In addition to playing the standard repertory, he often performed his own Violin Concerto in E Minor, a demanding virtuoso composition in the late-romantic style.[10] In 1912 he accepted an invitation to teach at the Canadian Academy of Music in Toronto. He formed the New Symphony Orchestra in 1923, a successful ensemble that in 1927 became the (revived) Toronto Symphony Orchestra.

---

10. The manuscript is deposited at the National Library of Ottawa.

*Emma Albani, shortly after her success
as Isolde in 1896.*

Emma Albani

The soprano Emma Albani was the first Canadian-born musician to achieve
an international reputation as a performer. Her autobiography, *Forty Years of
Song,* describes her long and successful career.[11]

She was born Marie Lajeunesse, in Chambly (near Montreal) in 1847. During
her early years she studied piano, harp, and voice with her father, and established
herself as a performer in Quebec and New York State before commencing her
vocal studies in Paris and Milan at age twenty-one. While in Europe she adopted
the stage name Emma Albani, and between 1870 and the early years of this
century she sang leading soprano roles in the best opera houses in Europe. In
1886 the critic Eduard Hanslick wrote of Albani, "By far the best singer at
Covent Garden this season, if not the only important one." She was greatly
admired by Liszt, Gounod, and von Bülow, and was one of the most celebrated
singers of the late nineteenth century. Once her singing career began she settled
in England and retired there in 1911.

Albani visited Canada in 1883 after being away for almost twenty years and
performed a series of three concerts. Later she made three tours of Canada, through
Quebec and Ontario in 1889, from Halifax to Vancouver in 1896–97, and a
farewell tour in 1906. Canadian audiences also heard her perform in *La Traviata*
and *Lucia di Lammermoor* in 1890, and in *Les Huguenots* and *Lohengrin* in
1892.

Canadians were very proud of this famous native: the Canadian Pacific Railway set aside a special car for her, and in Ottawa she stayed at the home of

11. Emma Albani, *Forty Years of Song* (London: Mills & Boon, 1911).

Prime Minister Sir John A. Macdonald. She was welcomed everywhere and treated as a celebrity. Unfortunately, not all towns were equipped with technical facilities, and in Calgary, for example, insufficient stage lighting made it necessary for the troupe to borrow a locomotive lamp from the railway to serve as the moon for the garden scene from Gounod's *Faust.*

A typical Albani concert programme on her 1896–97 tour consisted of both the Garden Scene and the Prison Scene from *Faust,* the aria "Ah fors'è lui" from *La Traviata,* and *Home Sweet Home.* She shared the programme with a mezzo-soprano, bass, tenor, solo violinist, and a piano accompanist. The Victoria *Times* recorded that the audience

> applauded and cheered when Canada's songstress made her appearance, they increased the applause when they heard her wonderful voice and they loaded her with beautiful floral tokens of their appreciation.[12]

Other Canadian musicians who established successful performing careers elsewhere include the organists Samuel Prowse Warren and Lynnwood Farnam, pianists William Waugh Lauder and Harry Field, and the violinists Oscar Martel, François Boucher, and Alfred De Seve. Field settled in London, the others in the United States.

The Business of Music[13]

Publishing and Instrument Building

Music publishing and instrument building, both firmly established by the mid-nineteenth century, continued to grow. The most successful music publishers were A. and S. Nordheimer, I. Suckling and Sons, and Whaley, Royce and Company in Toronto; Arthur Lavigne, and Lavigueur and Hutchison in Quebec; E. Archambault and A. J. Boucher in Montreal; and J. L. Orme and Son in Ottawa. The largest part of their output was sheet music, but they also published more ambitious collections of instrumental and choral music.

The production of instruments on a large scale continued to be confined mostly to organ and piano manufacturing, but there were a few Canadian string and brass instrument makers by the end of the century. One of the most renowned North American organ-building companies, Casavant Frères of St. Hyacinthe, Quebec, was formally established in 1880, although Joseph Casavant had been building organs since the 1840s. Many of the piano manufacturers that prospered into the twentieth century were founded during this period, including Mason and Risch, Les Pianos Lesages, Theodore Heintzman and Company, and Willis and Company.

12. Victoria *Times,* February 4, 1897.

13. Information for this section and the next on "Music Instruction" has been taken from Kallmann, *A History;* Clifford Ford, *Canada's Music: An Historical Survey* (Agincourt, Ontario: GLC Publishers, 1982); and the *EMC.*

Cartoon depicting the competition between the Toronto College of Music and the Toronto Conservatory of Music in 1893. Among those caricatured are (left top) F. H. Torrington, founder of the College and (top right) Edward Fisher, founder of the Conservatory.

A TORONTO MEDLEY.

Music Instruction

Private music instruction had been available in Canada for many years, but its quality was uneven. The first step in the regulation of teaching standards was the founding of the Académie de musique du Québec in 1868 under the leadership of prominent Quebec musicians, including Ernest Gagnon, Arthur Lavigne, and Antoine Dessane. While it did not offer instruction, the Académie established a graded repertory and set examinations. By 1890 several conservatories existed and music lessons were offered in Sackville, Halifax, Quebec City, Montreal, Toronto, and Hamilton; by 1900 similar teaching institutions could be found in most centres.[14]

Music instruction in the public school system began with the appointment of James P. Clarke to the Toronto Normal School in 1847. Halifax put music into the school curriculum in 1867, and by the end of the century schools in many of the larger cities offered music classes.

Universities began to offer courses in music in the mid-nineteenth century; the first to hold the academic title of professor of music was George W. Strathy in 1856, at Trinity College (now part of the University of Toronto). There was often a connection between the university departments of music and the conservatories, such as that between Trinity College and the Toronto Conservatory (now

14. For details about the dozens of conservatories, see Kallmann, *A History,* 189–92, and entries in the *EMC* under particular cities, universities, and conservatories.

the Royal Conservatory of Music), an association that contributed flexibility and breadth to both institutions. While separate faculties of music in the universities were not established until after World War I, music courses were available and undergraduate degrees in music were awarded much earlier.

Composers and Their Works

Shortly after Confederation a handful of serious musicians from both French and English Canada began to produce sophisticated compositions of a high calibre, and it is the works of these men—Calixa Lavallée, Guillaume Couture, Alexis Contant, W. O. Forsyth, and Charles A. E. Harriss—that constitute the roots of the Canadian composing tradition.

Calixa Lavallée

Canada's best-known composer of this period was Calixa Lavallée (Verchères near Montreal, 1842–Boston, 1891. In 1946 the area in which he was born was renamed Calixa-Lavallée). His father, Augustin Pâquet dit Lavallée, was a music teacher, sheet music dealer, bandmaster, and instrument maker and repairer. (He made more than two hundred violins, and was associated at one time with organ builder Joseph Casavant. It was reported that he repaired Frantz Jehin-Prume's Guarnerius violin after it had been crushed by a sleigh.)

Calixa studied instruments and composition with his father at home, and continued in Montreal with Paul Letondal and Charles Sabatier. (Later, in 1873–75, he studied composition in Paris, although it is not known with whom.) At the age of fifteen he left Canada and won first prize as a pianist, violinist, and cornetist in a competition in New Orleans. He remained in the United States and a few years later enlisted in the Rhode Island Regiment where he soon became first cornetist. It is believed that he fought in the Civil War and was wounded at the battle of Antietam. After his discharge in 1862, he worked in various places in the United States. At one time he was music director and superintendent of the Grand Opera House in New York City. Returning to Canada from time to time, he attempted to make a living as a composer, performer, choirmaster, and concert organizer, on occasion performing and teaching in both Quebec and Montreal with violinist Jehin-Prume and his wife.

In 1880 Lavallée moved permanently to the United States, where it was easier for him to find employment as a professional musician. He toured the United States as accompanist to the Hungarian soprano Etelka Gerster, and worked as pianist on a New York–Boston ferry. In 1882 he opened a teaching studio in Boston and taught harmony, orchestration, and composition at the Carlyle Petersilea Music Academy, served as choirmaster at the Cathedral of the Holy Cross, and performed widely. In 1886 he was elected president of the Music Teachers' National Association (MTNA).

Lavallée wrote a large number of modestly successful works, more than half of which have been lost. His compositions include the operettas *The Widow* and

Sheet music cover of **O Canada,** *first edition, featuring a portrait of Théodore Robitaille, the Lieutenant-Governor of the Province of Quebec.*

Tiq (The Indian Question Settled at Last); two lost operettas, *Lou-Lou* and *Le Jugement de Salomon;* a number of marches and other incidental compositions; cantatas, sonatas, songs, fashionable ballads, and salon pieces.

O Canada was not officially declared the national anthem until 1980, but it has been the most popular national song since it was written a hundred years ago.

The need for a national song had been felt for some time, and numerous people had tried their hand at it, beginning with Theodore Molt's *Sol canadien, terre chérie,* published in 1859. (Alexander Muir's *The Maple Leaf For Ever* was far too English-Canadian and a French translation has never been circulated.)

In early 1880 Lavallée was asked to write the music for a national song to be performed at the French Canadian National Festival in Quebec on June 24, the name day of the patron saint of Quebec, John the Baptist. When the music was completed, Ernest Gagnon, president of the festival music committee, asked Judge A. B. Routhier to write the text. (Gagnon is reported to have suggested the first line to Routhier: "O Canada, terre des nos aïeux." Even before its first public performance the Quebec press proclaimed: "At last we have a truly French Canadian National Song."[15]

The premiere of *O Canada* was scheduled for the morning of June 24, 1880, following a Mass held on the Plains of Abraham for forty thousand spectators. Unfortunately, plans went awry and it was not played until that evening at an

15. Trois Rivière *Le Constitutionnel,* 12 May, 1880, attributed to the *Journal de Québec,* from *EMC,* 685c.

imposing banquet. The ensemble for the first performance was comprised of the bands of Beauport, the 9th Battalion (Quebec Rifles), and a band from Fall River, Massachusetts, all conducted by Joseph Vézina. The next day the performance was repeated for an audience of six thousand.

Although originally intended for French-Canadians, *O Canada* became popular all over the country following its first English performance in Toronto in 1901. While there have been several English texts, the most widely used is that written in 1908 by Stanley Weir. More recently, since the official adoption of the song as the national anthem, a bilingual text has been officially sanctioned and widely used.

Lavallée's best-known work besides *O Canada* is a piano piece, *Le Papillon* (example IV–2), written while he was studying in Paris. It was placed on the study list of the Paris Conservatory, went through numerous editions in Europe and North America, and until recently appeared regularly in collections of piano compositions. Through *Le Papillon* Lavallée's name became well known to amateur pianists in Europe and North America.

Example IV–2: Calixa Lavallée, *Le Papillon,* mm. 1–6

In 1879 Lavallée wrote a cantata on a text by Napoléon Legundre for the official reception welcoming the Marquis de Lorne, new governor-general of Quebec. At the climax of the cantata, Lavallée ingeniously combined *God Save the Queen, Vive la canadienne,* and *Comin' thro' the Rye* to symbolize friendship between the English- and French-Canadians.

At the MTNA convention in 1890, he performed his cello suite[16] with cellist Charles Heydler for an enthusiastic audience. Afterward, when some teachers asked to see the score, Lavailée admitted that only the cello part was written; the piano part had not been written out.

His compositional style was often conservative in the manner of Gounod, Offenbach, and Sullivan. His works showed a fine creative talent, but the nature

---

16. This is one of Lavallée's lost works, and the form "suite" is a guess. It could also have been a sonata or a cello concerto (with the orchestral part reduced for piano).

of the career he chose and the public taste of the day dictated that he write lighter music with an immediate appeal to the public, although we can see in *Mouvement à la Pavane* that he used some of the more advanced harmonic practices of the time.

That Lavallée's music was more than a cut above the average salon music written at the time can be seen in his *Mouvement à la Pavane* (Anthology #4). The pavane was a stately and graceful procession dance and many were composed for amateur keyboard players throughout the century. But Lavallée's work must have given more than a few of them a bit of a start. The phrases are heavily chromatic, and although it is a simple, short dance, the harmonies move through several keys, making surprising chromatic turns. In the opening nine bars, for exmaple, the key of G minor is established and then chromatic changes are introduced beginning in bar 4. D major is strongly suggested in bar 7 (with G♯ in the treble and G♭ in the bass on the third beat), and in bar 9, G minor returns. In comparison with the *Grand Trunk Waltzes* (Anthology #3), a more typical salon piece, Lavallée's pavane is strikingly innovative. It demonstrates the composer's ability to bring to this genre elements of the more advanced nineteenth-century technique.

Lavallée's *The Widow* (libretto by Frank H. Nelson), written in 1881, is a good example both of an operetta of the period and of Lavallée's ability in that rather restricted form.

The work is similar to hundreds of operettas from that era, the best known of which are those by Lehar, Offenbach, and Gilbert and Sullivan. *The Widow* has an overture and thirty vocal number for ten soloists, chorus, and orchestra. The solos and duos are rather demanding, but the choruses have simple rhythms with easily sung intervals that could be performed by amateurs. Typically, the plot is one of silly amorous intrigue, intentionally lighthearted. "Single I Will Never Be" (Anthology #5) shows Lavallée's skillful treatment of the music, combining an inventive harmonic accompaniment with a light and charming melody.

"Single I Will Never Be" is typical of Lavallée's solo writing in *The Widow*. The song is built on a simple waltz format of four-bar phrases in ¾ time with a single chord for most measures, causing the music to move forward at a gentle one-to-the-bar pace. Even within this restricted format Lavallée has written an attractive and melodically creative song, with interesting and unexpected harmonic changes, as in the sequence from bars 17 to 22. The text, on the other hand, seems a bit stilted, and in sections such as bars 22–29, it seems strained to fit the melody. This has caused John Beckwith, in a 1982 performance of excerpts, to speculate that the text may have been added afterward to music Lavallée originally composed without a text.[17] In any case, there is little doubt that in "Single I Will Never Be," as in most of the other numbers, the text is not the equal of Lavallée's music.

17. Programme notes for "Music at Sharon," 1982.

Guillaume Couture

Guillaume Couture

Guillaume Couture (Montreal, 1851–1915) received most of his formal training at the Paris Conservatory (1873–75) where he studied with Théodore Dubois.
He supported himself throughout his career as a choirmaster and organist in a
number of churches in Montreal, and for a short while as choirmaster at Ste.
Clotilde in Paris, where the organists at the time were César Franck and Charles
Bordes. Couture had the opportunity to continue in the Paris position, but turned
it down to return to Canada out of a feeling of duty to his Montreal patron who
had supported him during his studies.[18] Before he left Paris in 1875, his choral
work *Memorare* was sung at the Salle Pleyel, and the Société nationale de musique
performed his *Rêverie* for orchestra, the earliest-known European performances
of compositions by a Canadian composer.

In Canada much of his time was spent as organizer and conductor of various
choruses and orchestras. He attempted quite ambitious works: with the Philharmonic Society he performed Beethoven's *Christ on the Mount of Olives,* Schumann's *Paradise and Peri,* and concert performances of Wagner's *The Flying
Dutchman* and *Tannhäuser.* To strengthen the orchestra he imported key players
from Boston; on one occasion he hired the entire Boston Festival Orchestra.
Couture was often adversely criticized for his work, but on the occasion of a
1892 performance of Saint-Saëns' *Déluge* and Gade's *Erlking's Daughter* with
orchestra, soloists, and a chorus of 250 voices, the *Montreal Gazette* gave him
credit for his efforts and revealed an interesting fact about the amount of rehearsal
time customary during those years:

18. Couture's patron was Léon Sentenne, curé of St. Jacques Church where Couture had served
from 1867 to 1873 as choirmaster. See *EMC,* 238b.

The greatest triumph of the evening was for the orchestra and for the conductor . . . few realize what a triumph of musical earnestness and ability is achieved by Mr. Couture in producing such an orchestral effect after one or, at the most, two rehearsals.[19]

Couture's own compositions are in the style of the mid- to late-nineteenth-century French composers, especially Franck and Saint-Saëns. His oratorio *Jean le Précurseur* (1907–09) was, in his own mind, his best work, but he never heard it; the premiere scheduled for 1914 was postponed because of the war. It was finally performed in 1923, eight years after his death. He also composed a Requiem Mass, a number of sacred and secular vocal works, and a few short instrumental works.

Several of Couture's compositions have been played in recent years—especially the oratorio, which was revived in 1928 and again in 1964. But Couture's most significant contribution to Canadian culture may well have been the ambitious orchestral programmes he presented which gave the citizens of Montreal an exposure to contemporary European repertory not available anywhere else in Canada in such quantity.

Alexis Contant

Alexis Contant (Montreal, 1858–1918) was the first composer of stature to study exclusively with Canadians. His early instruction was with Calixa Lavallée in Montreal in 1875 and in Boston in 1883. He also studied with Jehin-Prume and Guillaume Couture. With the exception of the six-month period in Boston, he spent his entire life in Canada.

Contant worked as a church organist and taught at various colleges and at the Conservatoire national de musique. His students included many of the important French-Canadian composers of the next generation: Victor Brault, Claude Champagne, J. J. Gagnier, Rodolphe Mathieu, and Wilfrid Pelletier.

Contant was unusual among the Canadian composers of his time in that he wrote for large ensembles. His major compositions, all written after 1897, are the second and third Masses, both with orchestral accompaniment; a piano trio; the oratorio *Cain;* a symphonic poem, *Les Deux Âmes*—in reality a second oratorio—and an unfinished opera, *Veronica*.

Other Composers: French Canada

Among the other composers active in Montreal at the turn of the century were Alphonse Lavallée-Smith, R. O. Pelletier, Achille Fortier, and Amedée Tremblay. Lavallée-Smith (1873–1912; he was related to Calixa Lavallée) studied in Paris with Dubois, Gigout, Guilmant, and Widor. He worked in Montreal as an organist and music teacher, and in 1905 founded the Conservatoire national de musique which he directed until his death. His compositions include operettas, cantatas, a Requiem Mass, and a number of shorter works.

Joseph Vézina (Quebec City, 1849–1924) was the most prominent musician in Quebec City. He was an organist and choirmaster, a bandmaster and com-

---

19. 1892, no day. Clipping in National Library, Ottawa.

poser. He studied composition for six months with Calixa Lavallée, but was otherwise self-taught. His works include several songs, a number of marches and light concert pieces written for the ensembles he conducted, and three operettas: *Le Lauréat, Le Rajah,* and *Le Fétiche.* Many of his works were printed by his own music publishing firm.

Napoléon Crépault (Kamouraska, Quebec, 1849–Quebec City, 1906) was a student of Dessane and Ernest Gagnon. Organist and choirmaster in Quebec at the church of St. Roch, he composed primarily for voice and piano. Several of his works were published in Quebec by Arthur Lavine, including *La Ruche harmonieuse,* a collection of approximately forty songs, and *Les Joies du foyer,* thirty salon pieces for piano.

Other Composers: English Canada

W. O. Forsyth (Markham, 1859–Toronto, 1937) studied in Toronto with Edward Fisher and at the Leipzig Conservatory. He spent most of his life teaching at the Toronto College of Music and the Toronto Conservatory of Music. From 1895 to 1912 he was the director of the Metropolitan School of Music. He was the first Canadian-born composer to see most of his works in print—they were published in both Germany and Canada. Most of his compositions are short, simple pieces in the style of Mendelssohn's *Songs Without Words* and Schumann's smaller works.

Charles A. E. Harriss (London, 1862–Ottawa, 1929) was an organist in Montreal and Ottawa early in his career, but marriage to an independently wealthy woman allowed him freedom to compose, organize concerts, and serve from 1904 to 1907 as the unpaid first director of the McGill Conservatorium. He brought a number of British artists to North America and arranged Emma Albani's 1896 cross-Canada tour. His passion was to organize and conduct extravagant musical presentations which he did in Montreal and in Ottawa. In England he conducted yearly performances of the "Imperial Choir," a massive group that appeared at the Crystal Palace. His London programmes included works by composers such as Bach, Elgar, Handel, Parry, and always at least one composition by Harriss, written specially for the occasion. His 1924 concert at the Empire Stadium in London utilized ten thousand voices and five hundred instruments!

Other composers from English-speaking Canada were Albert Ham (Bath, 1858–Brighton, 1940) and Edward Broome (Manchester, 1868–Toronto, 1932), both of whom worked in Toronto, and Robert Ambrose (Chelmsford, 1824–Hamilton, 1908) of Hamilton, whose sacred song "One Sweetly Solemn Thought" was published and widely circulated in the early decades of the twentieth century.

Clarence Lucas (Smithville, 1866–near Paris, 1947) achieved some level of success as a composer and arranger outside of Canada. Lucas studied in Paris with Dubois and, in his early twenties, worked in Canada for a few years as a music teacher and conductor. But most of his career was spent in New York, London, and Paris, where he transcribed, arranged, and composed music, and supplemented his income writing and editing for journals. His compositions include several overtures, a cantata, and a large number of salon pieces.

Summary

Confederation marked the beginning of a new stage in Canadian history. It signified that the country was now politically, economically, and culturally an entity separate from its colonial beginnings.

During this period Canadian music began to flourish, producing not only native performers and composers, but publishers and instrument makers as well. The music composed in Canada at this time was clearly derived from the European tradition with some influences from the United States; but it is clear that a distinctive Canadian musical identity was in the process of formation. Composers in Quebec adopted French models for their works; those in Ontario adopted English examples. All of them, however, took into account the tastes and needs of their public, and often chose topical Canadian subjects as their inspirations.

5

To The End of World War II, 1920–1945

The Canada that returning soldiers found at the end of the First World War was a different country from the one they had left. The social mores had changed: women had done men's work during the war and no longer silently accepted a domestic life; educational opportunities were widening for the general populace as technical and vocational schools developed; and the new labor movement was gaining strength in Canada as it was elsewhere. The population shifted from rural areas to the cities, and was augmented in the 1920s by the arrival of over one hundred thousand immigrants each year.

The economic adjustment following the war caused a recession as the nation changed to a peacetime economy, but by the mid-twenties unemployment began to decline as the discovery of natural gas and oil provided convenient and inexpensive fuel for enormous expansion in industrial centres. Soon the wheat crop brought new wealth to the prairie provinces; grain, lumber, and mining were responsible for rapid economic advances in the western provinces; and manufacturing provided similar results in Ontario and Quebec. Only the Atlantic region did not share equally in the growing prosperity of the Roaring Twenties: Nova Scotia and Prince Edward Island began to decline in population while New Brunswick grew far more slowly than the provinces to its west.

Canada did not escape the Great Depression of the early thirties, and the personal and economic hardships of those difficult years brought all these positive developments to a temporary halt. Nevertheless, the spirit of independence and sense of national identity that had grown since the turn of the centry did not falter. Canada recovered by the end of the decade, as did the rest of the world, and regained its economic strength.[1]

Culturally, Canada became a producer as well as a consumer on a much larger scale. The writings of Stephen Leacock and Bliss Carman, the paintings of the "Group of Seven," the compositions of Claude Champagne and Healey Willan, the singing of Edward Johnson, and the jazz of "Trump" Davidson are all examples of the artistic accomplishments of the newly productive Canadian society.

During the First World War, music making had continued on a small scale; since money, manpower, and energy were all needed for the war effort,[2] the

---

1. Material for the preceding paragraphs taken from Moir and Saunders, *Northern Destiny*, chs. 20–21.

2. Men formerly employed in making pianos, for example, were needed for the aviation industry.

large musical events of the late nineteenth century were no longer feasible. Shortly after the end of the war, however, the resumption and growth of those activities, spurred on by some significant new developments, led to essential changes in the Canadian music scene.

Radio and Phonograph

The most influential and far-reaching changes were brought about by the advent of the radio and the phonograph. Since both of these technological advancements had the capability of bringing entertainment directly into the home, an unprecedented influence on the taste of the entire nation was concentrated in the urban centres where radio programmes and record production originated. A certain amount of homogenization was inevitable since musical standards and programming were being determined by a relatively small special interest group. Nevertheless, the instant availability of many kinds of music to all citizens no matter how remote their communities made possible a national awareness of what was occurring in the major centres, and a kind of immediate cross-national communication network that had not existed previously.

The first broadcasting was begun on a regular basis in 1919 by the Canadian Marconi Company. By 1926 there were forty stations operating throughout the country. With the first nationwide radio broadcasts in 1927, on the occasion of the Diamond Jubilee of Confederation, the potential influence of radio became manifest. The three celebratory programmes included a Centenary Choir of one thousand voices and ten thousand schoolchildren, vocal soloists Eva Gauthier and Allan McQuhae, the Hart House String Quartet, the Bytown Troubadours, and the Chateau Laurier Orchestra. Prior to the broadcasts many of these musical ensembles were known only in their own regions. Afterward, the entire country

A rural Ontario scene, circa 1906.

was aware of them. These broadcasts, from Ottawa, Montreal, and Toronto, demonstrated that radio could disseminate culture on a national level.

Other nationwide radio concerts followed, presenting groups from various regions, and beginning in October of 1929, twenty-five performances of the Toronto Symphony were broadcast; the last concert of that series consisted entirely of music by Canadian composers such as Clarence Lucas, Claude Champagne, W. O. Forsyth, and Ernest MacMillan. Since that time, and especially since the founding of the Canadian Broadcasting Corporation (CBC) in 1936, radio, and later, television, have served both musicians and music by providing well-paid work for professional musicians, and by demonstrating to the entire nation the musical abilities of Canadian performers and composers. Radio was the first truly nationwide cultural unifying agent in the history of Canadian music.

Emile Berliner (1851–1929) was one of the pioneers in the development of recorded sound, and after some business setbacks in the United States, he moved his company to Montreal in 1899. The Berliner Gram-o-Phone Company thus became the first such enterprise in Canada. In later years it became the Victor Talking Machine Company of Canada, and in 1929, RCA Victor. The Columbia Graphophone Company (later CBS) established branch offices in Toronto, Montreal, and Brantford in 1904, and the Edison Speaking Phonograph Company had a distributor in Toronto beginning in 1913. Dozens of other companies, including branches of United States firms, operated in Canada in the twenties and thirties, although the largest volume of recording was done by Berliner, Columbia, and Edison (under various names and labels).[3]

The recorded repertory in Canada and the United States was virtually identical. Artists from both countries recorded on either side of the border, and the records were distributed both in Canada and the United States, with the exception of Canadian patriotic songs and the French language repertory produced for an exclusively Canadian audience. The Canadian companies prospered during the 1910s and '20s, but the depression of the '30s caused immense financial setbacks in the industry, and by the '40s the major record companies that survived were mostly in the United States. The smaller population of Canada and the problems of distribution over such a vast geographical area would not allow the Canadian companies to compete (a problem that to some degree still plagues the Canadian recording industry).

The most popular recorded music of the first decades of the century was a mixture of classics, ballads, and military band music. International artists such as Enrico Caruso and Ernestine Schumann-Heink recorded arias from *I Pagliacci, Rigoletto,* and *La Forza del Destino.* But just as popular were ballads such as *I Love a Lassie, She Is Ma Daisy,* and *Whistler and His Dog,* also performed by well-known artists; these included former Torontonian Herbert L. Clarke, conducting the band of John Philip Sousa. Specifically Canadian material included a number of patriotic wartime songs such as the marches *United Empire* and *Canadian Patrol* by Ontario composer Arthur Wellesley Hughes,

---

3. For additional details see Edward B. Moogk, *Roll Back the Years, History of Canadian Recorded Sound and Its Legacy* (Ottawa: National Library of Canada, 1975); and "Recorded Sound" in *EMC,* 796b–800b.

and *We're from Canada* by Irene Humble. Among the dozens of popular Canadian recording artists were Henry Burr (born Harry McClaskey), Willie Eckstein, Percy Faith, Guy Lombardo and his Royal Canadians, Harry MacDonough, Hector Pellerin, and the opera star Edward Johnson (see below, pp. 89–90), all of whom recorded dozens of pieces.[4]

Repertory

Music in North America in the first half of the twentieth century was far less compartmentalized than in the years following the Second World War. Operatic arias and art songs shared programmes with ballads, folk songs, and patriotic songs, just as they had in the nineteenth century. In the first decade of the twentieth century Emma Albani recorded both operatic arias and *Home Sweet Home,* the same repertory she had taken on tour a decade before. The Toronto Mendelssohn Choir recorded *Men of Harlech, Scots Wha Hae,* and Palestrina's *Adoramus Te.* Songbooks for domestic use included similar mélanges: *The Maple Leaf For Ever, The Maid from Algoma, The Minstrel Boy,* selections from Gilbert and Sullivan, songs of Stephen Foster, and various opera excerpts were combined in one volume.[5]

Popular Music

During the first half of the twentieth century some new popular music was added to the three types prevalent in the past century—folk music, salon music, and art music. The most original of the new forms were the several kinds of improvised music that fall under the general headings of ragtime and jazz. Both radio and phonograph gave impetus to popular music performed by professional ensembles—the so-called "dance bands" or "swing bands" that played for listening and dancing. The dance band repertory often included improvised (or pseudo-improvised) material related to jazz, thus including elements of both the popular music of the past and the new improvised forms.

Both ragtime and jazz are of Afro-American origin. The popularity of ragtime in Canada began in the late 1890s and involved a number of Canadian composers and performers. Shelton Brooks, pianist and composer of *Darktown Strutters Ball* and *Some of These Days,* was born in Amherstburg, Ontario. The most famous ragtime tune, *Maple Leaf Rag* by Scott Joplin, takes its title from the Maple Leaf Club in Sedalia, Missouri, which was owned by Will and Walker Williams from London, Ontario, and named for the symbol of Canada.

Jazz was introduced to Canada by touring groups from the United States some time after 1910. Jelly Roll Morton, the self-proclaimed "inventor" of jazz, performed in Vancouver in 1922. Shortly afterward, Canadian musicians formed their own ensembles and began touring Canada and the United States. In 1925 Jimmy (later "Trump") Davidson formed the Melody Five, modelled on the

---

4. Moogk, *Roll Back the Years.*

5. These selections found in the *University of Toronto Song Book* (Toronto: I. Suckling, 1887; many editions, many publishers). Other songbooks of the era contain a similar mixture.

Ben Hokea's Orchestra, Palace Theatre, Toronto, 1926.

popular United States band Red Nichols and the Five Pennies. The recording companies and the radio promoted these groups, and soon Canadian versions of the traditional jazz melodies were available; in 1926 the Gilbert Watson Orchestra recorded *St. Louis Blues,* the earliest jazz recording by a Canadian band. Many of the musicians did not restrict themselves to a single kind of popular music; in the thirties and forties Trump Davidson played a commercial form of Dixieland jazz for the general public, and a more adventurous form on special occasions.

Jazz groups, dance bands, and big bands performed experimental and conservative popular music across the country. Rex Battle, Cliff McKay, and Percy Faith were popular in Ontario; Steve Garrick, "Butch" Watanabe, and Maynard Ferguson in Montreal; and Dave Robbins in Vancouver. Oscar Peterson had his own radio show, "Fifteen Minutes Piano Rambling," on Montreal radio station CKAC in 1940, when he was fifteen. All of these performers were popular before 1950, and some are still working today.

Many professional popular musicians from Canada, like Gil Evans and Maynard Ferguson, found work in United States groups. One of the most popular arranger-conductors in Toronto during the twenties and thirties was Percy Faith, who moved to the United States in 1940, but returned frequently to Canada. Guy Lombardo first organized his orchestra in Canada, and it eventually became one of the most successful in the United States. His performance of *Auld Lang Syne* originated when he played in Scottish communities in Ontario, but became synonymous with the United States' New Year's Eve celebration.

Other groups remained more regional, performing more traditional music. Don Messer was perhaps the best-known performer of "old time" music from the thirties until the late sixties. His groups played traditional fiddle tunes and folk songs from the British Isles and new material in that style. By 1952 he had made more than thirty-five records (78s) of songs such as *Rippling Water Jig, High-*

level Hornpipe, and *Spud Island Breakdown*—all related to the old British folk tradition as it was preserved in the Maritimes.[6]

Instrumental Ensembles

In earlier times the local garrison band formed the nucleus of any group performing instrumental music. After the First World War, professional civilian musicians increasingly dominated music performance circles. The new radio stations and record companies as well as the theatres now offered regular employment and attracted musicians to the larger centres. (At the same time, of course, the availability of broadcast and recorded music diminished demand for live music provided by local musicians in the smaller cities and towns.) Encouraged by higher pay for concerts, large and small instrumental ensembles achieved more stability than they had in the past, and many of them grew into first-class groups capable of playing the most demanding repertory. Most of the professional orchestras in existence now were either founded or made major strides toward high professional standards and permanence during this period.

Orchestras

The only Canadian orchestra to survive the First World War was the Orchestre symphonique de Québec, founded in 1902 as the Société symphonique de Québec under Joseph Vézina. (It took its present name in 1942.) The Toronto Symphony Orchestra, established in 1906 by Frank Welsman, was disbanded during the war and was revived in 1923 (as the New Symphony Orchestra) under Luigi von Kunits. Von Kunits directed it until his death in 1931, and was replaced by Ernest MacMillan. In 1923 the Toronto orchestra performed its concerts at 5:00 P.M. so that the theatre musicians—who made up a major portion of the ensemble—could play in the evening shows. By 1933, when the talking motion pictures had displaced many of the theatre musicians (who then found daytime employment in radio and recording companies), the orchestra changed its concert time to the evening.

The present Montreal Symphony Orchestra had its beginning in 1934 as the Société des concerts symphoniques de Montréal, but there had been a strong orchestral tradition in Montreal since the last decades of the nineteenth century. The English-French rivalry within the city caused the formation of two competing orchestras for a short time—an English one in 1930 under Douglas Clarke, and a French one in 1934 directed by Wilfrid Pelletier. Over the years the personnel of the two groups became essentially the same, and in 1942 Clarke's orchestra finally ceased to exist.

The Calgary Symphony was begun in 1928, the Vancouver in 1931, and other

6. See Mark Miller, *Jazz in Canada: Fourteen Lives* (Toronto: University of Toronto Press, 1982); Ritchie Yorke, *Axes, Chops & Hot Licks, The Canadian Rock Music Scene* (Edmonton: M. G. Hurtig, 1971); "Jazz" and "Don Messer and His Islanders" in *EMC,* 469a–72a, 618c–19c.

orchestras using primarily professional musicians were formed during this period in Edmonton, Halifax, Ottawa, Winnipeg, and Regina.

The music offered by these ensembles included the standard repertory: Mozart, Beethoven, Schumann, and Tchaikowsky, with occasional performances of Richard Strauss, Debussy, and Sibelius by the larger groups. A sampling of some first performances by the Montreal Symphony under Pelletier (1934–39) and Désiré Defauw (1940–52) will provide an idea of the programming during this period:

1935—Poulenc	*Concert champêtre*	
1936—Respighi	*The Fountains of Rome*	
1937—Shostakovich	Symphony No. 1	
—Stravinsky	*L'Oiseau de Feu*	
1943—Copland	*Quiet City*	
1946—Shostakovich	Symphony No. 5	
—Milhaud	*Le Boeuf sur le toit*	
1947—Shostakovich	Symphony No. 9[7]	

In addition, the Montreal Symphony performed works by Canadian composers (most of them French-Canadian): Champagne, Contant, Coulthard, Couture, Daunais, Descarries, George, Gratton, Laliberté, Lavallée, Letondal, Mac-Millan, Mathieu, Miro, and Vermandere (Brother Placide).

Chamber Music

Many chamber music ensembles performed during these years on radio broadcasts and on tours of the large and small cities of Canada, and in the major concert halls of Europe and North America. Among those most frequently acclaimed were the Hambourg Trio, the Hart House String Quartet, the Toronto Conservatory String Quartet, the Parlow String Quartet, the Dubois Quartette, and the Canadian Trio (Nelson sisters Anne, Ida, and Zara. The last-mentioned gained international stature as the cello soloist Zara Nelsova).

Vocal Music

Choral Music

Concert choirs flourished in most communities. (In the early part of the century Toronto was known as the choral capital of North America because of the number and quality of the choral groups.)[8] As in the past, most community choirs began as extensions of church choirs. Their repertories included the large masterpieces of the eighteenth and nineteenth centuries and a few works by the more conservative early twentieth-century composers. Programmes usually centred around oratorios such as Handel's *Messiah,* Haydn's *The Creation,* and Mendelssohn's *St. Paul,* as they had for over seventy years. The more proficient groups performed cantatas, motets, and part-songs, and occasionally more avant-garde compositions.

7. I am indebted to Professor Elaine Keillor for this list.
8. *EMC,* 918a.

Opera

The First World War put an end to touring opera companies, and attempts to revive them after the war were only moderately successful. To replace the dwindling number of touring companies, local groups, both professional and amateur, sprang up in several communities. Many troupes would flourish for a few years and then perish (usually from a combination of internal artistic disagreements and financial problems), only to be replaced by another. In Montreal there were troupes that specialized in French light opera, such as La Société canadienne d'opérette (1921–33), and others that produced grand opera, like the Canadian Opera Company (1931–34) and the Société des festivals de Montréal (1936–65). Toronto had several groups devoted to English light opera: the Savoyards (1919–28) and the Eaton Operatic Society (1932–65); and to grand opera: Canadian Grand Opera Association (1935–37) and the Opera Guild of Toronto (1935–41).

In the early decades of the century operas were presented occasionally on privately owned radio stations, and after the formation of the CBC in 1936, they were increasingly broadcast nationwide. Since 1940 the CBC has carried the Saturday matinee performances of the Metropolitan Opera.[9]

Music Education

Opportunities for studying music in Canada expanded during this period. In addition to the conservatories that had been in existence since the end of the previous century, there were now professional performance staffs in the music faculties of many universities. The Registered Music Teachers' and the Canadian Federation of Music Teachers' associations were established in order to monitor teaching standards; competitive music festivals grew in number; and music was added to the school curriculum in most provinces.

The high calibre of music teaching that resulted from these developments allowed aspiring professional performers to remain in Canada for their entire training. The best of the students went on to establish national and international careers as performers, and many returned to staff the teaching institutions, thus more firmly establishing a Canadian tradition in music.

Outstanding Personalities

A number of talented Canadians achieved fame in the music profession as performers, conductors, and educators. A brief look at a few of the most outstanding will demonstrate the breadth of their activity during the years between the wars.

Edward Johnson

One of the most famous tenors of the first half of the twentieth century was Edward Johnson (Guelph, 1878–1959). He received his training first in Canada

9. See Cooper, "Opera in Montreal and Toronto," chs. 5 and 7.

Edward Johnson in 1950.

and then in New York, and began his career singing minor roles in operas and concerts in the eastern United States and Canada. In 1907 he was given his first important leading role in the Oscar Straus operetta *A Waltz Dream* and was widely acclaimed. He moved to Europe for several years where he called himself Edoardo Di Giovanni, and in 1912 made his opera debut in Giordano's *Andrea Chénier* at the Teatro Verdi in Padua. From that time until 1935 he sang the tenor roles in operas such as *Don Carlos, Aida, Pelléas et Mélisande, I Pagliacci,* and *Lohengrin* in Europe and the United States, and was a regular at the Metropolitan Opera in New York from 1922 until 1935. During the years 1935–1950 he was general manager of the Metropolitan Opera Company, and upon his retirement returned to Canada where he was chairman of the board of the Royal Conservatory until his death. The Edward Johnson Building that houses the Faculty of Music at the University of Toronto was named in his honour.

Harry Adaskin and Kathleen Parlow

Two exceptional violinists from this period were Harry Adaskin (Riga, Latvia, 1901) and Kathleen Parlow (Calgary, 1890–Oakville, Ontario, 1963), both of whom enjoyed successful careers as soloists and members of string quartets.

Adaskin studied in Canada with Luigi von Kunits and others in the United States and Europe. His solo career included tours of North America and Europe, frequently with his wife, pianist Frances Marr. He often played music by Canadian composers such as Champagne, Gratton, Smith, and Willan in the twenties and thirties, and later, works by Weinzweig, Pentland, Couture, and a number of the younger composers. He was a member of the Hart House String Quartet from 1923 to 1938, and taught at Upper Canada College and the Toronto Conservatory of Music.

Kathleen Parlow first studied in the United States, and, with the financial assistance of Lord Strathcona, Canada's high commissioner, worked with the famous Leopold Auer at the St. Petersburg Conservatory in Russia. After a long and successful career as a soloist (1907–27), she turned to chamber music, performing with Sir Ernest MacMillan and Zara Nelsova and the Parlow String Quartet. She taught in several places in the United States and at the Toronto Conservatory.

Percy Faith

Percy Faith (Toronto, 1908–Los Angeles, 1976) studied piano with Frank Welsman at the Toronto Conservatory and made his debut in Massey Hall at the age of fifteen performing Liszt's *Hungarian Fantasy*. He arranged music for the hotel orchestras of Luigi Romanelli and Rex Battle, and in 1927 began to appear regularly on radio and in concert as arranger-conductor. In 1940 he moved to Chicago as music director of an NBC radio programme, and soon was called upon to arrange and conduct for CBS radio and Columbia Records.

Faith also composed, and won a prize in 1943 for his operetta *The Gandy Dancer*. He wrote many popular songs in collaboration with several lyric writers, and one of his many film scores, *Love Me or Leave Me,* was nominated for an Academy Award.

Wilfrid Pelletier

The first career of Wilfrid Pelletier (Montreal, 1896–New York, 1982) was as percussionist in various groups and as pianist for the orchestra of the National Theatre, but he soon directed his major efforts toward opera and conducting. He won the Prix d'Europe in 1915, and went to Paris (in the midst of the war) to study. He moved to the United States in 1917 and became rehearsal pianist at the Metropolitan Opera; from 1929 to 1950 he was one of the regular conductors of the Metropolitan Opera orchestra.

Pelletier assisted in the formation of the Montreal Symphony Orchestra in 1934, and became its first artistic director. He was also the artistic director of the Quebec Symphony Orchestra (1951–66), and led the New York Philharmonic in its Children's Concerts series.

Composers

Although Canada was moving toward a national consciousness of the arts, composition retained, as it had in the past, either a French or an English orientation. The composers from French Canada usually took some of their training in Paris, while the English-Canadians either came from England or went there or to Germany to study.

Claude Champagne and Healey Willan are the two most famous composers from the first half of the twentieth century who represent these different traditions. Both men composed into the 1960s, but they were most active and influential between the wars. Their music and the music of others to be discussed in this chapter is almost entirely conservative when compared with the avant-garde works of Schoenberg, Stravinsky, or Varèse. They chose to continue along the melodic and harmonic lines of the late nineteenth-century tradition rather than to explore more experimental paths. In doing so they allied themselves with the likes of Rachmaninoff, Vaughan Williams, and d'Indy, to name a few of their famous contemporaries.

Claude Champagne

Claude Champagne (Montreal, 1891–1965) studied piano, violin, and theory at several schools in his native city, including the Conservatoire national, but began composing on his own without formal instruction. After his compositions had attracted some attention, the eminent Montreal music teacher Alfred Laliberté helped raise funds to send him to Paris in 1921 for studies with Raoul Laparra. While there, he was influenced by Paul Dukas and Vincent d'Indy. Returning to Montreal in 1928, Champagne began a career as teacher and administrator at various institutions, including McGill University and the Conservatoire de musique du Québec à Montréal. Some of his students were Violet Archer, François Brassard, Maurice Dela, Marvin Duchow, Serge Garant, Roger Matton, Pierre Mercure, François Morel, Clermont Pepin, Gilles Tremblay, and Robert Turner.

Champagne was much honoured during his lifetime. In 1946 he was awarded an honorary doctor of music degree by the University of Montreal. The year 1964 was declared "Claude Champagne Year" in Montreal, celebrated by a National Film Board production, *Bonsoir Claude Champagne,* the CBC television show "Hommage à Claude Champagne," and the inauguration of the Salle Claude-Champagne at the École Vincent-d'Indy in Outremont, Quebec.

Champagne's compositions are closely allied to early twentieth-century French works. One facet of his composition—and a very important one—is his ability to introduce a distinctly Canadian element into the French style. In his works we can hear the sounds, textures, and idioms of Fauré, Debussy, and Dukas, but applied with freshness to Canadian subject matter. Champagne's inspirations frequently come from French-Canadian folk music and various Canadian scenes, as his titles indicate: *Symphonie gaspésienne, Suite canadienne, Images du Canada français.* His own programme notes, following the title page of *Symphonie gaspésienne,* show both the orientation and organization of the work:

> This symphony opens with an "andante" which expresses the atmosphere of the Gaspé countryside—and the melancholy of its people. This is followed by an "allegretto" which describes the physical aspects of the landscape. A short "Interlude" in a pastoral vein leads to a restatement of the main themes of the "Andante" which is followed by a "coda" of large dimensions.

Further on he becomes even more specific: the final section suggests "the breaking of water upon the shore." Other descriptive passages are those in which the tubular bells and the celeste depict the chiming of the noonday village bells;

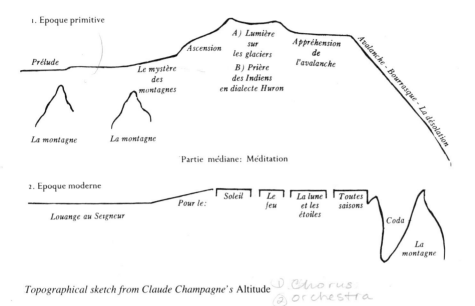

Topographical sketch from Claude Champagne's Altitude ① Chorus
② orchestra
③ + Ondes Martenot *

in other passages swirling figures in the violins recall the flight of seagulls over the Percé Rock, a well-known natural formation in the Gaspé.

In *Altitude*, a late work (1959) for orchestra, Ondes Martenot,[10] and chorus, he represents the Rocky Mountains in music; his subtitle is "Fresque sonore inspirée du spectacle des montagnes rocheuses." And to make the programmatic element as clear as possible, he includes at the beginning of the work a sketch that gives the scheme of the pictorial representation.

The score further explains the programme by including prose relating each section to parts of the topographical sketch. The music is in two sections: "The Primitive Era," in which the chorus sings a Huron Indian prayer (in the language of Canada's earliest inhabitants), and "The Modern Era," beginning with a prayer by Saint Francis of Assisi (representing the European settlers and their religion). The spirit of the entire composition is deeply religious in tone. As much as possible Champagne shapes the musical phrases to represent aurally the visual outline presented in the sketch.

Yet that was not Champagne's only style. In his smaller compositions he could be bright, charming, concise, and quite "folksy" as in his *Danse villageoise* (Anthology #6). Champagne wrote *Danse villageoise* for violin and piano in

10. The Ondes Martenot is an electronic instrument that allows control of pitch by either a keyboard or by the left-right movement of a ring worn on the finger. It was invented in 1928 by the Frenchman Maurice Martenot, and introduced to Montreal in 1950 in a recital given by the inventor's sister. Several performers of the Ondes Martenot now live in Montreal, and a number of French-Canadian composers have written compositions calling for that instrument. From *EMC*, 690a,b.

Example V–1: Claude Champagne, *Altitude,* coda, mm.174–85

The coda serves as both a graphic and musical summing up of the composition. The rising and falling melodic line represents the shape of the mountain as depicted in the sketch, and it also includes the principal melodic and rhythmic material.

It is in his large works that Champagne's music resembles that of the famous early twentieth-century French composers. The techniques of nonstandard scales, ethereal orchestration, and extremely long, wandering melodic phrases bring to mind the more famous compositions of Debussy and Dukas. The melody from *Hercule*, example V–

2, has a wandering and breathless indefinite shape that resembles the kind of line found in Debussy's *Prelude to the Afternoon of a Faun.*

Example V–2: Claude Champagne, *Hercule et Omphale,* opening theme

1929; he arranged it for string quartet in 1936, then for string orchestra somewhat later, and finally, sometimes after 1954, for full orchestra.

In complete contrast to the extended phrases of his romantic compositions, Champagne has based almost the entire composition on a single clear eight-bar melody in A major, that is made up of two four-bar phrases (example V–3).

Example V–3: Claude Champagne, *Danse villageoise,* opening theme

The second melody, at the beginning of page 174, is a variation of the first, in the key of E (dominant of A). All of the other sections are closely related to the original theme with the possible exception of that on p. 177, which is composed of some of the intervals of the original theme and its off-beat rhythm (compare bars 5 and 6 of G major section, with the first melody, bars 2 and 3). The charm of *Danse villageoise* is its attractive folklike theme and the off-beat rhythmic accents of the melody reflected in the accompaniment. Champagne recalls a rustic scene in old Quebec with the fiddler playing as the villagers dance a lively and ageless round dance.

Rodolphe Mathieu

The most adventurous of the composers of this time was Rodolphe Mathieu (Grondines, Quebec, 1890–Montreal, 1962), although his impact on the Canadian music scene was negligible. He studied with Alexis Contant and in Paris with d'Indy and Louis Aubert, but the strongest single influence on his writing was Scriabin, whose works were introduced to him by Alfred Laliberté. Mathieu wrote vocal compositions, chamber works including a string quartet and piano quintet, and a few pieces for piano.

Like Scriabin, Mathieu uses several compositional techniques. In Mathieu's works one can hear Wagner's harmonic ideas along with some of Debussy's techniques (e.g., a whole-tone scale). In compositions such as *Deux Poèmes* (1928) for tenor and string quartet, even the beginnings of serial technique are present, similar to that in works composed by Arnold Schoenberg and Alan Berg before 1910, that is, thick chordal motion with much chromaticism, suggesting the equality of all twelve tones.

Mathieu's music was far too modern for Canadian audiences and it evoked strong criticism. His reaction was to curtail his composing after the mid-thirties to concentrate on his son André's career and on his own teaching at the Canadian Institute of Music which he founded in 1929. In 1956 he made a final effort to write again—*Symphonie pour voix humaines,* for six-voice choir and brass—but it was never finished.

Mathieu was the first Canadian composer to introduce modern sounds into his writing; he was one of the most adventurous in the period before the Second World War (others were Colin McPhee and Léo-Pol Morin). Unfortunately, the audience was not yet ready, and Mathieu could not sustain the energy necessary to become a leader of contemporary composition.

Other notable composers in French Canada at the time were Hector Gratton (Hull, Quebec, 1900–Montreal, 1970) and Georges-Emile Tanguay (Quebec City, 1893–1964), both of whom wrote in the late nineteenth-century French style. Gratton was closely associated with folk music, and many of his works incorporate folk material. His compositions include incidental music for several radio productions.

In English-speaking Canada the greatest influence was exerted by teachers and composers who were trained in Britain and immigrated to Canada. Their music, predictably, was in the style current in Britain after the turn of the century: that of Elgar, Sullivan, Vaughan Williams, and Holst.

Healey Willan

Healey Willan (London, 1880–Toronto, 1968), the best-known Canadian composer, was most influential in English-speaking Canada as a result of his compositional productivity and his teaching at the Toronto Conservatory of Music and the University of Toronto. He studied composition in England and at age thirty-three came to Canada to instruct at the Conservatory at the invitation of its principal, A. S. Vogt.

Willan was organist at several churches over the years and conductor of various organizations, but he is best remembered as the organist and choirmaster at

Healey Willan

St. Mary Magdalene (1921–68), a church for which he wrote many organ compositions for service (e.g., chorale preludes) and hundreds of sacred vocal pieces, including eight of his fourteen *Missae brevi*. He also composed two symphonies, a piano concerto, two operas, music for plays and pageants, and dozens of other works for orchestra, band, chamber ensemble, choir, piano, and solo voice.

He wrote in a consciously conservative style, and in fact spoke out vehemently against more modern sounds on numerous occasions: "I hear only strange sounds which surprise and disturb me."[11] With so many compositions written over a period of sixty-five years (the *Healey Willan Catalogue* and its *Supplement*, compiled by Giles Bryant, list nearly eight hundred separate works), Willan developed numerous variations on his original style. But all of his works remain close to their turn-of-the-century British heritage. His most conservative works suggest Elgar, Stanford, and Parry, and the more adventurous contain the moderate dissonances of Gerald Finzi or Ralph Vaughan Williams.

Analysis of Willan's music by his biographer, F. R. C. Clarke, has shown that Willan wrote in two somewhat disparate styles: one for his secular and instrumental works, and another for his sacred choral works.[12]

Clarke sees in Willan's secular style the ideas of late-romantic and post-romantic composers (including Brahms, Tchaikowsky, Strauss, Franck, Holst, and Vaughan Williams) combined with the contrapuntal forms of Bach and other baroque composers. But no single composition shows traces of more than a few of these influences, and by constantly changing their combinations Willan produced quite a bit of variety within the framework of his conservative writing style.

---

11. *EMC*, 1000b.
12. F. R. C. Clarke, *Healey Willan* (Toronto: University of Toronto Press, 1983), 259.

Introduction, Passacaglia and Fugue (Anthology #7), one of his best-known organ works, is a good example of Willan's eclecticism. The work was written in 1916, shortly after he arrived in Canada. He was attending a concert in which Max Reger's *Passacaglia in D Minor* was performed, and a friend mentioned that the kind of composition could be composed only by a "German philosophical mind."[13] Willan took up the implied challenge and wrote *Introduction, Passacaglia and Fugue.*

We can see in this composition how Willan adopted the baroque forms of prelude, passacaglia (variations over a bass melodic pattern), and fugue, and added to them the colorful harmonies of the late nineteenth century. The Introduction is sectional, like a number of baroque preludes, alternating between a chordal, dramatic section in the first several bars and an arpeggiated figure over a slowly descending bass (page 180). The use of the tuba stop in the pedal (bar 5 of the "Maestoso" Introduction) takes advantage of that impressive stop on the organ at St. Paul's Anglican Church, where Willan held his first church position in Toronto.[14]

The Passacaglia consists of eighteen variations over the eight-bar ground bass presented at the beginning. The only direct thematic connection between the Introduction and the Passacaglia bass is the appearance in the Introduction of the interval of a fifth (see bar 7 and especially the highest voice six bars before the end). The melodic fifth assumes a prominent place at the beginning of the Passacaglia ground bass and in the fugue subject (which in turn is derived from the Passacaglia). Variations I, XI, and XII are contrapuntal; the others are rhapsodic (X), dramatic (XVI), or melodic (VII).

It is in the Fugue, built on a subject taken from the first four bars of the Passacaglia bass, that Willan demonstrates best his "philosophical mind," if what was meant by the remark is an ability to handle the exacting technical requirements of the fugal form. The fugue relentlessly gathers momentum from its beginning up to page 196. At that point Willan changes from duple to triple metre, introduces a quick-moving imitative section over a B♭ pedal (the dominant of the key), and triumphantly completes the work with a *nobilmente* canon at the sixth (similar to variation I of the Passacaglia). The composition has been hailed by many as Willan's finest instrumental work—an excellent example of baroque form in a late-romantic style.

Willan's major opera, *Deirdre,* has an involved history. The story began in 1941 as the radio drama "Conochar's Queen" by John Coulter, for which Willan wrote incidental music. In 1945 it was revised as a radio opera and renamed *Deirdre of the Sorrows,* and beginning in 1962 another extensive revision was made for the 1965 stage production at the University of Toronto Opera School, this time retitled *Deirdre.*

The subject of Coulter's libretto is an ancient Irish tale of the Red Branch Knights of Ulster, from the era of the Irish druids. The plot is typically complex for a tragic opera, revolving around the classic struggle between power and love. There are three acts, requiring nine soloists, a chorus, and orchestra.

13. *Ibid.,* 180.
14. *Ibid.*

The music for this vast work demonstrates Willan's musical relationship with the styles of a number of the composers mentioned above, as well as a close spiritual relationship with Wagner; the opera uses Wagner's idea of the leitmotif—a musical representation of characters and emotions. Example V–4 exhibits some of the major leitmotifs. Like those used by Wagner, these are quite short and moulded easily into a continuous melodic and harmonic fabric. In *Deirdre,* however, Willan does not use them as extensively as Wagner does in *Tristan und Isolde* and *The Ring of the Nibelung.* They rarely appear in long combinations, and there are large sections where no leitmotifs at all are employed. *Deirdre* was the first full-length opera commissioned by the CBC. Willan considered it his finest work.

Example V–4: Healey Willan, *Deirdre,* four leitmotifs

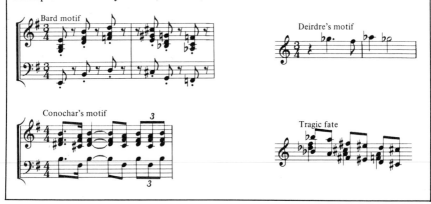

Willan's sacred style draws on plainsong, the polyphonic practices of the late Renaissance composers (Palestrina, Lasso), the sacred music of Parry and Stanford, and Russian church music of the late nineteenth century. Chant and the Renaissance compositions are part of the heritage of church music itself, and the Parry and Stanford models reflect Willan's English training. But the influence of Russian church music is indicative of Willan's appreciation of the sacred music of Gretchaninoff, Tchaikovsky, and Rachmaninoff. He was particularly attracted by its thick textures and prominent bass lines. All of these factors can be seen in *Rise Up, My Love, My Fair One* (Anthology #8), an Easter motet based on a text from the Song of Solomon.

In *Rise Up, My Love* Willan avoids the use of regular bar lines, preferring the free rhythmic flow of chant. The rippled separations on the vocal score remind the singers that the music is to flow without regular accent, rising and falling according to the contour of the lines. To express the mood and nature of the text, the individual voice lines are all melodic and often employ some form of imitation, and the phrase lengths are irregular. This style of writing is similar to the idea—but not the technique—of the Renaissance masters. The thick harmonic texture is characteristic of both the late nineteenth-century Anglican tradition and the Russian church composers. The texture becomes especially bass-heavy in the last few bars when the tenors descend and divide, producing a very dark vocal colouring. Willan's sacred works are frequently referred to as having a mystical aura, due, no doubt, to the mixture of the elements described above—especially that of the unmetrical flow and chantlike shape of the lines. *Rise Up, My Love* is probably Willan's most frequently performed work.

Willan was quite influential in English-speaking Canada, especially Toronto, during the first half of the century. His students included Patricia Blomfield Holt, Robert Fleming, Godfrey Ridout, Louis Applebaum, John Beckwith, Kelsey Jones, and John Weinzweig, all of whom have had distinguished careers as composers, although only a few of them followed in the style of their teacher. His honours have included a commission to write *O Lord, Our Governour* for the coronation of Queen Elizabeth II in 1953, a Lambeth Doctorate from the archbishop of Canterbury, and Companion of the Order of Canada.

Ernest MacMillan

Sir Ernest MacMillan (Mimico, Ontario, 1893–Toronto, 1973) was by far the most important musician in Canada in the first half of the twentieth century. His life story is one of storybook proportions—one would think three people would have been needed to lead it. MacMillan was a performer, composer, writer, ethnologist, conductor, administrator, and in general, spokesman for the music of Canada both at home and abroad. He had little formal training for many of his activities, but he carried on without concern, and succeeded in demonstrating his innate talents.

He gave evidence of musical ability early in life, beginning his performance career as an organist at age eight. His father, a Presbyterian minister with a strong leaning toward music (editor of *The Hymnary of the United Church of Canada*),[15] passed on to Ernest his love of sacred music and a wide interest in all music. Following his early training in Ontario, MacMillan went to Edinburgh, Scotland, for further organ studies and before his eighteenth birthday earned both his certificate as a Fellow of the Royal College of Organists (FRCO), and an extramural bachelor of music degree from Oxford University!

A bachelor of arts degree in modern history from the University of Toronto had to be awarded *in absentia* in 1915 because he was a prisoner of war at the time. He had been attending the Bayreuth Wagner Festival in the summer of 1914 when World War I broke out, and he was interned in a prisoner of war camp near Berlin until 1918. Even prison camp could not slow MacMillan. While there, he led a camp orchestra and composed several works, one of which was a setting of Swinburne's ode *England,* which he submitted to Oxford University through the Prisoners of War Education Committee. As a result, he received a doctor of music degree in 1918 upon his release from the camp. He returned to Canada as organist and teacher at the end of the war, becoming principal of the Toronto Conservatory in 1926 and dean of the Faculty of Music at the University

15. Toronto, 1931.

of Toronto a year later. In 1931 he became conductor of the Toronto Symphony orchestra (succeeding Luigi von Kunits), a position he held until 1956, and in 1942 he added to his duties the conductorship of the Mendelssohn Choir.

MacMillan travelled to all parts of Canada as an adjudicator and conservatory examiner, taught music courses, wrote keyboard training texts, and with Marius Barbeau collected and transcribed the music of Canada's native people. He was a guest conductor of orchestras in Australia, South America, and the United States. He promoted music as one of the initiators and first chairman of the Canadian Music Council, president of Composers, Authors and Publishers Association of Canada (CAPAC), founding member of the Canada Council, and president of the Canadian Music Centre and Les Jeunesses musicales du Canada. He wrote numerous articles and edited the first book of essays on Canadian music *(Music in Canada)* and an anthology of songs *(A Canadian Song Book).*[16] As a conductor he programmed a substantial amount of music by Canadian composers, including several pieces that he confessed were far too modern for his taste. He was honoured with a knighthood by King George V, received many medals of distinction from organizations in Canada and elsewhere, and was awarded nine honorary doctorates from Canadian and United States universities.

In addition to all this, MacMillan wrote some orchestral, choral, and chamber music in the conservative style common to British-trained musicians of the first half of the century. Many of his compositions contain folklike elements, and after discovering the Indian music of Canada in the late twenties, he incorporated some of those songs into his works.

Other Composers

Other composers in English Canada at this time include Leo Smith (England, 1881–Toronto, 1952) and Alfred Whitehead (Peterborough, England, 1887–Amherst, Nova Scotia, 1974), both trained in England. Smith wrote in an impressionistic style and sometimes used Canadian folk material. Whitehead was more oriented toward the late-romantic style of Brahms, and composed mainly sacred music.

Colin McPhee (Montreal, 1901–Los Angeles, 1964) was Canadian born, but worked mainly in the United States. He studied in Paris with Le Flem and in the United States with Varèse. In 1924 he performed his own Piano Concerto No. 2 with the Toronto Symphony conducted by Luigi von Kunits, and shortly afterward moved to the United States, where he achieved success as a composer and later as a teacher at the Institute of Ethnomusicology at the University of California in Los Angeles (1958–64) where he was a specialist in the culture of Indonesia. Many of his compositions incorporate musical ideas he was exposed to while living in Bali and Java from 1934 to 1939. Some of his works, however, demonstrate his Canadian heritage, for example his *Four Iroquois Dances* for orchestra.

---

16. *A Canadian Song Book* (London and Toronto: J. M. Dent, 1929; 2nd ed., 1948); *Music in Canada* (Toronto: University of Toronto Press, 1955).

Summary

In the period following World War I Canada's economic self-sufficiency was reflected in the arts. The period between the two world wars was by and large a time of great prosperity. Even the Great Depression brought only a temporary halt to economic growth, and the country became a major supplier of goods to other nations. Canadian music also grew quickly with the enlarging population, and musicians in every field were able to find competent training and employment at home. A large number of professional-level orchestras, choirs, chamber ensembles, and popular music groups developed, and the radio stations and phonograph industry provided employment for musicians and spread their reputations both inside and outside the country.

Two major composers, Claude Champagne and Healey Willan, emerged during this period, continuing the tradition of French- and English-oriented schools of composition. Along with their fellow composers and performers they provided a particularly Canadian contribution to Western music, from the symphonies of Champagne and the hymns of Willan to the jazz improvisations of Trump Davidson.

6

Recent Developments, 1945–1984

The years following the Second World War brought prosperity, population growth, and an ever-increasing sense of independence to Canada. Wheat, minerals, lumber, natural gas, and oil have continued to be mainstays of the economy, and manufactured products now rival natural resources as the major source of trade. The 1945 population of approximately twelve million more than doubled to nearly twenty-five million by 1980, and urbanization has continued: there are over two million people living in Toronto and the same in Montreal; one million in Vancouver and over a half million in several other cities. Canadians have been encouraged to retain the cultural integrity of their national and ethnic origins; the federal government works in both of the official national languages, French and English, and in all of the large cities Old World customs are celebrated by the entire population in annual fairs. In 1982 Canadian independence took another step forward when the constitution was brought from London to Ottawa; although some ties with Britain were retained, the document provided an important symbolic recognition of the Canadian sovereignty that had been a fact of life for many decades.[1] It is possible to see a telling comparison between these geopolitical developments and the evolution of a Canadian profile in music. In both cases change came about through a gradual process of recognition and consolidation over an entire century.

Since the end of World War II Canada has entered fully into the mainstream of Western music. In the major centres many first-class performing ensembles continue to be formed: orchestras, choral societies, popular music groups, chamber ensembles, and opera companies. Concerts by internationally known Canadian artists have become increasingly frequent. Music in the schools, universities, and conservatories has augmented in quality and quantity, and students no longer need to leave the country to be exposed to a variety of musical styles. In fact, Canadian musicians and schools of music attract students from other countries. Both the teaching and performance repertories in Canada comprise the same catholicity of taste evident in the rest of the Western world, and several Canadian composers have adopted avant-garde compositional techniques. Private and governmental support fosters the arts organizations of Canada in recognition of the need for a national artistic presence. In short, as a result of economic prosperity, advances in communications, and the adventurous experiments of a few excep-

---

1. Material above taken from Moir and Saunders, *Northern Destiny,* ch. 24.

tionally talented individuals, Canada now ranks with the rest of the Western world in all areas of music.

Multiculturalism

The present state of Canadian music is a result of the enrichment of an essentially French and British heritage by people of many other national backgrounds. Throughout history immigrants have retained elements of their native culture while assimilating a new one. But Canada is unique in the modern world in that the preservation of these cultures is consciously encouraged by such diverse means as cultural centres, radio broadcasts, and celebrations of music, dance, and crafts. Both the government and individual citizens support this effort.

There are entire communities in Canada still living much as they did in the old country. In other cases, certain Old World practices survive in tiny pockets amidst modern surroundings. Thus, a native culture may be perpetuated without change, like a living museum, although more often it is modified by the multitude of influences around it.

French- and English-Canadian Folk Song Today

The French folk tradition that took root in the area of Quebec when Canada was founded still survives. Thanks to the efforts of Ernest Gagnon in the nineteenth century, and Marius Barbeau and others in the twentieth century, much of the earliest repertory—both that which was brought from France and that newly composed in Canada—is preserved. Folk songs and dance tunes are still a major part of the social activities and folk festivals of the people of Quebec and the French-Canadian communities in Ontario and the Atlantic provinces.

English-Canadian folk music flourishes most in the Atlantic provinces, especially Newfoundland, where there is still a strong tradition of performing the tunes brought over from the British Isles and adding constantly to that repertory. The rhythmic and melodic style of Newfoundland's folk music is unmistakably that of England, Ireland, and Scotland, but it is not always possible to distinguish songs composed in Newfoundland from those brought over from the old country a century or more ago. The humorous ditty *Lukey's Boat* appears to be a local text, but to an imported tune (a Nova Scotia variant is *Loakie's Boat*). *We'll Rant and We'll Roar Like True Newfoundlanders* is clearly a local version of the English capstan shanty *Spanish Ladies; Jack Was Every Inch a Sailor* is an adaptation of the words of a New York music-hall song, possibly set to an original melody, whereas *The Kelligrew's Soiree* was entirely composed in Newfoundland.[2]

In the other Atlantic provinces—New Brunswick, Nova Scotia, and Prince Edward Island—the residents still preserve the folk music of their Scottish and English ancestors. Collectors such as Helen Creighton have found a great deal of folk material—both traditional and newly composed—in the smaller commu-

2. From *EMC*, 565c, 993a, 467a.

nities. The folk tradition extends to popular yearly events such as Highland festivals, which include athletic events, dancing, pipe bands, and folk music contests, thus reminding the people of their backgrounds. Scottish bagpiping is especially popular in Canada; Bill Livingstone of Ontario is a world champion bagpiper.

Collectors have also found Anglo-Canadian folk music in most of the other provinces. There, however, it is neither as intensely concentrated nor as often performed as in the Atlantic region. The folk music found in Ontario, the prairie provinces, and British Columbia, while dominated by songs or models from England, is mixed with Western songs from the United States.

Other Cultural Traditions

In the late nineteenth century several groups of Europeans came to Canada for religious reasons: the Doukhobors came from Russia; the Mennonites from Germany, Switzerland, and Russia; and the Hutterites from Austria. Instead of blending into existing communities in Canada, some of these groups established their own, and so preserved much of the way of life of the old country.

When the Doukhobors (spirit wrestlers) came to Canada in the 1890s, they established villages in the prairies near Yorkton, Saskatchewan. Those who arrived later, in the early years of the twentieth century, settled in the interior of British Columbia and Alberta. They all share a fundamentalist Christian belief and an opposition to what they consider corrupt practices in the Russian Orthodox church. The music of the Doukhobors is almost exclusively religious, with the exception of a few secular folk songs and children's songs. All of their music is vocal— they use no instruments—and relates directly to traditional Russian music, most of it brought with them from Russia. The sacred music is polyphonic and includes quite sophisticated counterpoint. An unusual aspect of this music is that it is transmitted orally, and even new compositions are not written down. The melodies are in the inner voices, accompanied above and below. The music is always sung slowly by choir—soloing is frowned upon in principle as a forbidden aspect of the cult of the personality—and staggered (alternating) breathing creates a continuous flow of sound in the psalms and hymns. Even the secular folk music includes improvised part-singing in the contrapuntal style.

The Mennonites came to Canada in the late eighteenth century, having first emigrated to Pennsylvania from Germany and Switzerland. Others arrived in the nineteenth and twentieth centuries, chiefly from Russia. The communities they established are all rural, and extend from Ontario to British Columbia.

The Hutterites moved from southern Germany and Austria first to the United States in the eighteenth and nineteenth centuries, and then to Alberta, Manitoba, and Saskatchewan in the twentieth century. Both denominations brought with them a strong choral tradition. In the strictest Mennonite sects the singing is all in unison and unaccompanied. The Hutterites and the more liberated Mennonite communities sing in parts and employ instruments, preserving the Old World traditions in their use of archaic dialects of the European languages and in the repertory which they brought with them.

Because of the excellence of their singing, Mennonites have been prominent in the performance of the more sophisticated repertory of vocal music in Canada. Choral groups with Mennonite background or sponsorship like the Mennonite Children's Choir and the Canadian Mennonite Bible College Choir of Winnipeg, have become known throughout the country.

Integrated Cultures

In contrast to communities that resisted assimilation, such as the ones described above, there were many other immigrant groups who settled in cities and towns, retaining some of their folk traditions, but for the most part accepting the culture of their new homeland. Ukrainian centres and Sikh temples, for example, can be found in both the larger cities and smaller towns. Japanese-Canadians who, until the Second World War lived in isolated western communities, now reside in the major cities; they mix with other citizens but preserve their national heritage in cultural centres where the language, customs, art, and music are cultivated and taught to the young.

In most cases the music of these various communities is a combination of the traditional and the current repertory of the home country. For example, the Chinese-Canadians are familiar with traditional Chinese songs and with the popular Chinese repertory, which is provided by new immigrants, visits to the old country, and touring artists (not only from mainland China, but also from Taiwan, Singapore, and Hong Kong). The Chinese-Canadians, therefore, keep in touch with their heritage—both past and present.

Some of the most interesting examples of cultural adaptation concern people from Caribbean nations, especially Jamaica and Trinidad. They have preserved their traditional music in a form modified to suit their new milieu: the large Canadian city.

The Jamaicans have brought with them their reggae, a stylized rock music in a slow tempo with a heavy bass line, and added to the repertory while in Canada. Reggae is associated with the Rastafarian religious movement which promotes justice and freedom from poverty, and the recent reggae songs express those ideas in a Canadian context.

The colourful calypso songs and steel band music of the Trinidadians have also been adapted to fit life in Canada. Calypso songs traditionally have improvised texts, and thus are easy to change. Typical ''Canadian'' calypso songs keep the melody and rhythm of the original but use new texts containing references to Canadian place names, situations, etc. The steel drum bands in Canada perform not only traditional music from the Caribbean, but also arrangements of Chopin, Strauss, and popular non-Trinidadian tunes!

The active preservation of so many cultures has kept vivid the colours of the Canadian artistic Joseph's coat. It provides all Canadians with a broad worldview and enriches and expands the Canadian culture.

Performing Groups

Orchestras

The symphony orchestras of Toronto and Montreal have risen to international status since World War II. After a long and difficult period of trial and error, they managed to achieve a good level of financial stability and to grow in size and quality, attracting first-rate performers and conductors.

The Orchestre symphonique de Montréal has always been adventurous in matters of programming (see pp. 87–8). Great strides were made in the development of repertory under Désiré Defauw who directed the orchestra from 1940 to 1952, and remained artistic director until 1958 while the orchestra was conducted by a number of guests. Beginning in 1958 under Igor Markevitch, the orchestra attained international importance, attracting resident directors Zubin Mehta, Franz-Paul Decker, and since 1978, Charles Dutoit.

The CBC Symphony Orchestra (1952–64), broadcasting from Toronto, was the leader in programming Canadian music. They have commissioned a number of works by Canadian composers, among them Matton's *L'Horoscope;* Somers' *Passacaglia and Fugue* and Piano Concerto No. 2; Symonds' Concerto Grosso; and Weinzweig's Violin Concerto and *Wine of Peace.*

Throughout his tenure as conductor of the Toronto Symphony Orchestra (1931–56), Sir Ernest MacMillan worked at raising the level of performance and encouraging the audience to accept a broader repertory. MacMillan's work was carried on by other internationally known musicians: Walter Susskind, Seiji Ozawa, Karel Ančerl, and Andrew Davis. The orchestra now performs a sizeable number of modern works, many of them by Canadian composers. It tours throughout the world and has a growing list of recordings.

Other noteworthy professional ensembles are the Atlantic Symphony (Halifax, Charlottetown, Saint John, St. John's), the Hamilton Philharmonic, the Vancouver Symphony, the Winnipeg Symphony, L'Orchestre symphonique de Québec, and the National Arts Centre Orchestra (Ottawa). Most communities also boast amateur orchestras of excellent quality. Prominent Canadian conductors include John Avison, Mario Bernardi, Alexander and Boris Brott, Victor Feldbrill, and Pierre Hétu.

Choral Music

The tradition of community choral ensembles has continued, highlighted by the remarkable success of the Festival Singers of Canada, a professional choir begun in 1954 by Elmer Iseler, and the Elmer Iseler Singers, which he founded in 1978. Iseler's groups have earned international reputations, and they are highly regarded for their performances of modern music (e.g., recordings by the Festival Singers of Schoenberg and Stravinsky). Iseler is a strong supporter of Canadian music; his choirs have commissioned a number of works by Canadian composers and regularly programme Canadian music. Other vocal ensembles that have met with critical acclaim in recent years include the Vancouver Cham-

Louis Riel, *by Harry Somers. Act I, Scene 1 in the Canadian Opera Company's 1967 production.*

ber Choir, the Mennonite Children's Choir (Winnipeg), and the Tudor Singers (Montreal).

Opera

The training of Canadian opera singers was greatly aided by the establishiment of an opera school in 1946 at the Royal Conservatory of Music in Toronto. Four years later this venture led to the formation of the Canadian Opera Company, a professional group that depends heavily on the Opera School (now a part of the Faculty of Music of the University of Toronto) for performers. Internationally recognized Canadian soloists, most of them Canadian-trained, include Pierrette Alarie, Victor Braun, Claude Corbeil, Maureen Forrester, Don Garrard, Raoul Jobin, Lois Marshall, Ermanno Mauro, Allan Monk, Maria Pellegrini, Louis and Gino Quilico, Léopold Simoneau, Teresa Stratas, Lilian Sukis, Heather Thomson, Bernard Turgeon, and Jon Vickers.

Opera continues to be a favourite attraction with Canadian audiences. Companies in Montreal, Vancouver, Edmonton, southern Alberta, and Manitoba, as well as smaller amateur and semiprofessional companies in many other places regularly present operas throughout Canada, including a significant number written by Canadian composers. There has been sufficient interest to warrant the publication of *Opera Canada,* a magazine founded in 1962 and devoted to opera news and reviews, both national and international.

Chamber Music

Chamber music can be heard in all major towns and cities and in a number of smaller places. Halifax, Ottawa, Montreal, Toronto, and Vancouver are visited by international touring groups, but most cities also enjoy performances by other small ensembles on a regular basis. For example, the Orford Quartet in residence at the University of Toronto, the Purcell String Quartet in residence at Simon Fraser University, and the Canadian Brass tour widely and enjoy international reputations; many other Canadian ensembles ranging from duos to chamber orchestras regularly tour at home as well as in other countries.

Currently active Canadian chamber groups of a more unusual nature include Nexus (percussion ensemble), GIML (Groupe d'interprétation de musique électroacoustique de Laval), the Canadian Electronic Ensemble (avant-garde performance on electronic instruments), and the Toronto Consort, Hortulanae Musicae, and Tafelmusik (Medieval, Renaissance, and Baroque music).

Popular Musicians

A number of Canadian musicians have established themselves both nationally and internationally in the field of popular or commercial music. There does not seem to be any specifically "Canadian" identity in the various areas of country, rock, jazz, or the other subdivisions of pop music making. To the public at large, Canadian artists blend in easily with the more numerous Americans. United States dominance of the Canadian pop market was abetted by the Canadian radio stations which, until 1970, played the recordings of United States musicians almost exclusively. Although there were numerous rock groups in Canada—Mark Miller estimates fourteen hundred by 1966[3]—few were recorded and even fewer received air time on the most popular radio shows. Canadian pop artists of the fifties and sixties included groups such as the Crew-Cuts, Rover Boys, Beaumarks, and Stampeders, and soloists Paul Anka, Bobby Curtola, Robert Goulet, Giselle McKenzie, and Hank Snow, most of whom achieved their fame in the United States.

In 1970 the Canadian Radio-Television and Telecommunications Commission (CRTC) established a requirement that 30 percent of all radio music programming have Canadian content. That regulation has given an enormous boost to both the Canadian recording industry and individual musicians. As a result of the high profile now given to outstanding Canadian artists, a number of them have achieved national and international fame. Some of the most popular have moved to the United States or keep residences in both countries, but others, like Anne Murray and Gordon Lightfoot, have stayed in Canada.

Some of the groups and artists mentioned above have continued to be popular through the seventies and into the eighties. New names in the rock field include Burton Cummings (originally with Guess Who), Randy Bachman (originally with Bachman-Turner Overdrive, more recently BTO), Terry Jacks (originally with the Poppy Family), and the groups April Wine, Rush, and Lighthouse. In the field of country music Canadian artists include Ian and Sylvia Tyson (separately since the mid-seventies), Tommy Hunter, Murray McLaughlin, and Carol Baker.

3. *EMC*, 815b.

Phil Nimmons in concert.

The popular songs of Frank Mills, the poet-singer Leonard Cohen, and Hagood Hardy are well known in both the United States and Canada.

Canadian jazz artists such as Trump and Teddy Davidson, Oscar Peterson, Phil Nimmons, and Harvey Silver were widely known in the forties or earlier, and some are still active. More recent (since the fifties) jazz performers in Canada include Jim Galloway, Rob McConnell (and his band Boss Brass), Sonny Greenwich, Ed Bickert, Moe Koffman, and Herbie Spanier. Both Paul Horn (from the United States) and Peter Appleyard (from Great Britain) have chosen to live in Canada.

Music Education

Music education of the highest quality has been available in Canada since the early 1930s. This has been manifest in the enormous growth of music education in the primary and secondary schools, a higher quality of instruction in the conservatories, and the establishment of departments and schools of music at many of the universities. While in the past Canada's most talented performers went to Europe and the United States for advanced work, they can now study in Canada. Among those who have been trained in Canada are Robert Aitken, Liona Boyd, James Campbell, the late Glenn Gould, Ofra Harnoy, André Laplante, Zara Nelsova, and Steven Staryk.

Talented students have numerous opportunities to supplement their school and conservatory programmes. Organizations such as the National Youth Orchestra (formed in 1960), the Banff School of Fine Arts (1933), the Toronto Symphony

Youth Orchestra (1974), and the summer camp of the Jeunesses musicales du Canada (1949) bring the young musicians into contact with internationally famous performers and teachers for intensive study and rehearsal.

Support Organizations

Canadian Music Centre

In 1959 the Canadian Music Centre (CMC) was established for the benefit of Canadian composers, providing a library and information centre for the dissemination and promotion of Canadian concert, operatic, educational, and church music. The centre's offices in Toronto, Montreal, Vancouver, and Calgary give out music and information about Canadian composers, function as a central repository for compositions written after 1940, and actively promote the music and the musicians through publications of catalogues, biographies, and scores.

Similar kinds of promotion of Canadian music and musicians are offered by two other organizations that originally were branches of United States groups: the Composers, Authors and Publishers Association of Canada (CAPAC), formerly the Canadian affiliate of the American Society of Composers, Authors and Publishers (ASCAP), and PRO Canada, formerly the Canadian subsidiary of Broadcast Music Incorporated (BMI).[4]

John Adaskin Project

In 1961 John Adaskin, while executive secretary of the Canadian Music Centre, initiated a scheme in which composers were encouraged to visit school music groups and to compose music for all educational levels. The John Adaskin Project has continued to provide a steady supply of contemporary music for young people, written by Canada's finest composers. Since the late 1970s the project, under the direction of Patricia Shand, has compiled a series of annotated lists of music suitable for educational use.[5]

Canada Council

The Canada Council was established in 1957 to support the arts, humanities, and social sciences. It is governed by a board of directors who are advised by specialists in particular fields. Among the many music programmes set up by the council are commissions for compositions, financial support for both amateur and professional performances and performers, scholarships for students, funds for scholarly research, and subsidies for Canadian publications of music and scholarship. Local arts organizations in some of the provinces have provided similar funding and services at the provincial level.

4. Additional information about these and other organizations available in *EMC,* and Ford, *Canada's Music,* 180–85.

5. Patricia Shand, *Canadian Music: A Selective Guidelist for Teachers* (Toronto: Canadian Music Centre, 1978). Other publications forthcoming.

CBC

The CBC radio and television networks give enormous support to Canadian composers and performers in a number of ways that go beyond providing the listening public with a wealth of fine music. Since its inception the national network has publicized music and musicians through personal interviews and by devoting entire programmes to Canadian musicians. A wide variety of music, both Canadian and foreign, is presented with informed commentary and without commercial interruption. Emphasis on music over CBC television varies greatly from year to year (and from budget to budget), but over the years works by Canadian composers have been commissioned and telecast, and Canadian musicians and ensembles of all types have been featured. The CBC also commissions concerts and recitals and has recorded several series of performances by Canadian artists. One of those series is devoted to representative works by the most distinguished Canadian composers.

Centennial Celebration

The Centennial year, 1967, brought a wealth of concerts and commissions all across the country. Following the federal government's lead, the provincial and local governments as well as the citizenry took a close look at the country and its arts. It was a year in which many people became familiar with the Canadian cultural heritage. As a part of the anniversary, Expo '67, the World's Fair in Montreal, served as a focal point for the celebration, and especially as a forum for the arts. The pavilions sponsored by the national and provincial governments prominently displayed Canadian arts for all the world to see.

During the Centennial year a number of Canadian musical groups toured the country. Financial assistance was given to encourage performances and composition (the CMC alone helped to commission 45 works). RCA and the CBC jointly released a seventeen-album series of discs, "Music and Musicians of Canada/Musique et musiciens du Canada," containing 42 compositions by thirty-two Canadians, performed by Canadian musicians. Altogether 130 works were

Man and Music Pavilion at Expo '67.

composed in honour of Canada's one hundredth birthday, including:

Stage works (opera, ballet, puppet works)	16
Radio opera	4
Orchestral works	34
Fanfares	4
Chamber music	23
Choral	26
Vocal	14
Keyboard	7
Film sound tracks	2[6]

Because of the nature of the occasion the subject matter of a majority of these compositions was in some way nationalistic. The stage works, especially, dwelt on episodes from Canadian history, like the operas by Murray Adaskin, *Grant, Warden of the Plains* (Métis leader Cuthbert Grant); Kelsey Jones, *Sam Slick* (fictional Yankee clockmaker from nineteenth-century Nova Scotia); Harry Somers, *Louis Riel* (see below, pp. 132 ff.); and Robert Turner, *The Brideship* (the 1862 shipment of orphan girls to Victoria to become wives for the miners); and ballets by Harry Freedman, *Rose Latulippe* (set in 1740 Quebec); and Srul Irving Glick, *Heritage* (Jews in Canada).

The Centennial year provided an impetus for many Canadian composers to focus on national themes. The composers provided alternative views of the national heritage, and many Canadians became much more aware of the fine music being written in their country.

Composition

In the late forties a number of the younger Canadian composers (most of whom had studied abroad) achieved prominence and secured positions of importance that enabled them to exert an influence on the direction of music in their country. There was almost a revolutionary fervor about the way in which some of them broke with the older generation. They studied with Americans as well as Europeans, and had a stronger allegiance to the international school of experimental music than to the Old World traditional leanings of the more established Canadian composers. The strongest influence was exerted by those composers who taught at the universities, where they began in earnest to train Canadians in modern compositional styles and techniques. The new appointments included John Weinzweig to the University of Toronto; Barbara Pentland to the University of British Columbia; Murray Adaskin to the University of Saskatchewan; István Anhalt to McGill; and Jean Papineau-Couture to the Université de Montréal.[7] The music they espoused utilized the broad panorama of modern sounds found in the most advanced cities of the Western world (this included electronic com-

6. From George Proctor, *Canadian Music* (Toronto: University of Toronto Press, 1980), 151.
7. *Ibid.*, 34.

The twentieth anniversary conference of the Canadian League of Composers at the University of Victoria, 1971. Among the composers present were John Weinzweig (3rd from left) and Barbara Pentland (2nd from right).

position once a full-fledged electronic studio was established in Toronto in 1959—the second one in North America).

In 1951 the Canadian League of Composers was formed with John Weinzweig as its first president. It immediately set about obtaining performances and publicity for Canadian composers—not only for the most avant-garde, but for all. (The audience's reluctance to listen to music by local composers extended to all of them, regardless of style.) From its inception, the League encompassed the widely varied approaches of the serialists (Weinzweig, Pentland, Papineau-Couture), the more traditionally oriented (Ridout, Prévost), and the avant-garde experimentalists (Schafer, Anhalt, Somers). The single source of unity among them has been the need to promote their own music in a society that prefers the music of the past from other countries. With the cooperation of the other organizations mentioned above, the League has succeeded extremely well in a relatively short time. None of the composers is a household name, but few modern composers anywhere are. The League has obtained hearings for contemporary works, and it is now possible for the public—which the League have helped to educate—to experience the artistic creations of Canadian composers. As Barbara Pentland wrote in the *Northern Review* in 1950:

> It looks as if we will at long last grow up as a community of people, and begin to realize our potential. . . . The long dependence on a "mother" country has allowed our resources of native talent to be stifled or exported, with the same indifference that has seen our Indian art scattered to Europe and the United States. . . . In looking back over the last twenty years I can most happily note a vast change for the better in the Canadian scene. Young composers now have an opportunity of learning their creative craft without going beyond the border . . . Handel is finally dethroned as the model for the composition student. . . . At least we've started something, even if it still leaves our generation in the difficult role of pioneer.

The music written in Canada since the Second World War is astonishingly rich. Every modern trend is represented and many composers strive for wide diversity within their own output. To get some idea of the variety of compositional styles current today, we shall look at some of the more influential composers who are representative of the varied approaches to music in the last forty years. What will become evident from the following discussion is that Canada has developed a musical profile with quality and variety comparable to that found anywhere in the Western world.

There have been three main sources of influence that have helped shape contemporary Canadian composition in recent years: the major directions taken by members of the international school (i.e., electronic or synthesized music, aleatoric music, serialism, etc.); the inheritance of an early twentieth-century French and English orientation (post-Debussy, Ravel, Delius, Vaughan Williams, etc.); and the compositional characteristics of foreign-born or foreign-trained composers who have settled in Canada and there created for themselves a unique stylistic amalgam, blending background with surroundings (i.e., Anhalt, Morowetz, etc.).

Composers in French-speaking Canada—especially those from Montreal—have, for the most part, carried forward the French-Canadian heritage described earlier in the discussion of Claude Champagne (see chapter 5). Each composer in turn has renewed the French influence by studies abroad. Nadia Boulanger, Olivier Messiaen, Arthur Honegger, Pierre Boulez, and Edgard Varèse have all helped shape an entire group of Canadian composers.

Jean Papineau-Couture

Jean Papineau-Couture was born in Montreal in 1916, a grandson of Guillaume Couture (see chapter 4). He studied with Quincy Porter in the United States and with Nadia Boulanger in Paris, and was greatly influenced by Stravinsky. An instructor at Brébeuf College and the University of Montreal, his pupils included Jacques Hetú, François Morel, André Prevost, and Gilles Tremblay.

Papineau-Couture's works from the forties and fifties exhibit some of the impressionistic tendencies of French composers during the early years of the century; his *Suite pour Piano* (1943) and Concerto Grosso (1943, revised 1955), for example, remind one of Debussy and Ravel. His forms are neoclassic, with clearly distinct and contrasting sections, and he derives entire phrases from tiny variations of a small motive. The Prelude (Anthology #9) from his *Suite pour Piano* is an example of his early style. The entire composition is derived from the motive ♩. ♪♩ ♩ found at the very beginning of the composition. Throughout the short movement, this motive supplies the basic rhythm. (It can be found in the contrasting second melodic section in bar 5 as ♫ ♫ .) He uses dissonances in nearly every chord, but by widely separating the dissonant notes (notice the separation of G and A♭ in the first chord), he minimizes the clash and produces a rich harmonic sound.

His harmonic practices changed over the decades; the late-romantic and impressionistic sounds of his early compositions from the forties became more dissonant in the fifties. By 1967 when he wrote his String Quartet No. 2, he had made a significant change, adopting the strong harmonic clashes reminiscent of late Stravinsky and Bartók, along with sharper rhythms and more frequent changes of texture and pace.

Papineau-Couture's music has continued to evolve into the late seventies, uniting the light impressionism[8] of his early works with a highly personal use of the more atonal harmonic elements,[9] thereby producing emotional compositions such as *Le Débat du coeur et du corps de Villon* (1977), for narrator, cello, and percussion, in which the principal motive is a rhythm symbolic of a heartbeat ♪♩ (see example VI–1). Throughout the composition the narrator reads from a text by François Villon while the instruments punctuate the spoken phrases and separate them with short passages, all united by a relationship to the heartbeat motive.

Example VI–1: Jean Papineau-Couture, *Le Débat du coeur et du corps de Villon*

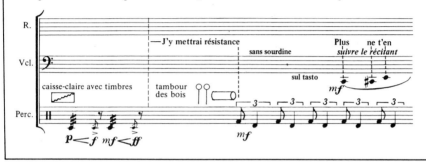

Gilles Tremblay

Gilles Tremblay (Jonquière, Quebec, 1932) studied in Montreal with Papineau-Couture and Champagne, and in Europe with Messiaen, Boulez, and Pousseur. He is active as both composer and performer (on the Ondes Martenot).[10] He is also an active board member of the Société de musique contemporaine du Québec (SMCQ, founded in 1966), an organization that promotes contemporary music through an annual series of six to eight concerts featuring new works by Canadian and foreign composers. Tremblay's compositions show the influences of Messiaen, Boulez, and Varèse in their complex mixtures of sound and rhythmic shapes.

In "Phases" (Anthology #10) from *Pièces pour piano,* Tremblay has composed a work entirely based on contrasts at every level of the music: volume, motion, rhythm, range, texture, colour.

8. "Impressionism" is the name usually used to describe a style of composition at the turn of the twentieth century designed to create descriptive impressions by evoking mood through rich and varied harmonies and timbres. The term is most often applied to the music of Claude Debussy and other French composers of his era. For additional description, see Joseph Machlis, *The Enjoyment of Music,* 5th ed. (New York: W. W. Norton, 1984), 441ff.

9. "Atonal," "serial technique," or "twelve-tone composition" are roughly equivalent terms for the technique developed in the early years of the twentieth century by Arnold Schoenberg, in which all twelve tones of the chromatic scale are given equal emphasis and arranged in a basic set. For additional information, see Machlis, *Enjoyment of Music,* 471–73.

10. See chapter 5, note 10.

The basic elements of the piece are all revealed in the first three bars. "Phases" is based on a twelve-tone row that is presented one note at a time. The row has built into it the pitch contrasts of half steps sounded close together, for example in bar 2, B and B♭, followed by F and G♭. In bar 1 he has set two pairs of notes against one another in the same manner—E♭, C in one octave, and E, C♯ in the other. By the end of the first three bars he has established the following contrasts:

1. notes played in similar range (bar 1), separated range (bar 2), and widely separate ranges (bar 3)
2. soft vs. loud
3. smooth vs. accented
4. held notes (bar 1) vs. detached notes
5. even vs. abrupt motion

The rest of the composition can be seen as a working-out of all these contrasts, causing the piece to shimmer with mysterious excitement. The diamond-shaped notes (seen for the first time in bar 8) indicate keys depressed without striking, producing sympathetic vibrations. This technique illustrates Tremblay's concern with harmonics and the overtone system, an interest which has persisted since he took a course in acoustics with Papineau-Couture.

Tremblay's orchestral and ensemble compositions exhibit the same kind of interest in pure sound. He frequently explores unconventional sounds, such as blowing into wind instruments without making a tone, or unusual harmonics from the string instruments.

Others

Other influential composers from French-speaking Canada include Serge Garant, André Prévost, and Clermont Pépin, whose works are all based to some degree on French models, although the three composers have different styles and musical goals.

Serge Garant (Quebec City, 1929) studied with Champagne and Messiaen, and was much influenced by the music of Anton Webern. He is active as a conductor of modern music in Montreal. At the founding of SMCQ in 1966 he was appointed music director and has conducted the group regularly both in North America and Europe. Garant's early compositions show the sweeping sounds so typical of Messiaen and the pointillistic influence of Anton Webern's music (e.g., *Asymetries No. 1*), while in his more recent compositions he has demonstrated an interest in variation of sonority, texture, and pace (e.g., . . . *chant d'amours*).

Clermont Pépin (St.-Georges-de Beauce, Quebec, 1926) studied in Montreal with Claude Champagne, in Toronto with Arnold Walter, in Paris with Arthur Honegger, and in Philadelphia with Rosario Scalero. He began writing in the late-romantic style of his teachers. In Quartet No.1, dedicated to Honegger, the melody is built on a *soggetto cavato* on Honegger's name (i.e., constructed from the vowels of his name as they correspond to solfège syllables), and his teacher's influence is clearly present. In later works he has moved toward more dissonance and some use of serial technique, as in *Guernica* (1952) and Symphony No. 3 *Quasars* (1967), but his compositions are still oriented toward the large colourful gestures and sweeping lines connected with the post-romantic movement. He thinks of himself as "sentimental at heart and very romantic."[11]

André Prévost (Hawkesbury, Ontario, 1934) was a student of both Papineau-Couture and Pépin before going to Paris from 1960 to 1962 to study with Messiaen and Dutilleux. He employs elements of the serial technique in many of his works, but he favours long lyrical lines and repetition of musical elements. His compositions often have extra-musical connotations and relationships: *Fantasmes* describes "the unwelcome and desperate vision of a nightmare," and in *Chorégraphie I* he reacts to the senseless murder of the Olympic contenders at Munich in 1972.[12]

The music of the composers in English-speaking Canada is more varied than that of their French-speaking counterparts and exhibits a broad variety of backgrounds and influences. Their teachers include the most noted composers from Europe and North America. Their compositions range from conservative to highly experimental, exhibiting almost every style current in the Western world. We shall single out a few of the more influential composers in order to sample their diversity.

One phenomenon unique to the twentieth century is the composer who writes entirely in an earlier style. Nearly all of the Canadian composers in the first half of this century chose conservative models for their works; that avenue has remained a valid stylistic choice.

Three quite different conservative approaches have been taken by Godfrey Ridout, Violet Archer, and Oskar Morawetz. Ridout favoured the sounds of the English composers from early in the century; Archer writes in the neoclassic style of her teacher Paul Hindemith; and Morawetz's works reflect the Eastern European and Russian styles reminiscent of Shostakovich and Prokofiev. Each composer has established a distinctive style and a considerable reputation.

Godfrey Ridout

Godfrey Ridout (Toronto, 1918–1984) was the best and most unabashed representative of the English musical heritage in Canada. He studied with Healey Willan and continued to compose along the same traditional lines as his teacher, although his works are more varied and draw frequently on Canadian material. In his many journal articles and in his courses at the University of Toronto (1942–82) he indicated his allegiance to Sullivan, Elgar, and Vaughan Williams. This loyalty is substantiated in the titles of compositions such as *Three Preludes on Scottish Tunes* (1959), *Festal Overture* (1939), and *Music for a Young Prince* (1959). Some of his compositions contain Canadian material, like *Folk Songs of Eastern Canada,* in which he followed the tradition of Holst and Vaughan Wil-

---

11. *EMC*, 740a.
12. Proctor, *Canadian Music,* 112–13, 176.

liams by providing a rich harmonic setting for folk tunes. In 1963 he reconstructed Canada's first opera, Joseph Quesnel's *Colas et Colinette* (1788), by filling out the orchestration from the surviving vocal score and second violin part, and providing an overture in Quesnel's style. In this form the opera has been performed a number of times and produced on CBC radio and television.[13]

Ridout employed the lush tonal harmonic vocabulary of the early twentieth-century British post-romantics such as Vaughan Williams, Holst, and Elgar, with a bit of dissonance as found in Walton and Britten.

> For the most part, he confined his writing to the formal designs of the neoclassicists—nearly all of his works have clearly marked sections. His music consists of short recurring motives, both rhythmic and melodic, as in the opening melody of *Fall Fair* (example VI–2). The melody is clearly in D major, and uses the rhythm ♩ ♩ ♪♩ ♪ (bar 1) and its reverse ♪♩ ♪♩ ♩ (bars 2 and 3). The fanfare-like rhythm and the opening intervals of a third and fifth give the melody a strong character and clear identification. Like many of the British post-romantics, Ridout was able to invent melodies that resemble folk songs.
>
> Example VI–2: Godfrey Ridout, *Fall Fair,* opening melody
>
>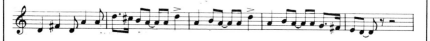

His *Music for a Young Prince* was written to celebrate the opening of the St. Lawrence Seaway, and Ridout composed it with young Prince Charles in mind. The four movements are meant to conjure up vivid childhood fantasies: I. "Dreams," II. "From the Caboose," III. "The Cowboy and the Injun," IV. "Pageantry."

In "From the Caboose," Ridout recreates the impression of riding on a train. The steam engine can be heard starting up with jolting sounds that finally achieve a regular pace. When the train later slows to a stop, the trombone players blow into their mouthpieces—not to make a musical sound, but to simulate the sound of a train releasing steam from its brakes. (The train is understandably an image used by many Canadian composers, including Alexander Brott, R. Murray Schafer, and John Weinzweig.)

> Ridout's more contemporary technique can be seen in the second of *Two Etudes* for string orchestra (1946, revised 1951; Anthology #11). In this work the melodic phrases are less regular and folklike than those in *Fall Fair* and *Music for a Young Prince*. The melody itself is chromatic and the harmonies contain strong dissonances (for example in bar 2, C♯ against D). The movement illustrates his method of constructing an entire piece from several short motives. The principal ones are introduced near the beginning of the movement: a triplet figure, first seen in bar 2; the rhythm 𝄽 ♩ ♩ ♩ (later ♩. ♩ ♩) in bars 3–4; the syncopated rhythm and the arpeggio, both in bar

13. See chapter 2, note 33.

7; and the turn-like melodic figure in example VI-3, introduced by the first violins in bars 9–10. The rest of the composition consists of variations formed by combining and altering these motives. The arpeggio figure from bar 7, for example, appears again in bar 47 accompanied by the turn-like figure (at double speed); and the relaxed lyrical section from rehearsal numbers 11 to 15 can be traced to the aggressive rhythm of bars 3–4. Ridout continually recombines his basic motives to spin out a vigorous movement that propels itself forward with great variety and enthusiasm.

Example VI–3: Godfrey Ridout, Etude II from *Two Etudes,* mm. 9–10

For the most part, Ridout's music looks back, both in style and intent. The composer assumed the role of the village storyteller, conjuring up images of the Canadian past. His friend and colleague Harvey Olnick wrote of him: "Essentially an eclectic, Ridout yet does not lack for individuality. His music, though intensely felt, is prevailingly sunny and affirmative . . . Ridout in the end may be perceived to be more original than many innovators and one of the determined communicators of our day."[14]

Violet Archer

Violet Archer (Montreal, 1913) began her studies with Claude Champagne at the McGill Conservatorium, and her earliest compositions reflected Champagne's interest in folklike melodies and rhythms and late-romantic harmonies. After studying in New York with Béla Bartók in 1942 and at Yale University with Paul Hindemith in 1949, she changed her style of composition completely.

Example VI–4: Violet Archer, Prelude and Allegro, mm. 61–65

Archer's approach since the early fifties can be described as neoclassic: she chooses classic forms with clear and well-shaped melodies. Her harmonies are determined by intervals, rather than keys, following the practice of Hindemith. Her music is marked by reserved emotional content, as can be seen in the excerpt from her Prelude and Allegro for piano and violin.

---

14. *EMC,* 810b.

In this "allegro scherzoso" Archer has skillfully constructed three lines of counterpoint based on a clear idea of consonance and dissonance, which frequently change tonal orientation. The opening suggestion of a tonal centre around A is weakened by the violin D♯ in bar 4, and again in the fifth bar where the bass line finishes its scale on G♯. The two outside lines proceed completely in contrary motion, while the middle line has material similar in some ways to the violin part. The middle voice in bars 1 and 3 begins with the second note of the violin part, and for seven notes traces the same pattern. By a clever change in the rhythm pattern, Archer gives to the middle line a lighter dance pattern—rebarred it would look like an Italian *giga:* ♫♩♫♩ | ♩ ♪♪♪♪ | —which provides a contrast to the more intense outside voices.

In her later works Archer used more dissonance than can be seen in example VI–4 (as in *Plainsongs,* 1977), and in some works she has included electronic sounds.

She has taught theory and composition at several universities in the United States and Canada, and in 1962 joined the faculty of the University of Alberta, where she served as chairman of the theory and composition department and guided many aspiring composers from the western provinces.

Oskar Morawetz

Oskar Morawetz (Svĕltá nad Sázavou, Czechoslovakia, 1917) immigrated to Canada in 1940 after studying theory and piano in Prague, Vienna, and Paris. He received both bachelor and doctor of music degrees from the University of Toronto, but is for the most part a self-taught composer. George Proctor states that he "stands out as the main exponent of late Romanticism. His penchant for chromatic wanderings, long developments and virtuoso display link him with Franck and Reger on the one hand and Liszt and Rachmaninoff on the other."[15]

Morawetz's connection with late romanticism lies more in the spirit of the music than in the actual techniques employed. His melodic lines are comparatively long and disjunct, and the texture is thick and rich with colour. His harmonies suggest those of Richard Strauss in that they shift their basic orientation from section to section, but remain quite stable within any one long phrase. His two most distinctive characteristics are a high degree of emotionalism in everything he writes, and irregular changes of pace as a composition unfolds. For an audience familiar with the romantic repertory, Morawetz's music is not difficult to listen to. His non-tonal harmonic ideas are softened by the sweeping sentiment of the lines. The subjects of his compositions tend to be international: *Carnival Overture, Memorial to Martin Luther King, Fantasy on a Hebrew Theme, From the Diary of Anne Frank.*

One of his most successful compositions is *From the Diary of Anne Frank* (1970) for soprano and orchestra; the work is an excellent example of Morawetz's style. The subject of the composition is the diary written in the 1940s by

15. Proctor, *Canadian Music,* 38.

a young Jewish girl in Amsterdam who, for over two years, hid in an attic with her family and several others in order to escape the Nazis. They were finally found, and Anne Frank died in a concentration camp before her sixteenth birthday.

Morawetz was drawn to the subject both by his own experience as a Jew fleeing Hitler, and by Anne Frank's unshakable belief in human decency. Morawetz corresponded with the father, Otto Frank, travelled to Europe several times to hear of the family's experiences firsthand, and followed up every detail of the story.

For the text, he used sections of the diary in which Anne reflects on the fate of a friend who had been captured. These passages demonstrate Anne's fears, uncertainties, hopes, and strength. ''I am not more virtuous than she; she too, wanted to do what was right, why should I be chosen to live and she probably to die? . . . And when I pray for her, I pray for all the Jews and for all those in need!''

Example VI–5: Oskar Morawetz, *From the Diary of Anne Frank*, excerpt

The music portrays these powerful sentiments with a variety of strong and emotional lines. The passage below begins with a plea for help that Anne has imagined comes from her friend: ''Oh help me, rescue me from this hell.'' Morawetz has set this cry to an irregular, descending vocal line, emphasizing the anguish and the hopelessness of the plea. For the next passage, as Anne reflects on her inability to assist her friend, the rhythm is slow, regular, and the notes somewhat static. The accompaniment for both passages supports the emotional message. For the friend's cry for help the accompaniment is short and abrupt—a rather disjointed musical punctuation. For Anne's reflection, the accompaniment is sustained to emphasize both the futility of her position and the narrative character of the statement.

Others

Conservatism can be found in the different styles of several other composers: Maurice Dela (Montreal, 1919–1978) and Robert Turner (Montreal, 1920) both studied with Claude Champagne. Their music is somewhat modeled along the conservative ideas of their teacher. Jean Coulthard (Vancouver, 1908) shows in her music the English romantic influence of her teachers R. O. Morris, Vaughan Williams, and Gordon Jacobs. Murray Adaskin (Toronto, 1906) has consciously chosen a more conservative mode of neoclassic composition than that of his teacher, John Weinzweig.

Other composers worthy of mention here are Sophie-Carmen Eckhardt-Gramaté (Moscow, 1902–Stuttgart, 1974); Arnold Walter (Hannsdorf, Moravia, 1902–Toronto, 1973); and Talivaldis Kenins (Liepaja, Latvia, 1919). The last-mentioned has, since the early seventies, moved away from conservatism, exploring the techniques of chance music and tone clusters.

Modern Directions

A number of Canadian composers began their experimental efforts with Schoenberg's serial technique,[16] but none of them have remained totally within that area. The seven composers treated in some depth here—Weinzweig, Freedman, Pentland, Beckwith, Anhalt, Somers, and Schafer—have been chosen to illustrate the widest possible variety of style and approach found in English-speaking Canada today (electronic music is treated separately, beginning on p. 138).

☀ John Weinzweig

John Weinzweig (Toronto, 1913) is probably the most influential composer in present-day Canada because of the success of his compositions, the large number of students who studied with him at the Toronto Conservatory and the University of Toronto, and his position as first president of the Canadian League of Composers. He is generally considered the first Canadian to use the twelve-tone row (1939), although he drifted away from that system in the 1960s.

Weinzweig studied in Toronto with Willan and MacMillan and at the Eastman School with Howard Hanson and Bernard Rogers. He has been profoundly influenced by the music of Sibelius, whose concept of sweeping, romantic melody has stayed with him throughout his career. Described by his biographer, Elaine

---

16. See note 9.

Keillor, as a "romantic melodist," he composes within a very spare framework, placing a few well-chosen sounds in silence. In many of his works the elements of jazz—especially blues—can be heard in the rhythms and melodic phrases. Most of Weinzweig's music is instrumental, and includes a number of film scores written early in his career for the National Film Board on various Canadian subjects. In those works and in many of his other programmatic compositions his Canadian orientation (e.g., *The Red Ear of Corn*) or his Polish-Jewish ancestry (e.g., Cello Sonata *Israel*) are reflected.

Over a period of many years he has written a series of nine divertimenti, all but the last for solo instruments, which resemble classical concertos. These pieces demonstrate the various stages in Weinzweig's development as he moved from serialism to an interest in timbre as the major formative element.

The first movement of his *Divertimento No. 1* for flute and string orchestra (Anthology #12) is a good example of Weinzweig's early style. Begun in 1945 while he was in the Royal Canadian Air Force, it won for him the highest award for chamber music at the London Olympiad in 1948 and has remained one of his most frequently performed works.

The first movement contrasts the short detached (bouncing bow) strokes of the string instruments with the more lyrical sounds of the flute. The piece begins with an almost neoclassic motive, reminiscent of the kind of line found in some Stravinsky works. But as the movement proceeds, Weinzweig's unemotional theme expands, becoming more lyrical (bars 20–28, 40–49). The movement is based on a melodic tone row. Weinzweig allows himself the freedom of repeating notes of the row so that the flute does not complete its row until the G in bar 10. He did not intentionally use a row harmonically, but by bar 21 all twelve tones are used in the accompaniment parts as well. In this case, as in many of his serial compositions, the row is used principally to avoid any feeling of tonality, but Weinzweig found that he could accomplish that goal and still repeat notes as his lyrical muse dictated.

Many of Weinzweig's compositions on Canadian subjects contain folklike melodies, although none is an actual folk tune. It is said that when he wants to write that kind of melody, he first listens to a number of folk songs and then composes his own personal distillation of what he has heard.

In 1967 he wrote Concerto for Harp and Chamber Orchestra, a one-movement piece with six interconnected sections. This is his most heavily serialized composition, extending the serial concept to all elements, in the style of Webern. In attempting to write in a unique style for harp he became interested in timbre, and since that time he has frequently abandoned the serial technique in favour of using sound contrasts as the formative or organizing element in his writing.

Weinzweig's students include a large number of the most active composers in English-speaking Canada: Murray Adaskin, Norma Beecroft, Brian Cherney,

Samuel Dolin, Harry Freedman, Srul Irving Glick, Bruce Mather, R. Murray Schafer, and Harry Somers.

Harry Freedman

Harry Freedman (Lodz, Poland, 1922) emigrated to Canada (Medicine Hat and Winnipeg) early in life, and studied composition with Weinzweig. His early works, especially *Divertimento for Oboe and Strings,* show the influence of his teacher. He has written a number of film scores *(Pale Horse, Pale Rider* and *Act of the Heart),* incidental music for plays *(Much Ado About Nothing* and *As You Like It* for the Stratford Festival Theatre), and compositions for ballet.

Freedman's music is always richly scored, and tends toward long, broad phrases. He occasionally incorporates nontraditional sounds in his works, as in *Pan* for soprano, flute, and piano, where the performers stamp their feet, whisper, and shout into the piano.

Inspiration for his works sometimes comes from paintings and other nonmusical sources. The three movements of *Images* for orchestra all have titles of paintings: "Blue Mountain," by Lawren Harris, "Structure at Dusk," by Kazuo Nakamura, and "Landscape," by Jean-Paul Riopelle, all twentieth-century Canadian painters. The Harris painting is *Lakes and Mountains* (now in the Art Gallery of Ontario), a stylized representation of a blue mountain, but the other two paintings are nonobjective. Freedman attempts to reflect the moods and shapes

Lake and Mountains, *an oil by Lawren S. Harris (1885-1970) which served as inspiration for Harry Freedman's "Blue Mountain" from* **Images.**

of the paintings in the compositions. ''Blue Mountain'' has long lines and strong chordal motion connoting grandeur; ''Structure at Dusk'' is made up of many short, quick, and even melodic motions over a sustained accompaniment; and ''Landscape'' has long and short lines, smooth and halting motion, large and small phrases.

Barbara Pentland

Barbara Pentland (Winnipeg, 1912) was strongly affected by the works of Paul Hindemith and her teacher Aaron Copland, but by the late fifties she, too, utilized serial technique as a way of organizing her compositions.

One of her earliest works in this technique is *Symphony for Ten Parts,* a work that clearly shows the influence of Anton Webern (see example VI–6). Here Pentland has adopted Webern's economy of statement and pointillistic technique of breaking up the melodic line among a number of instruments. In the example below, the opening melody of movement I of the symphony can be seen to jump from instrument to instrument before it reaches the end of the short first phrase in bar 3.

Example VI–6: Barbara Pentland, *Symphony for Ten Parts,* first movement, mm.1–3

By the late sixties Pentland had begun to include aleatoric (chance) sections in some of her works *(Trio con Alea, Mutations),* and by the end of the seventies she had become interested in sonority and colour contrast as a focus of organization. In her two latest dramatic works she makes strong social comment: sarcasm is directed at violence and war in *News* and at male domination in *Disasters of the Sun.* Her compositions since the forties have been marked by short, concise phrases and rhythmic figures, by an avoidance of sentimentality, and often by humour.

John Beckwith

John Beckwith (Victoria, 1927) is one of the most important musicians in Canada today. He is a nationalist who, through his writings, composition, teaching, and other activities, has been a central force for Canadian music since the fifties. The increased interest in Canada's music that is now apparent across the country is a product of this devotion. He has written extensively about his country's music scene and edited and co-edited various source books on Canadian music. His article "About Canadian Music: The PR Failure"[17] was the inspiration for the *Encyclopedia of Music in Canada*. He has written and narrated music programmes on CBC radio, was the first secretary of the Canadian League of Composers, and served on the board of the Canadian Music Centre. Since 1955 he has taught music history, theory, and composition at the University of Toronto, where he served as dean of the Faculty of Music from 1970 to 1977.

Beckwith studied composition in Paris with Nadia Boulanger. Most of his works have Canadian content—either in the form of source material, as in *Sharon Fragments* (referring to music at the Sharon Temple; see p. 58), or as extra-musical subjects (e.g., *Gas!* and *Canada Dash—Canada Dot*). His most successful works are those for voice, especially the operas *Night Blooming Cereus* and *The Shivaree* (both on texts by James Reaney), his radio dramas (e.g., *Canada Dash—Canada Dot*, a documentary also by Reaney), and *The Journals of Susanna Moodie* (a poem cycle by Margaret Atwood). The titles of some of his compositions, such as *All the Bees and All the Keys* (a children's tale for narrator and orchestra, text by Reaney) and *Elastic Band Studies* (for concert band) suggest the tongue-in-cheek aspect of many of his works.

Example VI–7: John Beckwith, *The Shivaree*, prologue

---

17. *Musicanada* (1969), 4–7, 10–13.

The subject of his opera *The Shivaree* is the North American tradition of a pots-and-pans serenade to newlyweds on their wedding night. Reaney's script takes a number of unusual and unexpected twists in which a rejected suitor actually succeeds in winning back the bride on her wedding night. Beckwith's music moves between short lyrical passages and quasi-recitative.

In his compositions on historical subjects, Beckwith quotes from older music or composes sections in a traditional style to evoke images of another era. For example, in *Keyboard Practice,* for four players and ten keyboard instruments, he quotes from sources such as the Fitzwilliam Virginal Book (seventeenth century) and the suites of François Couperin (eighteenth century). The net impression is a partially tongue-in-cheek mixture of music from the concert hall and from the practice rooms, together with experimental sounds more frequently associated with John Cage or Steve Reich.

István Anhalt

István Anhalt (Budapest, 1919) also has turned increasingly to Canadian subject matter. He studied with Zoltán Kodály and Nadia Boulanger, and since his immigration to Canada in 1949, he has been influential as composer and teacher at McGill University and Queen's University. Although Anhalt's early works were based on the serial technique, his later works involve serialism only to a degree and do not follow that system with any regularity. He has experimented with electronic music, and many of his compositions include electronically produced sound.

Anhalt's major works are theatrical in size and design, like *La Tourangelle* for solo voices, chorus, tapes, and instruments. *La Tourangelle* (The Woman from Tours) concerns Marie de l'Incarnation, an Ursuline nun who settled in New France in the seventeenth century. It is a work of large proportions, in which the voices, instruments, and tape are woven together in a lyrical but complex manner.

Harry Somers

Harry Somers (Toronto, 1925) uses a number of modern elements in his work. He studied with Weinzweig and Milhaud and his compositions reflect their styles, as well as those of Bartók and Copland. The subject matter of his works varies greatly. There are compositions with generic titles such as string quartet and sonata, written in the neoclassic style he learned from Weinzweig; works on nationalistic subjects such as *Louis Riel* and *Northern Lights;* and works inspired by international subjects such as *Picasso Suite* and *Zen, Yeats and Emily Dickinson.* All his compositions exude vitality and rhythmic drive whether they are written in the serial technique, quasi-diatonic style, or an eclectic mixture.

North Country, an early work (1948), demonstrates Somers' method of painting a scene in music. The subject is northern Ontario, and the four movements depict ruggedness, tranquillity, majesty, and energy. The opening bars of the first movement (see example VI–8) demonstrate, in miniature, Somers' approach to phrase and drama: the melody, played by the first violin, consists of several short phrases (three are reproduced in the example) that as a group constitute a somewhat long line punctuated by shorter accompanying lines in the remainder of the orchestra. It is Somers' habit to build tension like this and to release it by swift rhythmic punctuation—whether a single, dramatic chord as in this composition, or a rhythmic figure of two or three notes.

Example VI–8: Harry Somers, *North Country,* first movement, mm.1–8

We can see also his technique of building a melody from small rhythmic and intervallic motives (possibly a Weinzweig influence). The first bar contains a fifth (G to D) and a fourth (A to D). Bar 3 has the same intervals, but backward—F♯ to B, and E to B. And the rhythmic cell found at the beginning of the first bar— ♩ ♫ —can be seen in bar 3. In bars 5–6 the material of both the preceding subphrases has been combined: the rhythmic cell and the intervals of a fifth and fourth are both present. The isolation of the slow, irregularly moving melody accompanied by such dramatic and dissonant chords (notice in bar 2 the clash of E♭ and B♭ against the melodic B♮, finally relieved by the melody note D♯-E♭ paints a picture of loneliness, ruggedness, and stark beauty: Somers' impression of the North Country.

Among Somers' many concerns is that good music reach young people. His *Theme for Variations* was written for school use as a part of the John Adaskin Project (see p. 112). He was invited to spend the year 1968–69 as a special consultant to the schools of North York (Toronto) where he helped students create musical ideas and become aware of the natural sounds around them. His composition *Improvisation*, a product of that year, shows his creativity in using material not usually thought of as part of a musical composition. *Improvisation* includes dropping tennis and Ping-Pong balls on the piano strings, and requires the performers to react to one another within a general framework of music and movement. His purpose was to include in the music objects and situations familiar to the students.

In 1969 Somers was asked to speak at a symposium of student composers on his use of the voice in composition. He responded with a demonstration of the variety of vocal sounds—an area he was exploring in the schools. His 1971 composition *Voiceplay* (example VI–9), commissioned by the CBC for soprano Cathy Berberian, incorporated the ideas he had developed in the school experience and his symposium "address." His notes to the soloist make it clear that much of what is performed is subjective and open to a wide array of personal interpretations:

> The piece is a display of vocal range and possibilities of each particular soloist. The piece is a musical "composition." The piece is a work for theatre. The piece will sometimes seem clear in intent to the audience, sometimes an enigma, sometimes ambiguous, sometimes seeming to move in and out of "focus".[18]

The soloist attempts to communicate with vocal sounds and physical actions rather than words. An accompanist acts as master of ceremonies, introducing

Example VI–9: Harry Somers, *Voiceplay,* excerpt

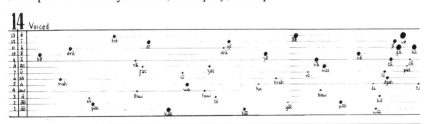

18. From Somers' notes to *Voiceplay,* quoted in Brian Cherney, *Harry Somers* (Toronto: University of Toronto Press, 1975), 147.

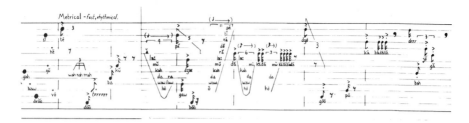

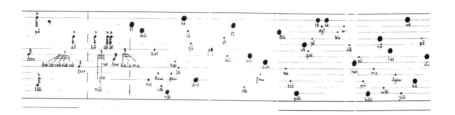

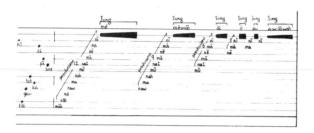

and thanking the performer, and also assists in some of the activities called for in the score.

The opera *Louis Riel* (1967) is considered by many to be Harry Somers' most important work and the finest Canadian opera of the century. Commissioned during Centennial year, it was performed first in Toronto by the Canadian Opera Company in September 1967, and a month later at Expo '67 in Montreal. It has had several performances since then and was televised in 1969.

Somers' opera, on a libretto by Mavor Moore, requires twenty-six soloists, chorus and orchestra, and a tape of electronic sounds created by Somers and Lowell Cross. The characters sing in English, French, Cree (Indian), and Latin. The opera was appropriate for the Centennial year: it concerns two dramatic chapters in the formation of Canada, and one of the major characters is the first prime minister, Sir John A. Macdonald.

The plot has two main focal points: the 1869 execution of Thomas Scott by Métis leader Louis Riel, and the execution of Riel in 1885 by the Canadian government. At the heart of the conflict in the opera is Riel's belief in his God-given destiny to lead his small band of Métis followers in spite of all opposition.

Example VI–10: Harry Somers, *Louis Riel*, Act I, Riel's soliloquy

In setting the text, Somers employed a wide range of techniques and styles. He used actual native song, and created his own folk and popular songs modeled on those of the period. There is dissonant atonal writing in dramatically intense scenes and diatonic writing in the relaxed and lighthearted sections. The vocal line assigned to the various characters underlines their personalities: Riel's music is usually lyrical (and often unaccompanied) to emphasize the romantic, visionary aspect of his character, while Macdonald, the pragmatist, is most often given a line of heightened or inflected speech. Most of the lengthy solos involve a variety of melodic writing rather than a single style, as in the soliloquy (example VI–10) above. Passages alternate simple melody with elaborate and difficult sections; they often draw upon a wide range of vocal sounds, occasionally resembling speech.

Riel's character is brought out most clearly in his soliloquy at the end of Act I (example VI–10). The librettist describes Riel's character as a "personification of some of the great liturgical themes of mankind . . . the idealist driven mad . . . the thinker paralyzed by his thinking, the Hamlet syndrome . . . the half-breed, the schizophrenic outsider."[19]

An example of Somers' adoption of existing material can be seen in his use of the native song "Kuyas" (Cree for "long ago") for Marguerite's soliloquy in Act III, scene 1 (example VI–11). (Later he extracted this song from the opera and released it separately, scored as in the original for voice, flute, and percussion.)

Example VI–11: Harry Somers, *Kuyas,* opening

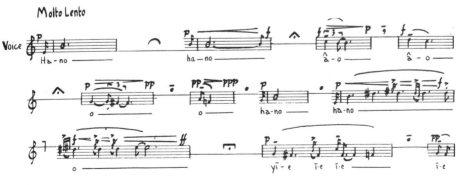

19. *Ibid.,* 130.

The orchestra in *Louis Riel* serves two roles: as the portrayer of the message, and as accompaniment for the singing. When the orchestra is playing alone, the music is emotionally evocative, sometimes emphasizing conflict through strongly dissonant and clashing passages, or suggesting the simplemindedness of government officials through simple melody set to diatonic harmonies. When accompanying vocal passages, the orchestra plays in various styles, but always very lightly, more as punctuation or support than in partnership with the singers.

Louis Riel is a summary of nearly all of Somers' compositional techniques. It has been widely praised by the public and the critics as an exceptional work of art.

R. Murray Schafer

R. Murray Schafer's (Sarnia, Ontario, 1933) sources of inspiration extend beyond his studies of composition with Weinzweig and Peter Racine Fricker to his interest in painting, his contact with the writer Marshal McLuhan, his study of medieval German at the Vienna Academy, and his journalistic efforts (his list of articles and booklets is nearly as long as his list of compositions). While teaching at Simon Fraser University (1965–75), Schafer established the "World Soundscape Project," dedicated to the study of man's relationship to his acoustical environment. The subject matter of this project includes all sound, both natural and man-made, its representation of man and nature, and its effect on both. The massive scope of such a multifaceted and interdisciplinary project accurately reflects Schafer's concerns.

The titles of his works further suggest the breadth of his interests: *Brébeuf, Requiems for the Party Girl, In Search of Zoroaster, Epitaph for Moonlight, Adieu Robert Schumann,* the more humourously titled *Son of Heldenleben* (based on the orchestration and occasionally on the themes of the Richard Strauss tone poem) and *No Longer than Ten Minutes* (a spoof on the specifications of a commission he received from the Toronto Symphony).

It is difficult to summarize Schafer's compositions because they are so diverse. They range from those with a purely abstract orientation like String Quartet No. 1 to those with extra-musical content, such as *Ra* (1983), an all-night vigil for the Egyptian sun god that includes song, dance, and prayer, and requires audience participation.

Schafer's works draw upon a wide range of compositional techniques to achieve the musical images: conventional notation, graphic scores, and electronic sounds. His sources of inspiration are just as diverse, including the poetry of Ezra Pound, the Tibetan Book of the Dead, and various subjects emerging from his interest in the environment.

Requiems for the Party Girl (Anthology #13) shows Schafer in a compositional mood similar to that of John Cage (although using quite different techniques). In this case he employs only traditional forces—a mezzo-soprano and a chamber orchestra—but the treatment is anything but traditional. The accompanying instruments serve a number of functions: they accentuate the text, as on the first page, when harp and tom-tom supply an emphasis separating the first sentence from the second; they set the mood throughout the piece, illustrating the emptiness and loneliness of the ''party girl;'' and they create sounds of confusion, the mixed noises heard at a party.

Schafer's music reflects the world he sees around him. He is interested in everything from minor social encounters to commentaries on war and the sounds of the sea.

Sun God's mask from **Ra** *by R. Murray Schafer.*

Electronic (Electroacoustic) Music

Electronic composition began on a permanent basis in Canada with the establishment of studios at the University of Toronto in 1959, at McGill University in 1963, and at the University of British Columbia in 1964. Some of the earliest work on the development of the electronic instruments was done by Hugh LeCaine (Port Arthur, 1914–Ottawa, 1977), a physicist and composer. He developed instruments for the studios at Toronto and McGill, and for the Hebrew University in Jerusalem. His work provided the foundation for commercial synthesizers, and he advised a number of the better-known synthesizer manufacturers.

LeCaine's 1955 composition *Dripsody* is still one of the most frequently played pieces of Canadian electronic music. It is an excellent introduction to the possibilities of electronic music making—the composition consists entirely of electronic manipulations of the sound of a single drip of water![20]

A number of Canadian composers have used the electronic medium. Most of them consider electronically produced sound to be only one of a number of possible sound sources, but a few compose extensively in that medium, for example Gustav Ciamaga, David Keane, Barry Truax, and the members of the Canadian Electronic Ensemble.

Gustav Ciamaga

Gustav Ciamaga (London, Ontario, 1930) studied composition in Toronto with John Beckwith and John Weinzweig, and in the United States with Arthur Berger, Harold Shapero, and Irving Fine. He joined the Faculty of Music at the University of Toronto in 1963, became director of the Electronic Music Studio in 1965, and from 1977 to 1984 served as dean of the faculty. Ciamaga has been active in the development of electronic instruments, most notably the Serial Sound Structure Generator. His compositions are for the most part short, contrapuntal studies with neoclassic formal designs, e.g., *Two-Part Inventions*. In *Solipsism While Dying* (text by Margaret Atwood) he combines electronic sounds with soprano, flute, and piano.

David Keane

David Keane (Akron, Ohio, 1943) is director of the Queen's University Electronic Music Studio which he founded in 1970. He studied composition at Ohio State University, but was influenced more by listening to a wide selection of music, especially medieval and Renaissance music. His compositions have won a number of international awards, including a prize at the Bourges (France) Festival competition in 1979 for *In Memoriam, Hugh LeCaine*.[21] In addition to vocal and instrumental music, he has created some forty electronic works for stage, television, film, and the concert hall. Keane's talents also include writing

---

20. Recorded on Folkways, FM 34360.
21. Recorded on Music Gallery ed. #29.

about music; he has published many articles on musical aesthetics, and a book, *Tape Music Composition*.[22]

Barry Truax

The electronic works of Barry Truax (Chatham, Ontario, 1947) usually have programmatic associations, such as *Tapes from Gilgamesh,* and *Children* for soprano and tape (text by e. e. cummings). Truax studied mathematics and physics at Queen's University, and composition with Courtland Hultberg at the University of British Columbia and with G. M. Koenig and Otto Laske in Utrecht. While in Utrecht he developed the programmes POD-6 and POD-7 for use in computer music. He replaced R. Murray Schafer as director of the World Soundscape Project at Simon Fraser University. In 1977 he won first prize in the competition at Bourges for *Sonic Landscape No. 3.*

Other Electronic Composers

István Anhalt has written a number of large electronic compositions, and more recently has incorporated electronic tape into compositions such as *La Tourangelle* (see p. 129). R. Murray Schafer mixes electronic sounds with orchestra in *Lustro.* Other composers who have used electronic sounds in their works include Norma Beecroft, Serge Garant, Udo Kasemets, Pierre Mercure, and Harry Somers.

Other composers active in the field of electronics include Micheline Coulombe-Saint-Marcoux and Yves Daoust, both of whom have won prizes in the Bourges competition; Jean Piché, whose *La Mer à l'Aube* won the CBC National Radio Competition for Young Composers in 1975–76 and has been recorded;[23] Marcelle Deschesnes who combines electronic composition with mime, dance, film, and light in multimedia presentations; Bruce Pennycook who attracted national attention with his *Speeches for Dr. Frankenstein* based on a poem by Margaret Atwood; and William Buxton who has received international recognition for his development of computer music programmes and devices for composition.

Space will not permit lengthy discussion of the many other Canadian composers who have made major contributions to the music repertory since the mid-forties, but their names should be mentioned as composers well worth listening to: Robert Aitken, Louis Applebaum, Walter Buczynski, Brian Cherney, Samuel Dolin, John Hawkins, Derek Healey, Jacques Hétu, Otto Joachim, Kelsey Jones, Lothar Klein, and Robert Turner.

Now would seem to be the moment to mention some of the younger generation of Canadian composers whose works we are bound to hear in the near future: Michael Baker, Walter Boudreau, Denys Bouliane, Patrick Cardy, Stephen Gellman, Mark Hand, Peter Paul Koprowski, Alexina Louie, Elma Miller, Marjan Mozetich, John Rea, Paul Théberge, and Claude Vivier.

22. London, 1980.
23. Recorded on Melbourne, SMLP 4045.

Summary

The enormous growth in the population and the economy of Canada since the end of the Second World War has had a parallel in the proliferation of musical activities. There has been a great increase in performance, composition, and teaching, all of the highest quality and on a scale much larger than the country's overall population would suggest.

We have seen that there have always been two strong and usually quite separate bases of composition in Canada—French and English. In the period since the Second World War, additional influences have been brought to bear by immigrant musicians from many countries, by Canadians who studied abroad, and by the interchange of music from all over the country and the world brought about by improved communications. Now, composers can assimilate many different influences without leaving their native soil. As a result, the traditional English and French poles of musical orientation may soon amalgamate or become influenced by one another and by additional styles from elsewhere, so that distinctions according to European national characteristics may not be possible in the future. The evidence from recent compositions by the young composers suggests that, at least to some degree, this is already true.

In our survey we have seen that the music of Canada has followed the same pattern as other aspects of the country's history. Folk songs of the early settlers, salon pieces from a developing nineteenth-century society, jazz of the Roaring Twenties, and avant-garde experiments of the recent decades have all reflected the needs, hopes, dreams, and accomplishments of the people.

To tell the story of the music it has been necessary to relate something of the general history of the country, for one cannot be understood without the other. The history of music in Canada is that of the millions of people who over the centuries have turned a wilderness into a modern civilization; as they changed, and as the country changed, so did the music. And just as the musical picture of the various eras becomes clearer when set in context, so too, it is hoped that the entire picture of Canadian history will have a clearer focus in the light of the discussion of the music.

7

Music of the Original Canadians

In previous chapters, we have discussed the musical traditions brought to Canada by the various national groups who settled in this part of the New World. We have examined the acculturation of those traditions—how they were transmuted and changed by their removal to a new environment. In this chapter we will look at the music of the people who were here for hundreds of years before the European settlers arrived—at the traditions that have remained much the same for centuries, and at the changes that have resulted from the contact of these earliest Canadians with the civilization of the settlers.

Anthropologists tell us that the original inhabitants of Canada came from Asia by way of the Bering Strait, and moved across what is now Canada and the United States. The earliest were the Indians, who arrived at least twenty-five thousand years ago, followed approximately twenty thousand years later by the Inuit. ("Eskimo," the more commonly used name for Inuit, comes from the Cree Indians and carries a pejorative meaning—"Eaters of raw flesh." We shall use the name they call themselves.) Not only are there genetic differences between the Indians and Inuit, but they inhabit different areas of the country and have separate cultures.

The traditional music of both Indians and Inuit share several general characteristics. The most striking of these—and an important point to remember—is the role of music in their cultures, which differs from its European counterpart. In the native cultures much of the music is associated with religious ritual and is viewed as an essential part of life, whereas most European-descended music is secular. Many centuries ago, music undoubtedly occupied a place in European life similar to that of the Indians and Inuit. But the major role that music plays in present-day Western culture is merely recreational. In contrast, only a portion of the traditional music of the Indians and Inuit is for entertainment. Most of it is embedded in rituals designed to achieve some purpose such as good health, a successful hunt, rain, or contact with the spirit world. The descriptions of that music, therefore, will necessarily involve descriptions of the tribal rituals.

The arrival of the European settlers in the seventeenth century had a strong influence on the native cultures. The Indians, especially, soon changed many of their living habits as the Europeans encroached upon their land and their lives. Nomadic tribes were forced to give up their way of life, and ancient beliefs had to coexist with Christianity. In more recent times television, radio, and tourists have made Western culture easily available to the Indian reservations and Inuit settlements, increasing the threat to the old way of life.

The native people are aware that their old traditions are in danger of totally disappearing, and efforts have been made to preserve what is left.[1] In many cases these have resulted in a cultural ''compartmentalization'' in which Euro-American customs are adopted while the old traditions are still observed. In terms of music this means that the Indians and Inuit listen to and perform modern popular music as well as their native music, keeping the two quite separate from one another, with little observable influence of one style on the other.

We will discuss the indigenous ways of the Indians and Inuit, but they must not be considered representative of what exists now among those people in all areas. Much of what is presented here is history, no longer relevant to the daily lives of Canada's oldest citizens.

Canadian Indians[2]

The Indian tribes within each of the following geographic areas (see map) are related:

1. Eastern woodlands, nomadic (Algonkian)
2. Eastern woodlands, sedentary (Iroquoian)
3. Plains—Canadian prairies
4. Mackenzie River—along the Mackenzie River, and woodlands north of the Churchill River
5. Plateau—interior plateau of British Columbia and the Yukon
6. Pacific Coast—British Columbia coastal areas

We shall discuss the groups of each of these areas in turn, noting their characteristics, the role played by music within the group, their instruments, and their song types. But first we shall look at those things common to most Indian cultures and music (although the reader should note that very little is common to *all* tribes in *all* areas; we present here those customs that persist in a large number of tribes).

In general, Indian music consists mostly of songs. Some have words and tell a story, express a prayer or a wish, or describe an emotion. But many songs have only vocables—syllables and exclamations—rather than words, while others have a combination of words and vocables. Apparently some of the vocable-type songs once had words that have been either forgotten or altered over the centuries. Others may never have had real words, their meaning having been transmitted in other ways, such as tone of voice, or general melodic-rhythmic characteristics, or by the occasion itself.

Instrumental solos are rarely found, but instruments are often used for accompaniment, especially in dance music. Whistles, drums, and rattles of a wide variety of types and sizes (exhibiting much imagination in design) are used to define rhythm and mood. Exactly which ones are used depends on the tribe, the season, and the occasion.

1. Since the beginning of the twentieth century serious efforts have been made to record the traditional culture of the native people.
2. I am indebted to Elaine Keillor for much of the factual material included in this section.

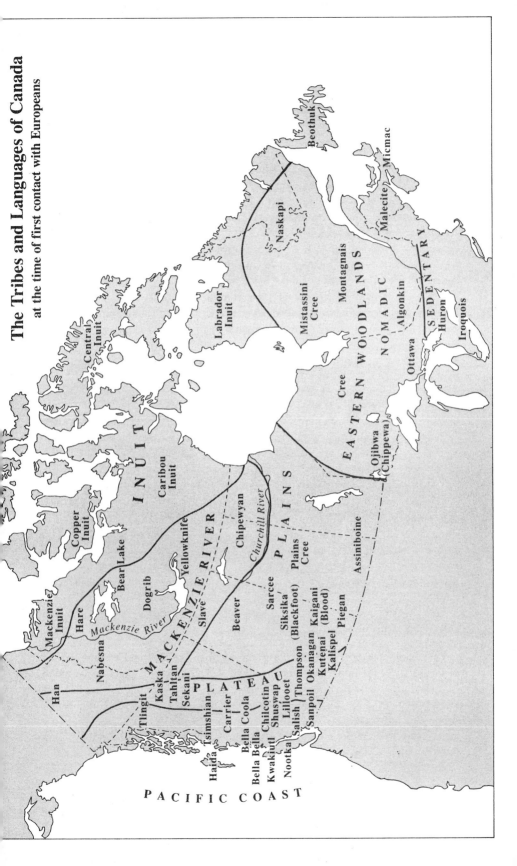

The Tribes and Languages of Canada
at the time of first contact with Europeans

PACIFIC COAST

INUIT

Central Inuit

Labrador Inuit

Copper Inuit

Caribou Inuit

Mackenzie Inuit

Hare

Bear Lake

Dogrib

Yellowknife

Nabesna

Mackenzie River

MACKENZIE RIVER

Slave

Chipewyan

Churchill River

Han

Kaska

Tahltan

Sekani

Beaver

Sarcee

PLAINS

Plains Cree

Assiniboine

Cree

Mistassini Cree

Naskapi

Beothuk

Montagnais

EASTERN WOODLANDS

NOMADIC

Ojibwa (Chippewa)

Algonkin

Ottawa

SEDENTARY

Huron

Iroquois

Malecite

Micmac

Tlingit

PLATEAU

Tsimshian

Carrier

Bella Coola

Chilcotin

Shuswap

Lillooet

Thompson

Sanpoil

Okanagan

Salish

Kutenai

Kaigani (Blood)

Kalispel

Piegan

Siksika (Blackfoot)

Haida

Bella Bella

Kwakiutl

Nootka

Basic to any discussion of traditional Indian music is the notion of ownership. In those places where this is an important issue, a song belongs to the person who composed or "received" it, which means that he is the only one who may sing it. But if he composes it for his tribe, for members of his family, or for someone else, then they may sing it as well. Ritual songs rarely come into the "public domain," but on the death of the composer his songs can be inherited by family members or close friends, although even then there are restrictions on who may perform them. This tradition becomes more understandable if we remember that each song is a personal expression of the composer, and that it has a purpose within the tribal ritual.

An Indian usually does not compose many songs, often only one in a lifetime. He may compose deliberately, like Western composers, or, more commonly, he "receives" his song while in a trance, or from a vision or a dream. The experience is considered to be a special reward for him, or evidence that he has contacted a spirit who "gives him the song." For these reasons each song is believed to possess supernatural powers, and it is sung only under special circumstances. Inherited songs are thought to embody the personal strengths of the former owner(s), thus accumulating power from one generation to another. In other areas, however, songs circulate freely without consideration of ownership. And in some tribes there are special writers, often women, who supply many songs for entertainment.

There is also, among the Indians, a strong sense of appropriateness: a song for a winter ceremony would not be sung in summer; and a song for one clan would not be sung by another. Many songs for particular occasions include dancing as an integral part of their meaning. Lengthy ceremonies involving songs, dances, and other events (speeches, prayers, etc.) are central to the rituals of all North American Indian tribes, and are performed at various important times of the year or when the group or an individual faces a problem—illness, for example. At significant rites of passage like puberty or death, or social events such as intercommunity meetings, many songs and dances honour the special event or person. The function of music on these occasions is at the very heart of Indian culture. (Ethnologists refer to the music as "validating" the events.) The ceremonies serve to reaffirm the religious beliefs of the tribal members, to educate the young, and, because of traditions governing who sings what to whom, to reinforce the social structure of the tribe.

Eastern Woodlands, Nomadic (Algonkian)

The Algonkian area covers a vast section of the central and eastern portions of the country, including the east coast and the central woodlands which extend from the coast west past the Great Lakes (except for the Iroquois area in southeastern Ontario). The languages spoken are all dialects of the Algonquian language family: Micmac, Malecite, Ojibway (Chippewa in Ontario), Cree, Algonkin, Montagnais, Abenakis, Naskapi, Potawatomi, Delaware, and Ottawa. These Indians traditionally lived a migratory life, hunting, fishing, and gathering wild fruit, with no permanent settlements. The small northern bands are rather loosely

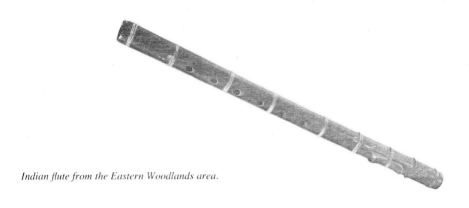

Indian flute from the Eastern Woodlands area.

organized, with a leader chosen for the task at hand. In the larger bands of the southern area there is a stronger political system with leaders chosen for longer periods of time.

In the Algonkian culture there are ritual songs associated with medicine societies, songs within myths, and songs to ensure good hunting. There are also entertainment songs associated with dancing, and songs for choosing a chief and preparing for war. Some are sung by a soloist, while others involve a leader and chorus; the latter are often accompanied by dancing.

Musical instruments used by the Algonkians include several kinds of rattles: some of birch bark containing pebbles; some disc-shaped, made of skin with seeds or pebbles inside; and some made of animal horn with seeds or pebbles (tin cans now occasionally replace the traditional containers). Several different kinds of drums include water drums, and frame drums with one or two heads (tambourine-like). The Algonkians also have wind instruments made of rolls of birch bark, conch shells, and vertical whistle flutes.

The whistle flute is found in many of the Indian cultures in Canada, mainly in the Algonkian, Iroquoian, and Plains areas. It is unusual in that it has an external block—a piece of wood placed on the outside of the flute that directs the air into the chamber. The flute is commonly played by young men when courting, although in the Plateau area it is also used as a signal in horse-stealing raids, and in the Plains area it functioned as a war signal.

Example VII–1 is an Algonkian flute song called *Don't Leave Me*. It exhibits many of the characteristics found in most flute melodies: a range of an octave, a tonal centre based on the lowest note, and frequent use of the interval of a major second. The song has a pentatonic (five-note) scale, E♭, F, A♭, B♭, D, and a musical structure: A B A B.

The transcription below can only approximate the sounds of the flute song. Change of tone colour and variation in speed, pitch, and accent are all important musical values in this culture. Flute songs often contain birdcalls, and sometimes entire sections of birdcall imitations are added at the end in a manner quite unrelated to the rest of the song.

Example VII–1: Algonkian flute song, *Don't Leave Me*

Eastern Woodlands, Sedentary (Iroquoian)

The Iroquoian area covers the territory in southeastern Ontario and several of the northeastern United States. The dialects of the Iroquoian language spoken are Huron, Cayuga, Mohawk, Oneida, Onondaga, Seneca, and Tuscarora. In contrast to the migratory Algonkians, Iroquoian culture is based on agriculture and permanent villages, and has produced a highly developed political system and fostered religious societies.

The music of the Iroquoian tribes is organized around the cycle of the agricultural year, with songs to accompany the rituals for planting and harvest. In addition, there are songs belonging to certain societies; shaman songs (shaman = medicine man or witch doctor) like the important False Face Society Dance with its elaborate masks; social entertainment songs that usually are accompanied by dancing; and songs for the life cycle, the most important of which is for the Feast of the Dead. Various kinds of rattles are used: some are made of rawhide, gourds, or horn, with tortoise and turtle rattles reserved for specific ceremonies. The Iroquois also use water drums, one- and two-headed drums, and the vertical whistle flute.

The traditional ceremonies still take place in the Longhouse, a rectangular building that at one time was a communal residence for a number of families. During a ceremony the women and men sit separately (specific seating arrangements change depending upon the ceremony), with a fire near each end of the Longhouse. When the dances begin, those who lead it occupy a bench in the

The Great Defender, a false face mask from the Iroquois tribe of the Eastern Woodlands area.

centre of the Longhouse; the dancers circle first around one of the fires or the central bench, and then, as the remainder of the tribe members join in, they circle the entire interior periphery of the building.[3]

The Iroquois usually wear costumes relating to the nature of the dance, and carry feathers, sticks, or other small hand-held "props." These help to convey the idea of some of the dances like the Duck Dance, Robin Dance, Fish Dance, and Grinding-an-Arrow. (Other dances depict fertility, strength, expertise at hunting and fishing, and longevity.)

The Corn Dance (example VII–2) was originally addressed to the female corn spirit and obviously was an important part of the agricultural rites. It could also be used for social dancing. The sections of the dance are sung by a leader while the others respond "wiha" in rapid alternation—a performance characteristic that is unique to the Iroquois—providing a very rhythmic and exciting performance (the group response is marked by the words above the staff).

Example VII–2: Iroquoian Corn Dance

3. From Gertrude Kurath, *Dance and Song Rituals of Six Nations Reserve, Ontario,* National Museum of Canada Bulletin no. 220 (Ottawa, 1968), 8–9; and Michael Foster, *From the Earth to Beyond the Sky: An Ethnographic Approach to Four Longhouse Iroquois Speech Events,* National Museum of Man Mercury Series, Canadian Ethnology Service Paper no. 20 (Ottawa, 1974), 24–28.

Example VII–2, an extract from the dance song (only sections a, b, and d are reproduced), illustrates that Iroquoian songs are sectional in contrast to the strophic structure found in songs from other areas, for example in the Algonkian song, example VII–1. The melody of the Corn Dance song is contained within a five-note range (D-A) with use of the lower octave only in the opening section.

The Drum Dance ceremony is still performed on the Six Nation Reserves in Ontario and in several places in the eastern United States, although it is no longer the central religious expression it once was. The ceremony lasts several hours and includes a preacher who delivers short prayers combined with chants sung on a single pitch (similar to psalm-tone settings), and a number of ritual songs and dance songs. The ceremony is led by a drum leader who plays while he sings, and his assistant who plays a horn rattle. Each song type has its own characteristic text (thanksgiving, supplication, personal reflection), and is distinguished by a different drum beat (steady, irregular, etc.) and certain melodic characteristics. In dance songs with choruses a group of up to five women join in the singing.

The Iroquois ritual dances all proceed in the same manner. First only one or two male leaders begin to dance. Gradually, the other participants line up behind one another, and move in a circle counterclockwise—considered by the Indians to be "against the motion of the sun." All dances have fairly simple movements—slow or fast, jumping or shuffling—but all allow a great deal of individual expression. There are two basic dance steps, the stomp, which is what its name implies, and the fish step, which requires placing the ball of the foot down first, then the rest of the foot. The fish step is done rapidly, while twisting the body and the feet first to one side and then the other.

Example VII–3: Iroquoian Drum Dance

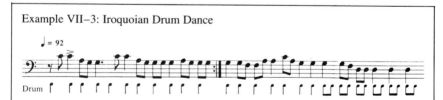

Example VII–3 is a portion of a ritual Drum Dance. The example seems to be a rather simple combination of rhythms and melodic motives. The notes in the transcription, however, cannot convey the many subtleties of the song—changes in vocal tone, addition of quick vocal ornaments, and use of quarter-tone and microtone variants and inflections which add to the complexity of the song (compare to recording).

A drum of the Blood (Blackfoot) band of Plains Indians.

We can only imagine the significance of the sounds, the dance steps, and the personal involvement in the ancient tradition of the Indian tribes where this ceremony was considered an essential part of life.

Plains

The Plains Indians inhabit the Canadian prairies, and speak dialects of three major language groups: the Algonquian dialects Ojibway, Cree, and Blackfoot; the Athapaskan dialects Beaver and Sarcee; and the Siouan dialects Assiniboine (Stony in Alberta), Sioux, and Dakota. These Indians once lived a migratory life, following the buffalo herds on which they depended for food and clothing. The bands have close political bonds with one another.

There are a number of rituals in this culture, most involving many songs. The All Smoke ceremony of the Blood (Blackfoot) band, for example, has over one hundred songs that must be performed accurately and in the proper context and order to produce the desired result. One important feature of the rituals concerns the Medicine Bundles—special pouches containing ceremonial objects such as pipes and rattles. Specific songs accompany the use of each object, and must be sung when the object is removed from the pouch. Some of the songs are the property of special societies.

The most important initiation ritual is the Sun Dance, which is sponsored by the medicine woman and takes place in a lodge specially constructed for the purpose. A central pole is erected in the centre of the ceremonial lodge to symbolize the joining of earth and heaven. The ritual differs in details from tribe to tribe, but in many the ceremony begins at the first full moon after the summer solstice (in late June or early July), and can last for two weeks. This is the first big social event of the warm season, and so the ceremony also serves as a time to renew old acquaintances. Some of the many songs express the Indians' dependence on the people of the earth for food, and other songs accompany the distribution of gifts. During lulls between portions of the ritual the people perform social dances. The most popular of these is the Owl Dance with its accompanying ♩ ♪ rhythm.

Example VII–4: Blackfoot Indian Song

[ ] denotes vocables

akeeyé	wiinootáamoket	takxkyaaowimíinii
woman	don't worry about me	I'm going back home to eat berries

Example VII–4 is a Blackfoot song demonstrating the type of melody composed by Plains Indians, and showing a combination of vocables and text. This song, characteristic of the Plains style, has a range much wider than the songs we have already looked at. Its melodic structure is often referred to as "terraced," that is, a high phrase at the beginning is followed by a medium-range phrase, and finally by a low phrase at the end of each section. The song is sung by men very loudly at an extremely high pitch with a strained voice. The occasion for the song is not known.

The Plains Indians have a large assortment of musical instruments, including rattles of rawhide in several shapes and sizes, buzzers made from buffalo hooves, bull-roarers, rasps, bells, drums both large and small with one or two heads, a large powwow drum with two heads which is suspended by four stakes driven into the ground and drummed usually by four men with sticks,[4] single-headed medium-size drums painted with a special design from the drummer's spirit helper, water drums, vertical whistle flutes, and whistles made from the long bones of eagle's wings. Whistles are used to accompany the Sun Dance (a specific dance within the Sun Dance ceremony), sounded rapidly in syncopation with the song. This song goes on for days at a time and induces trances.

Mackenzie River

The Mackenzie River cultural area encompasses the Mackenzie River system and the woodlands north of the Churchill River. The languages spoken are all dialects of Athapaskan: Hare, Beaver, Chipewyan, Slave, Dekani, Nahane, Loucheux, Dog Rib, Yellowknife, and Tutchone. The Indians here once lived a migratory life like the Algonkians—hunting, fishing, and gathering wild fruit—with temporary leaders and no political unity between bands.

---

4. There are recent instances of groups of three and six drummers involved in this activity.

The Drum Dance ceremony of the Slavey Indians is one of the most important events in their culture.[5] At the present time, it is performed upon the arrival of important people or the return of a tribal member. In the past, however, it took place in summer as the first occasion for the renewal of friendships after a long winter of semi-isolation. Like the Drum Dance of the Iroquoian, this one employs a special group of drummers who sing while beating on frame drums. The celebration begins with either a speech by one of the drummers stating the reason for the celebration, or with a religious song in which the drummers ask for help in drumming and singing. The event can last anywhere from three hours to two days, and has five specific social events calling for music: the Rabbit Dance, the Tea Dance, the Round Dance, a religious ceremony involving only the drummers, and a solo ceremony involving only a single singer-drummer.

The song types are differentiated by rhythm patterns, formal structures, and dance formations. The Rabbit Dance *Beyond Me* (example VII–5) is one kind of dance song from this cultural region. Note once again the range of a fifth. The two sections of this song have a parallel construction with identical opening and closing sections.

Example VII–5: Rabbit Dance song, *Beyond Me*

During the singing of the Rabbit Dance the dancers (everyone except the very young and the infirm) line up behind one another and form a circle. When the dance begins, the circle moves clockwise.

All of the songs have titles like *Beyond Me* and *Toward My Friend,* a hint that they probably once had words, although now most are sung only with vocables. Happy songs are now performed on any happy occasion as entertainment, but may well have had a ritual function in the past. They accompany social dances involving ten to thirty men and women in a circle. These songs, too, are mostly sung with vocables, but include some spoken exclamations, which in recent years have included English words such as "New Year" and "fire fighting."[6]

Mackenzie River Indian instruments include rattles made from skin, plank drums, mostly single-headed tambourine drums (some tribes use snares), and a tambourine drum with a handle, similar to one used by the Inuit. Flutes and whistles are rare in this group.

Plateau

The Plateau Indians occupy the interior plateau of British Columbia and the Yukon. They fish and hunt and live in semipermanent settlements. There is very

5. Michael Asch, "Social Context and the Musical Analysis of Slavey Drum Dance Songs," *Ethnomusicology* 19 (1975): 145–57.

6. *Ibid.*

little political organization. They speak the Salishan dialects of Shuswap, Lillooet, Ntlakyapamuk, and Okanagan; the Tagish dialect of Tlingit; and the Kutenai dialect of Kutenaian.

Very little is known about the music of the Plateau Indians, but the information available indicates that the eastern bands are quite similar to the Plains Indians in their cultural practices, while the western bands are like the Pacific Coast Indians.

Pacific Coast

The Pacific Coast area encompasses the large number of Indian bands that occupy coastal British Columbia. Their languages include the Tsimshian dialects Gitksan and Niska; Haida; the Salishan dialects Bella Coola, Songish, Cowichan, Puntlatch, Squamish, Comox, Sechelt, and Semichmoo; and the Wakashan dialects Heiltsuk, Nootka, Kwakiutl, and Haisla. These Indians have established permanent settlements with several levels of society, including slaves. They have a highly developed trade with interior bands.

The music of the Pacific Coast Indians accompanies their very elaborate theatrical-dramatic rituals. The Bella Coola band, for example, has a Mystery Dance that mimics the springtime regeneration of nature in which the dancers take the part of trees, shrubs, and Mother Nature.

The instruments of the Coastal Indians include split-log drums, square wooden boxes, planks, sticks, rattles carved from wood, strings of shells or bear's claws or bird's bills, and various whistles. The Coastal Indians are especially artistic, and their instruments, as well as their masks and costumes, are elaborately decorated.

The Potlatch is the most important of the Pacific Coast Indian ceremonies. It is a very involved ritual which can last up to several weeks, consisting of songs, dances, and prayers that summarize the tribes' social customs and religious beliefs.

The principal event during a Potlatch involves the distribution of gifts as an indication of the personal wealth and power of the host chief. Example VII–6 is sung by a Potlatch host of the Niska band while he distributes food to his guests: at first he taunts a stranger who is receiving the gifts; later he apologizes. The song has a few spoken words and a complex variety of rhythms against a steady drum beat.

Example VII–6: Potlatch host song

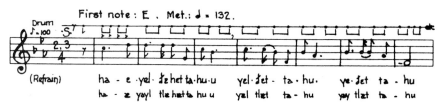

Two Indian rattles from the Pacific Coast area:
(left) Kwakiutl; (below) Tsimshian.

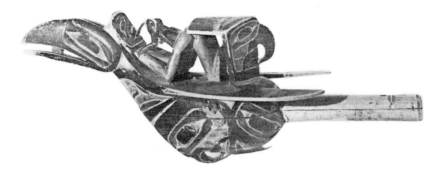

A mask from the Pacific
Coast area.

A sea monster mask from the Tsim-
shian Indians of the Pacific Coast.

A refrain begins and ends the song. Within the refrain there is an internal repeat section. Pacific Coast songs tend to have an undulating arch shape (see example VII–6, line 7).

A Contemporary Powwow Ceremony

As indicated at the beginning of this chapter, many of the rites of the Indians have changed in response to modern civilization. These ceremonies now often combine traditional elements with contemporary Canadian activities. The following summary of Robert Witmer's account of a modern Powwow ceremony held by a Blood (Plains area) tribe demonstrates how the Indians accommodate both the old and new ways of life:

The Powwow is the most important of the current ceremonies among the Blood Indians, replacing the Sun Dance (which is still occasionally performed, however) but using some of its elements. The Powwow is a totally social occasion, consisting of dancing, speeches, and partying over a period of several days. Like the Sun Dance, it is an opportunity to gather clans together and renew old acquaintances. New to this ceremony are the visits of tourists, the use of recordings and voice amplification, and the presence of food concessions—all common elements adopted from the summer fairs of the non-Indians.

The Powwow reported by Witmer took place during the annual Indian Days celebration in July 1968, in a field opposite the Red Crow Memorial Stadium in Standoff, Alberta. Indians and tourists arrived by car and camper and lived in the campers, modern tents, and tipis. The central area was fenced off to form the dancing area, with an electric light standard in the centre, around which the dances circled (in the traditional counterclockwise direction). The ceremony was presided over by a "dance announcer" who kept up a constant commentary, encouraged the people to enjoy themselves, and made public service announcements over the public address system.

Music and dancing was provided by a large number of singers, instrumental-

Medicine Pipe Stem Dance *an oil painting by Paul Kane.*

ists, and dancers who performed the traditional music and dances (War Dances, Owl Dances, Sioux Dances, Grass Dances). Dancing was not restricted to Indians, and of the Indians who did dance, many (perhaps half) were from tribes other than the Blood, who travelled the summer Powwow circuit. There was a nucleus of professional dancers who performed throughout, distinguishable by their elaborate costumes, face and body paint, and superior dancing ability. The musicians and the professional dancers were paid for their services.[7]

The Indians have accommodated some of their traditional life to the comforts and expediencies of the white man's civilization. But by means such as those described above, they preserve their heritage and pass it along to the next generation.

Inuit[8]

The Inuit inhabit the northern bays and plains all across North America—including Alaska, Arctic Canada, and Greenland (see map on page 143). Traditionally they have lived a nomadic life, hunting seal at their breathing holes in the ice during winter, and caribou during August and September when the large herds begin to migrate south. They live in close contact with nature and the land, and are quite clever in eking out an existence in an unfriendly climate. Their food includes muskox, polar bear, fox, and fish, in addition to seal and caribou. The animals they hunt also provide their clothing, heating fuel, and tools. Contact with the Europeans in the last fifty years has affected some of their culture—for example, their lives are not as nomadic as in the past—but much of their traditional culture has been preserved, much more than that of the Indians.

The Inuit in Canada can be divided into three main geographical groups: those of the Yukon and Mackenzie Delta; the Copper, Netsilik, Caribou, and Iglulik of the central Arctic; and those of Baffinland, northern Quebec, and Labrador. There are a number of differences among the cultural practices of the people in the various areas, and even from one community to another. Nevertheless, there are a surprising number of similarities, and in this study we shall note both the broader aspects of the common Inuit practices that involve music, and some local variants.

In traditional practice, depending on the area, music can play a part in either formal rituals or informal events. But in either case, most of it is related to ancient beliefs. In this sense Inuit music functions much like that of the Indians. Further similarities can be found in the nature of the rituals themselves and the topics of the ceremonies, which are closely connected with the earth, the seasons, and the spirit world. There are songs for healing sickness, like example

7. The description is taken from Robert Witmer, *The Musical Life of the Blood Indians,* National Museum of Man Mercury Series, Canadian Ethnology Service Paper no. 86 (Ottawa, 1982), 26–30.

8. Most of the information for this section is taken from Beverley Cavanagh, *Music of the Netsilik Eskimos: A Study of Stability and Change,* 2 vols., National Museum of Man Mercury Series, Canadian Ethnology Service Paper no. 82, (Ottawa, 1982); and from the *EMC* article ''Inuit,'' 458b–60c, also by Cavanagh.

VII–7, and a song for the return of the sun in late January in those areas where there is total darkness during the winter months. Songs are also occasioned by strong emotions like joy, fear, or despair.

Example VII–7: Song for healing sickness

The narrow range of example VII–7 (a fourth) is typical of many Inuit songs, as is the recitative-like melody with small archlike contours and a steady pulse.

Although some Netsilik composers produce several songs in a lifetime, most compose only one. In contrast to the Indian, the Inuit deliberately intends to compose. And in most cases, while Inuit tradition keeps a song in a personal or family repertory, it differs from the Indian concept of ownership. Other people may occasionally sing a particular song, for example, a chorus accompaniment to a solo drum dance, but it is acknowledged to be the composer's song, and usually involves him in some way (in the case of the solo drum song, he would be the one dancing).

Drum dancers Donald and Alice Suluk from Eskimo Point, North West Territories.

Inuit Drum Dance

The Drum Dance ceremony is traditionally the most important of all, and can be found in most Inuit communities of the central and western Canadian Arctic. Originally it was the central Inuit ritual, and functioned both to reinforce common religious beliefs and as a major social occasion. The Drum Dance would be held to welcome visitors (a western Mackenzie Delta "inviting-in"), and at those times of the year when many people would come together (for example at the annual sea-ice camp of the Netsilik people).

Depending on the area, the Drum Dance ceremony is performed either indoors or out. In those areas where it is an indoor activity, special houses were once erected for just that use. The ceremony always includes a number of monophonic songs, dances, and dance competitions and usually lasts several hours. Again, depending on region, the song texts are made up either of vocables or meaningful words. The texts of the Caribou Inuit have short stanzas, while the Netsilik songs are long narratives, usually about hunting. Almost all Inuit Drum Dance songs are strophic (including those with vocable texts), and most have refrains on vocables. The vocable "ajaija" is a popular refrain, and in some locations a Drum Dance song is actually called an "ajaija."

One of the earliest accounts of an Inuit Drum Dance is that of Roald Engelbregt Gravning Amundsen, who led a famous expedition to the Arctic region in 1903–06. His description offers an excellent view of one of those ceremonies.

One night, after seal-catching had commenced, I was invited to witness the "kelaudi," the Eskimo's favourite festival, held in order to propitiate the higher powers to induce them to favour a good catch. The air was clear and frosty, and the vast silent desert was lit up by the moon so brightly that one could easily have read by her rays. In the midst of the many igloos of the camp, a large gala igloo, erected for the occasion, towered above the rest, with bright light streaming invitingly from all its ice-windows. The hut looked very well inside, being brilliantly illuminated with "Light pastilles." A large ring of snow-blocks had been set up in the centre of the floor. Some of the men of the colony had already arrived, and entertained us as well as they could. They were decked tonight in their brightest and most elegantly ornamented reindeer clothing. Some of these were actual masterpieces of taste and skill. By and by the rest of the audience arrived—Anana, Kabloka, Onaller, Alerpa, Alo-Alo, and whatever names the others are called by, not to forget "Nalungia," there being at least ten of that name. "Orna" (the she-eagle) was the last of a row of at least twenty women, who all sat down silently and demurely on the snow-blocks arranged in a circle. They certainly did not look as if they were in a festive mood, any of them. The men took up their places at random around the women, and there was soon a full muster of them. In contrast to the women, they were all lively and full of fun and laughter. It looked as if they were the only ones who were to enjoy themselves. At last the leading "senior" appears. To-night it is Kachkochnelli who acts in this capacity. He is arrayed in a light embroidered reindeer-skin dress, but he is wearing a cap and gloves. He brings with him the precious "kelaudi," the musical instrument of the tribe, which consists of a hoop or wood like a barrel hoop, covered with thin tanned reindeer skin, and fitted with a handle; the drum-stick is a small club of wood, covered with sealskin.

The entertainment now begins. Kachkochnelli enters the ring; thereupon Anana lifted up her voice and started something which I suppose I must call singing, though I find it rather hard to use the word in this connection, and the other women joined in. I have never heard anything so monotonous, its effect is still worse when chanted in chorus. But there must be some sort of fixed tune in this chanting of four notes, because they all manage to keep together. As the other women join in, Kachkochnelli commences to dance and beat the drum. It was not exactly a graceful dance. Keeping in one spot, he raises first one, then the other leg, and sways his body forward and backward, uttering loud yells. All the time he vigorously belabours the drum with his drumstick, striking it not on the skin, but on the frame. The result of all these efforts is a deafening din. Kachkochnelli's dance gradually becomes less and less energetic, and after about twenty minutes he stops. The women's chant, which has been keeping time with the dancer's movements, dies away simultaneously with the cessation of the dance. Then the next man enters the ring. There does not appear to be any order of precedence among the Nechilli, whoever happens to sit nearest, and is willing to perform comes up unceremoniously into the ring, and the same dance, the same yells, and the same chant are repeated, without a shade of variation. But I noticed that the women took turns in leading the singing. When Kirnir, and Ichyuachtorvik Eskimo was dancing, it was a woman of his tribe who acted as precentor, and when Nulieu, the Ogluli Eskimo performed, an old cross-eyes Ogluli woman led the singing. It also seemed to me as if the tune varied slightly for the various tribes, but I should not like to be certain on this point. As I have already hinted, I have not a good ear for music.

I have seen this dance and chant described in several books of travels, and all the authors are unanimous in declaring that the performers worked themselves into a state of frenzy. This I cannot endorse. According to my very careful observation they were all quite normal and in their full senses during the whole dance, even when it was at its height. From the descriptions, I had expected something far wilder, and was therefore disappointed. It is altogether incomprehensible to me in what the pleasure of this performance consists. The performers looked bored, particularly the poor women, who had to repeat the same notes ad infinitum. In fact, they seemed quite delighted when there were no more volunteers, and immediately disappeared from the hut. This performance lasted about three hours, and had I known that it all consisted in a repetition of the first "turn," I should have come away much earlier.

These dances were performed throughout the winter. Frequently even after a fatiguing day at seal-hunting, after ten hours' toil on the ice in storm and cold, they would proceed direct to the dancing igloo for this mad exercise.[9]

The melodies of the Drum Dance songs usually have a five-note scale and do not contain any semitones. The melodies are made up of a number of short melodic formulas or motives that are common to that particular area. The same set of motives can be found in various combinations in all of the songs from that area. Microtones are often used as ornaments.

Example VII–8, a Drum Dance song from the Netsilik area, has a range of a sixth, and the tonal centre is in the middle of the range rather than at the bottom end. The structure is quasi-strophic. The songs all have a definite pulse, but the rhythm patterns do not repeat exactly. In the western areas the accompanying drum beat is usually the same as the song pulse, but in the eastern Arctic region the tempo of the drum can be independent of the pulse of the song.

Example VII–8: Drum Dance song

9. Roald E. G. Amundsen, *The Northwest Passage*, 2 vols. (London, A. Constable, 1908), 2:23–26.

The drums, all with an attached handle, are of two types: west of the Mackenzie Delta they are small and made of a whale-liver or walrus-stomach membrane covering a narrow wooden frame. They are beaten either on the frame, or with a stroke that takes in both the frame and the head. In the central and eastern areas the drums are larger, have a wider frame, and are covered with caribou skin.

The dance songs frequently concern daily activities, such as fishing, hunting, and paddling. The dancers often wear loonskin headdresses (Copper and Western) or dance mittens (Alaska and Mackenzie Delta), and mime animal behavior (Alaska Delta) or otherwise act out the topic of the dance. There is a humourous whaler's skin-toss dance in Alaska in which one person is bounced into the air by a group of approximately thirty people holding a large skin. While in the air he must pass a pole over his head and under his feet.

Among the Inuit of the central Arctic and Copper regions there is a tradition of solo drum dancing. In some communities this activity is restricted to men, but there are places where both men and women dance solo. While the soloist dances, striking his frame drum first on one side and then the other, a chorus (often of women) chants a narrative song composed by the solo dancer or one of his relatives.

Another custom is the singing duel in which individual singers (usually from different communities) dance and sing a song mocking each other. In these cases music serves as an important part of a dispute between the two men. Each states his side of the story while insulting the other, and when the song is finished the community decides who has made the best case for himself.

Other songs among the Inuit communities include story songs, game songs, and affectionate songs for one's family members—in Greenland these are known as "petting songs." Story songs include the adventures of various legendary figures and songs about humanized birds and animals that incorporate their cries. Oddly enough, story songs often resemble European-style psalm tones, with pitch repetition and a range of only two or three notes.

Songs accompany many Inuit games such as juggling, hide-and-seek, string-figure, and chasing games. The string-figure games are usually performed in autumn because it is believed that they will capture the sun and keep it from disappearing. The song that accompanies the game is short and is sung to aid the player in the execution of the string web.

Some of the most unusual games are those played by women in the eastern Arctic region, known as vocal (or throat) games. Most of these are played by two women who face each other, standing or squatting with their faces only a few centimeters apart. They direct loud rhythmic guttural and breathing sounds at one another in rapid exchange. Sometimes real words are used with texts that are meaningless or riddles. The object is to be able to continue without interruption. The women sometimes intensify their sounds toward one another by holding household objects such as pans, kettles, or parka hoods next to the face.

Summary

The music of the Indians and Inuit is colourful, varied, and—to those brought up on European-based music—unusual. Through a conscious effort to retain their identity both groups are actively preserving their ancient traditions and making their past a part of their present. When added to the rest of the Canadian musical landscape the music of the Indians and Inuit puts Canadians in touch with music of enormous variety, encompassing styles and traditions spanning thousands of years.

ANTHOLOGY

1. JOSEPH QUESNEL (ca. 1746–1809), "Rions chantons" from *Colas et Colinette* (1788)

2. JAMES P. CLARKE (1807–77), "The Emigrants Home Dream" from *Lays of the Maple Leaf, or Songs of Canada* (1853)

4. CALIXA LAVALLÉE (1842–1891), *Mouvement à la Pavane* (1886)

5. CALIXA LAVALLÉE, "Single I Will Never Be" from *The Widow* (1882)

Or I have made up my   mind,....   That my husband I   will find.   Sil - ly maid,   be

not afraid,   For   joy   will   soon a - wait you ;   Hope repeat   what bosom beat, No

vi - sion shall   cheat   you.   you.

D.C.

6. CLAUDE CHAMPAGNE (1891–1965), *Danse villageoise* (1929)

7. HEALEY WILLAN (1880–1968), *Introduction, Passacaglia and Fugue* (1916)

Used by arrangement with G. Schirmer, Inc.

Passacaglia

Andante moderato (♩ = 66)

*p Ch. to Ped. with soft 32′

* Ch. p 8′

Sw. p 8′ Lieblich

Sw.

* Theme in canon at the sixth above.

* Theme divided between voices marked ⌐.

* Theme divided into small sections and used in imitation in pedal.

8. HEALEY WILLAN, *Rise Up, My Love, My Fair One* (1929)

199

the flowers ap - pear_____ up - on___ the

cres.

the flowers ap - pear_____ up - on the

cres.

the flowers ap - pear_____ up - on the

the flowers_____ ap - pear_____ up - on the

cres.

earth; the time of the sing - ing of birds is come; a -

earth; the time of the sing - ing of birds is come; a -

earth; the time of the sing - ing of birds is come; a -

earth; the time of the sing - ing of birds is come; a -

9. JEAN PAPINEAU-COUTURE (1916–), Prelude from *Suite pour Piano* (1943)

10. GILLES TREMBLAY (1932–), "Phases" from *Pièces pour piano* (1956)

✻ Enfoncer silencieusement les notes losangées un peu avant la fin des sons ordinaires (m. 10), ou un peu avant le frappé (m. 8).

Used by permission of Berandol Music, Ltd., Toronto.

Paris, 1955/56

** L'ondulation doit avoir la même vitesse que la ♪ de la musique qui précède.

11. GODFREY RIDOUT (1918–1984), Etude II from *Two Etudes* (1946, revised 1951)

12. JOHN WEINZWEIG (1913–), Movement No. 1 from *Divertimento No. 1* (1945)

13. R. MURRAY SCHAFER (1933–), Part V from *Requiems for the Party Girl* (1966)

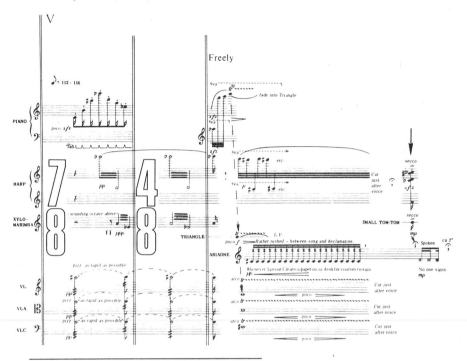

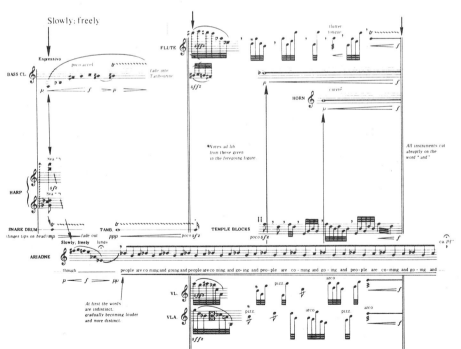

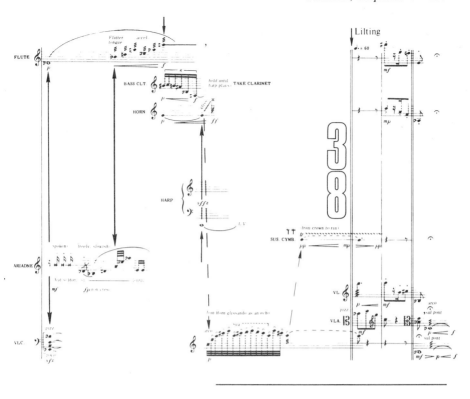

APPENDIX

Readings, Recordings, and Films

General

Bradley, Ian L. *A Selected Bibliography of Musical Canadiana.* Rev. ed. Agincourt, Ontario: GLC Publishers, 1976.

Canadian Broadcasting Corporation. *Radio Canada International Transcriptions Catalogue / Catalogue des transcriptions de Radio Canada international.* Montreal: CBC, 1946–.

Ford, Clifford. *Canada's Music: An Historical Survey.* Agincourt, Ontario: GLC Publishers, 1982.

Gillis, Frank, and Alan P. Merriam. *Ethnomusicology and Folk Music: an International Bibliography of Dissertations and Theses.* Middletown, CT: Wesleyan University Press, 1966.

Hall, Frederick A., et al., comps. *A Basic Bibliography of Musical Canadiana.* Toronto: University of Toronto Press, 1970.

Kallmann, Helmut, Gilles Potvin, and Kenneth Winters, eds. *Encyclopedia of Music in Canada.* Toronto: University of Toronto Press, 1981.

Kallmann, Helmut. *A History of Music in Canada 1534–1914.* Toronto: University of Toronto Press, 1960.

———. "Toward a Bibliography of Canadian Folk Music," *Ethnomusicology* XVI (1972): 499–503.

MacMillan, Ernest. *Music in Canada.* Toronto: University of Toronto Press, 1955.

Morey, Carl, and Roxanne Connick Carlisle. "Canada," in *The New Grove Dictionary of Music and Musicians,* ed. Stanley Sadie, vol. 3, pp. 667–675. London: Macmillan, 1980.

Proctor, George A. *Sources in Canadian Music: a Bibliography of Bibliographies.* 2nd ed. Sackville, New Brunswick: Ralph Picard Bell Library, Mount Allison University, 1979.

Toomey, Kathleen M., and Stephen C. Willis. *Musicians in Canada: a Bio-bibliographical Finding List / Musiciens au Canada: Index bio-bibliographique.* Ottawa: Canadian Association of Music Libraries, 1981.

Walter, Arnold, ed. *Aspects of Music in Canada.* Toronto: University of Toronto Press, 1969.

Chapter 1

General

Amtmann, Willy. *Music in Canada 1600–1800*. Montreal: Habitex, 1975.
Lescarbot, Marc. *The History of New France*. (tr. W. L. Grant). New York: Greenwood Press, 1968 (repr. of 1907 ed.).
Champlain, Samuel de. *Works*. (ed. and tr. H. P. Biggar). 6 vols. Toronto: The Champlain Society, 1922–26.

Folk Songs

Barbeau, Marius. "Canadian Folk Songs," *University of Toronto Quarterly* XVI (1947): 183–187.
Laforte, Conrad. *Le catalogue de la chanson folklorique français*. Quebec: Les presses de l'université Laval, 1958.

Folk Song Collections

Arsenault, Georges. *Complainte acadiennes de l'île-du-Prince-Edouard*. Ottawa: Leméac, 1980.
Barbeau, Marius. *A la claire fontaine*. Quebec: Comité de la survivance français, 1946.
———. *Allouette! Nouveau recueil de chansons populaires, avec mélodies choisies*. Montreal: Éditions Lumen, 1946.
———. *Folk Songs of Old Quebec*. (tr. Regina Lenore Shoolman). National Museum of Canada Bulletin 75, Anthropological Series No. 16, 2nd ed. Ottawa, 1964.
———. *Jongleur Songs of Old Quebec*. Toronto: Ryerson Press, 1962.
———. *Romancero du Canada*. Montreal: Beauchemin, 1937.
———. *Le Rossignol y chante*. Musée national du Canada, Série anthropologique, bulletin 175. Ottawa: Imprimeur de la Reine, 1962.
Gagnon, Ernest. *Chansons populaires du Canada*. Montreal: Beauchemin, 1968 (repr. of 1880 ed.).
MacMillan, Ernest, et al. *Vingt-et-unes chansons canadiennes / Twenty-one Folk Songs of French Canada*. Oakville, Ontario: Frederick Harris, n.d.
Also consult listings in Bradley. *A Selected Bibliography*, and the bibliography following the entry "Folk Music, Franco-Canadian" in Kallmann et al. *Encylopedia of Music in Canada (EMC)*.

Voyageurs

Nute, Grace. *The Voyageurs*. St. Paul: The Minnesota Historical Society, 1955 (repr. of 1931 ed.).
Reference to the Voyageurs and their music can be found in MacMillan. *Music in Canada* and in various encyclopedias.

Dancing

Fournier, Hélène. "Examen comparatif des quadrilles charentais et québecois," *Culture & Tradition* 6 (1982): 52–72.

Theatre

The "Theatre of Neptune" can be found in Lescarbot, Marc, *Les Muses de la Novvelle-France*. Paris, 1886.

Sacred Music

Gallat-Morin, Elisabeth. "Le livre d'orgue de Montreal aperçu d'un manuscrit inédit," *Canadian University Music Review / Revue de musique des universités canadiennes* 2 (1981): 1–38.

Gallat-Morin, Elisabeth, and Antoine Bouchard. *Témoins de la vie musicale en Nouvelle-France*. Quebec: Archives nationales du Québec, 1981. Discusses all of the extant sources.

Schwandt, Erich. "The Motet in New France: 17th and 18th Century Sacred Music in Quebec," *L'orgue à notre époque*. Montreal, 1982: 71–82.

Sacred Music Collections

Schwandt, Erich. *The Motet in New France: Twenty Motets, Antiphons and Canticles from the Archives of the Ursulines and the Archives of the Hôtel-Dieu of Quebec*. Victoria: Jeu Éditions, 1981.

Le livre d'orgue de Montréal. Montreal: Fondation Lionel-Groulx, 1981.

Recording of Work Discussed in the Text

A la claire fontaine in *Folk Songs of French Canada*. Folkways FG 3560, 1957. Sung by Jacques Labrecque.

Chapters II and III

Individual Communities

Amtmann, Willy. *Music in Canada 1600–1800*. Montreal: Habitex, 1975.

Blakeley, Phyllis. "Music in Nova Scotia 1605–1867," *Dalhousie Review* 31 (1951): 94–101, 223–230.

Crysler, Elizabeth. "Musical Life in Present Day Niagara-on-the-Lake in the Late Eighteenth and Nineteenth Centuries." MA thesis, Carleton University, 1981.

Hall, Frederick A. "Musical Life in Eighteenth-Century Halifax," *Canadian University Music Review / Revue de musique de universités canadiennes* 4 (1983): 278–307.

Harris, Reginald, V. *The Church of Saint Paul in Halifax, Nova Scotia: 1749–1949*. Toronto: Ryerson Press, 1949.

McGee, Timothy J. "Music in Halifax, 1749–1799," *Dalhousie Review* 49 (1969): 377–387.

McIntosh, Robert D. *A Documentary History of Music in Victoria, British Columbia.* Vol. 1, *1850–1899.* Victoria: University of Victoria, 1981.

Sale, David. "Toronto's Pre-Confederation Music Societies, 1845–67." MA thesis, University of Toronto, 1968.

Schau, Ann. "Sacred Music at Sharon, a Nineteenth-Century Canadian Community." MA thesis, Carleton University, 1983.

Commentaries on Music and Social Life

Innis, Mary Quayle. *Mrs. Simcoe's Diary.* Toronto: Macmillan, 1965.

McMillan, Barclay. "Music in Canada 1791–1867: A Travellers Perspective." MA thesis, Carleton University, 1983.

Sacred Music

Appel, Richard G. *The Music of the Bay Psalm Book, 9th Edition (1698).* New York: Institute for Studies in American Music 5, 1975.

McMillan, Barclay. "Tune Book Imprints in Canada to 1867: a Descriptive Bibliography," *Papers of the Bibliographical Society of Canada* 16 (1977).

Sonneck, Oscar. *Francis Hopkinson and James Lyon.* New York: Da Capo, 1967 (repr. of 1905 ed.).

Sacred and Secular Music Collections

Publications of the Canadian Musical Heritage Society, Ottawa:
Vol. 1 Keillor, Elaine, ed. *Piano Music I,* 1983.
Vol. 2 Ford, Clifford, ed. *Sacred Choral Music I,* 1984.
Vol. 3 Hall, Frederick, ed. *Songs I to English Texts,* 1985.
In Preparation:
Organ Music
Hymn Tunes
Piano Music II
Songs II, to French Texts
Music for Orchestra I
Sacred Choral Music II
Opera and Operetta Excerpts
Songs III, to English Texts
Chamber Music

French-Canadian Folk Songs

See listings for Chapter I

English-Canadian Folk Songs

Doucette, Laurel, and Colin Quigley. "The Child Ballad in Canada: a Survey," *Canadian Folk Music Journal* 9 (1981): 3–19.

Fowke, Edith, comp. "A Reference List of Canadian Folk Music," *Canadian Folk Music Journal* 11 (1983): 43–60.

Fowke, Edith, and Carole Henderson Carpenter. *A Bibliography of Canadian Folklore in English*. Toronto: University of Toronto Press, 1981 (repr. of 1956 ed.).

Mercer, Paul. *Newfoundland Songs and Ballads in Print 1842–1974: A Title and First-Line Index*. Folklore and Language Publications, Bibliographical and Special Series no. 6. Saint John's: Memorial University of Newfoundland, 1979.

———. "A Supplementary Bibliography on Newfoundland Music," *Canadian Folk Music Journal* 2 (1974): 52–56.

Folk Song Collections

Cox, Gordon S. A. *Folk Music in a Newfoundland Outport*. National Museum of Man Mercury Series, Canadian Centre for Folk Culture Studies Paper no. 32. Ottawa: National Museums of Canada, 1980.

Creighton, Helen. *Folksongs from Southern New Brunswick*. Publications in Folk Culture no. 1. Ottawa: National Museum of Man, 1971.

———. *Maritime Folk-Songs*. Toronto: Ryerson Press, 1962.

———. *Songs and Ballads from Nova Scotia*. New York: Peter Smith, 1966 (repr. of 1932 ed.).

———. *Twelve Folk Songs from Nova Scotia*. London: Novello, 1950.

Creighton, Helen, and Calum MacLeod. *Gaelic Songs in Nova Scotia*. Ottawa: National Museums of Canada, 1979 (repr. of 1964 ed.).

Creighton, Helen, and Doreen H. Senior. *Traditional Songs from Nova Scotia*. Toronto: Ryerson Press, 1950.

Dibbles, Randall, and Dorothy Dibbles. *Folksongs from Prince Edward Island*. Summerside, Prince Edward Island: Williams and Crue, 1973.

Doyle, Gerald S. *Old-time Songs and Poetry of Newfoundland*. Saint John's: Gerald S. Doyle, 1978 (repr. of 1927 ed.).

Fowke, Edith. *Lumbering Songs from the Northern Woods*. American Folklore Society, Memoir Series, Vol. 55. Austin and London: University of Texas Press, 1970.

———. *Ring Around the Moon*. Toronto: McClelland and Stewart, 1977.

———. *Sally Go Round the Sun: 300 Songs, Rhymes and Games of Canadian Children*. Toronto and Montreal: McClelland and Stewart, 1971 (repr. of 1969 ed.).

———. *Sea Songs and Ballads from Nineteenth-Century Nova Scotia: the William H. Smith and Fenwick Hatt Manuscripts*. New York: Folklorica, 1981. Does not contain music.

———. *Traditional Singers and Songs from Ontario*. Hatboro, Pa.: Folklore Associates, 1965.

Fowke, Edith, and Richard Johnston. *Folk Songs of Canada*. Waterloo: Waterloo Music Co., 1954.

Fowke, Edith, and Keith MacMillan. *The Penguin Book of Canadian Folk Songs*. Harmondsworth: Penguin, 1973.

Karpeles, Maud. *Folk Songs from Newfoundland*. London: Faber and Faber, 1971.

Peacock, Kenneth, ed. *Songs of the Newfoundland Outports*. 3 vols. Bulletin no. 197, Anthropological Series No. 65. Ottawa: National Museums of Canada, 1965.

MacKenzie, Roy W. *Ballads and Sea-songs from Nova Scotia*. Hatboro, Pa.: Folklore Association, 1965 (repr. of 1928 ed.).

Ryan, Shannon, and Larry Small. *Haulin' rope & gaff: Songs and Poetry in the History of the Newfoundland Seal Fishery*. St. John's: Breakwater Books, 1978.

Thomas, Amby. *Songs & Stories from Deep Cove, Cape Breton*. Sydney, Nova Scotia: College of Cape Breton Press, 1979.

Also see *EMC* entry "Folk Songs, Anglo-Canadian."

Opera

Cooper, Dorith. "Opera in Montreal and Toronto: A Study of Performance Traditions and Repertoire 1783–1980." Ph.D. thesis, University of Toronto, 1984.

Morey, Carl. "Pre-Confederation Opera in Toronto," *Opera Canada* 10 (1969): 13.

Publishing

Calderisi, Maria. *Music Publishing in the Canadas: 1800–1867*. Ottawa: National Library of Canada, 1981.

Recordings of Works Discussed in the Text

Quesnel, Joseph. "Cher protecteur" from *Colas et Colinette* (example II-5). RCI 234 / Select CC.15.001 and SSC-24-160.

Far Canadian Fields: Companion to the Penguin Book of Canadian Folk Songs. Leeder LEE 4057, 1975. Recorded by Edith Fowke.

Additional Recordings of Early 19th-Century Music

Piano Music by Torontonians 1834–1984. WRCI 3315. Available from 102 Rykert Cres., Toronto, Ontario M4G 2S9.

Musical Toronto—A Concert Party. Marquis Records 104.

Early Music from Quebec. CBC SM 204.

Music at Sharon 1831–1981. Melbourne SMLP 4041.

Chapters IV and V

Bibliography

Canadian Association of Music Libraries. *Canadian Musical Works 1900–1980: A Bibliography of General and Analytical Sources*. Quebec City: University of Laval, 1983.

Phonograph

Moogk, Edward B. *Roll Back the Years: A History of Canadian Recorded Sound and its Legacy*. Ottawa: National Library of Canada, 1975.

Jazz

Miller, Mark. *Jazz in Canada: Fourteen Lives*. Toronto: University of Toronto Press, 1982.

Music Collections

See listings for Chapters II and III, especially publications of the Canadian Musical Heritage Society.

Opera

Morey, Carl. "Canada's First Opera Ensemble." *Opera Canada* 11 (1970): 15.

Memoirs

Gottschalk, Louis Moreau. *Notes of a Pianist.* (ed. Jeanne Behrend) New York: Alfred A. Knopf, 1964.

Albani, Emma. *Forty Years of Songs.* London: Mills & Boon, 1911.

Performance and Composition

Adaskin, Harry, *A Fiddler's World.* Vancouver: November House, 1977.

Beckwith, John, and Keith MacMillan, eds. *Contemporary Canadian Composers.* Toronto: Oxford University Press, 1975.

Begg, Debra. "A History of Orchestras in Ottawa from 1894 to 1960." MA thesis, Carleton University, 1981.

Bourassa-Trépanier, Juliette. "Rodolphe Mathieu (1890–1962)." D. Mus, thesis, Laval University, 1972.

Bradley, Ian. *Twentieth Century Canadian Composers.* 2 vols. Toronto: GLC Publishers, 1977, 1979. Volume 1 contains discussions of Willan, Champagne, MacMillan, Adaskin, Weinzweig, Papineau-Couture, Turner, Freedman, Mercure, and Schafer. Volume 2 contains discussions of Coulthard, Pentland, Archer, Morawetz, Ridout, Somers, Garant, Tremblay, Prévost, and Mather.

Bryant, Giles. *Healey Willan Catalogue.* Ottawa: National Library of Canada, 1972; Supplement, 1982.

Clarke, F. R. C. *Healey Willan.* Toronto: University of Toronto, 1983.

Compositeurs au Québec: Claude Champagne. Montreal: Canadian Music Centre, 1979.

Edinborough, Arnold. *A Personal History of the Toronto Symphony.* Toronto: Rothmans, 1971.

French, Maida Parlow. *Kathleen Parlow: A Portrait.* Toronto: Ryerson Press, 1967.

Kallmann, Helmut, ed. *Catalogue of Canadian Composers.* Toronto: Canadian Broadcasting Corporation, 1952. Reprint, Ann Arbor: 1972.

Keillor, Elaine. "Wesley Octavius Forsyth 1859–1937," Les cahiers canadiens de musique /Canadian Music Book 7 (1973): 101–121.

McCready, Louise G. *Famous Musicians: MacMillan, Johnson, Pelletier, Willan.* Toronto: Clarke, Irwin & Co., 1957.

Mercer, Ruby. *The Tenor of His Time.* Toronto: Clarke, Irwin & Co., 1976. A discussion of Edward Johnson.

Thirty-Four Biographies of Canadian Composers / Trente-quatre biographies de compositeurs canadiens. Montreal: Canadian Broadcasting Corporation, 1964.

Instruments

Kallmann, Helmut. *Canadian-Built 19th-Century Musical Instruments: A Check List.* Toronto: Canadian Music Library Association, 1965, Rev. Ottawa, 1966.

Discographies

Litchfield, Jack. *The Canadian Jazz Discography 1916–1980.* Toronto: University of Toronto Press, 1982.

Moogk. *Roll Back the Years.* Complete documentation of Canadian recordings up to 1930. Arranged by performer and composer / arranger—approximately 7,700 performer items; 860 recordings of 224 Canadian compositions.

Recordings of Works Discussed in the Text

Champagne, Claude. *Altitude* (example V-1). CBC RCI 179.
——— *Symphonie Gaspésienne.* Radio-Canada Transcription 213, 213S.
Lavallée, Calixa. *Le papillon* (example IV-2) in *O Canada: Calixa Lavallée et son temps.* CBC RCI 513.
———. *The Widow* in *O Canada: Calixa Lavallée et son temps.* CBC RCI 231 and 513.
Seitz, Ernest. *The World is Waiting for the Sunrise* in *Musical Toronto—A Concert Party.* Marquis Records MAR 104.

Recordings of Other Works

Albani, Emma. "The Art of Bel Canto." *The Great Prima Donnas.* Vol 2. Belcantodisc BC 208.
Canadian Centennial Issue. Vol. 2. Rococco 5255.
Early Music from Quebec. CBC SM 204.
Light Canadian Orchestral Classics. Capitol ST 6261. Works by Lavallée, Couture, Vezina, Lucas, Gagnier, and Leo Smith.
MacMillan, Ernest. Deutsche Grammophon Gesellschaft SLPM 139900; Columbia MS 6962.
Music at Sharon 1831–1981. Melbourne SMLP 4041.
O Canada: Calixa Lavallée et son temps. CBC RCI 231 and 513. Works by Couture, Vezina, Lavigne, and Contant.
Piano Music by Torontonians 1834–1984. WRCI 3315. Works by Clarke, Strathy, Harrison, Lucas, Forsyth and Anger.
Healey Willan. RCI Anthology of Canadian Music / *Anthologie de la musique canadienne.*

Chapter VI

Multiculturalism

Bégin, Carmelle. *La musique traditionnelle pour violon: Jean Carignan.* National Museum of Man Mercury Series, Canadian Centre for Folk Culture Studies Paper no. 40. Ottawa: National Museums of Canada, 1981.
Brednich, Rolf W. "Hymns and Folksong Tradition," In *Mennonite Folklife and Folklore: A Preliminary Report,* 69–76. National Museum of Man Mercury Series, Canadian Centre for Folk Culture Studies Paper no. 22. Ottawa: National Museums of Canada, 1977.
Cohen, Judith R. "Judeo-Spanish Traditional Songs in Montreal and Toronto," *Canadian Folk Music Journal* 10 (1982): 40–47.
Cormier, Charlotte. *Écoutez tous, petits et grands: chansons de Pré-d'en-haut.* Moncton: Éditions d'Acadie, 1978. Includes two 7″ discs of musical examples.

Dostie, Bruno. "Understanding the Role of Folk Music on Quebec's Scene Today," *Canadian Composer* 131 (1978): 4–9.

Feldman, Anna. "Yiddish Songs of the Jewish Farm Colonies in Saskatchewan, 1917–1939." MA thesis, Carleton University, 1983.

Gibbons, Roy W. *As It Comes: Folk Fiddling in Prince George, British Columbia.* National Museum of Man Mercury Series, Canadian Centre for Folk Culture Studies Paper no. 42. Ottawa: National Museums of Canada, 1982.

———. *Folk Fiddling in Canada: A Sampling.* National Museum of Man Mercury Series, Canadian Centre for Folk Culture Studies Paper no. 35. Ottawa: National Museums of Canada, 1981.

Glofcheskie, John Michael. *Folk Music of Canada's Oldest Polish Community.* National Museum of Man Mercury Series, Canadian Centre for Folk Culture Studies Paper no. 33. Ottawa: National Museums of Canada, 1980.

Hall, Leslie. "Turkish Musical Culture in Toronto," *Canadian Folk Music Journal* 10 (1982): 48–52.

Haywood, Charles. *A Bibliography of North American Folklore and Folksong.* 2nd rev. ed. New York: Dover, 1961, with index of performers and arrangers.

Hendrickson, Cheryl J. "English Language Folk Music in Alberta," *Canadian Folk Music Journal* 10 (1982): 34–39.

Johnston, Thomas F. "Black Blues, Soul, and Rock Music in Western Canada," *Anthropological Journal of Canada* 18 (1980): 16–24.

———. "Black Canadian Ethnic Identity," *Ethnologische Zeitschrift Zürich* 1 (1978 [1979]): 117–125.

———. "Caribbean Music in Western Canada," *Viltis* 37 (1978): 11–15.

———. "Change in Black Music in Canada," *Anthropological Journal of Canada* 17 (1979): 9–12.

———. "Music and Blacks in 18th and 19th Century Canada," *Anthropological Journal of Canada* 18 (1980): 19–21.

Klymasz, Robert Bogdan. " 'Sounds You Never Before Heard:' Ukranian Country Music," in *Ukrainian Folklore in Canada,* 91–107. New York: Arno Press, 1980.

Kolinski, Mieczyslaw. "Malbrough s'en va-t-en guerre: Seven Canadian Versions of a French Folksong," *Yearbook of the International Folk Music Council* 10 (1978 [1979]): 1–32.

MacGillvray, Allister. *The Cape Breton Fiddler.* Sydney, Nova Scotia: College of Cape Breton Press, 1981.

MacKinnon, Richard. "Cape Breton Scottish Folksong Collections," *Culture & Tradition* 4 (1979): 23–39.

MacLeod, Margaret. *Songs of Old Manitoba.* Toronto: Ryerson Press, 1959.

MacMillan, Ernest. *A Canadian Song Book.* Don Mills, Ontario: J. M. Dent and Sons, 1948.

———. *Northland Songs.* Toronto: G. V. Thompson, n.d.

Medwidsky, Bodhan. "A Ukranian Assassination Ballad in Canada," *Canadian Folk Music Journal* 6 (1978): 30–37.

Michaud-Latrémouille, Alice. *Chansons de grand-mère.* Ottawa: Éditions de l'Université d'Ottawa, 1980.

Ornstein, Lisa. "Instrumental Folk Music of Quebec: an Introduction," *Canadian Folk Music Journal* 10 (1982): 311.

Peacock, Kenneth. *Songs of the Doukhobors: An Introductory Outline.* Bulletin no. 231, Folklore Series No. 7. Ottawa: National Museums of Canada, 1970.

———. *Twenty Ethnic Songs from Western Canada.* Ottawa: National Museums of Canada, 1965.

Pelinski, Ramón. "The Music of Canada's Ethnic Minorities," *The Canada Music Book* 10 (1975): 59–86.

Perkowski, Jan L. *Gusle and gange among the Hercegovinians of Toronto*. Ann Arbor: University Microfilms for the Center for Russian and East European Studies, University of Virginia, 1978.

Phillips, Gordon. "The Northumbrian Small Pipes in Ontario: A General Field Survey Concerning Their Popularity and Dispersal," *Canadian Folklore canadien* 2 (1980): 54–56.

Song, Bang-Song. "The Korean-Canadians: a Consideration of Their Musical Behaviour in Canadian Society," *Korea Journal* 19 (1978): 32–41.

Thomas, Philip J. *Songs of the Pacific Northwest*. Saanichton, British Columbia: Hancock House, 1979.

Violette, Nicole. "French-Canadian Folk Dancing," *Ontario Folkdancer* 10 (1979): 8–13.

Opera

Opera Canada. Edited by Ruby Mercer. Toronto, 1962–

Popular Music and Jazz

Hopkins, Anthony. *Songs from the Front & Rear: Canadian Servicemen's Songs of the Second World War*. Edmonton: Hurtig Publishers, 1979.

Miller. *Jazz in Canada: Fourteen Lives*.

Yorke, Ritchie. *Axes, Chops & Hot Licks: The Canadian Rock Music Scene*. Edmonton: Hurtig, 1971.

Repertory Lists

Specific lists available from Canadian Music Centre offices.

Shand, Patricia. *Canadian Music: A Selective Guidelist for Teachers*. Toronto: Canadian Music Centre, 1978.

Centennial Celebration

"Festival Canada Highlights," *Opera Canada* 6 (1967): 14–17.

Composition

General

Beckwith and MacMillan, eds. *Contemporary Canadian Composers*.

Canadian Musical Works 1900–1980: A Bibliography of General and Analytical Sources. Canadian Association of Music Libraries Publication 3, n.p., 1983.

Publicity pamphlets on composers available from: Canadian Music Centre offices; and PRO Canada, 41 Valley Brook Drive, Don Mills, Ontario.

Individual Composers

Adams, Stephen. *R. Murray Schafer*. Toronto: University of Toronto Press, 1983.

Bail-Milot, Louise. *Jeane Papineau-Couture*. Montreal (in preparation).

Bradley. *Twentieth Century Canadian Composers*.

Cherney, Brian. *Harry Somers*. Toronto: University of Toronto Press, 1975.

Eastman, Sheila, and Timothy J. McGee. *Barbara Pentland*. Toronto: University of Toronto Press, 1983.

Hepner, Lee. "An Analytical Study of Selected Canadian Orchestral Compositions of the mid-20th Century." Ph. D. thesis, New York University, 1972.

Napier, Ronald. *A Guide to Canada's Composers*. rev. ed. Willowdale, Ontario: Avondale Press, 1976.

Proctor, George. *Canadian Music of the Twentieth Century*. Toronto: University of Toronto Press, 1980.

Skelton, Robert A. "Weinzweig, Gould, Schafer: Three Canadian String Quartets." D. Mus. thesis, Indiana University, 1976.

Such, Peter. *Soundprints: Contemporary Composers*. Toronto: Clarke, Irwin, 1973. Discusses Weinzweig, Somers, Beckwith, Beecroft, Buczynski, and Shafer.

Electronic Music

Keane, David. *Tape Music Composition*. London: Oxford University Press, 1980.

Record Catalogues

Catalogues of CBC and RCI recordings by contemporary Canadian composers available from the CBC.

Centrediscs catalogue available from the Canadian Music Centre, 20 St. Joseph Street, Toronto, Ontario M4Y 1J9.

Melbourne catalogue available from PRO Canada, 41 Valley Brook Drive, Don Mills, Ontario.

Recordings of Works Discussed in the Text

Papineau-Couture, Jean. *Le débat du coeur et du corps de Villon* (example VI-1). RCI Anthology of Canadian Music / Anthologie de la musique canadienne.

Ridout, Godfrey. *Fall Fair* (example VI-2) in *The Toronto Symphony 1922–1972*. Audat 477–4001, and CAPAC QC 1185.

Archer, Violet. *Prelude and Allegro* (example VI-4). RCI Anthology of Canadian Music / Anthologie de la musique canadienne.

Morawetz, Oskar. *From the Diary of Anne Frank* (example VI-5). RCI Anthology of Canadian Music / Anthologie de la musique canadienne.

Weinzweig, John. *Concerto for Harp and Chamber Orchestra*. RCI Anthology of Canadian Music / Anthologie de la musique canadienne.

Freedman, Harry. *Images* in *Canadian Music in the 20th Century*, Columbia Odyssey Y31993, and RCI Anthology of Canadian Music / Anthologie de la musique canadienne.

Pentland, Barbara. *Symphony for Ten Parts* (example VI-6). RCA CCS 1009; RCT 215 / 215-S.

Anhalt, István. *La Tourangelle* in *Sonics*. Centrediscs CMC 0382 WRCI 1976.

Somers, Harry. *North Country* (example VI-8) and *Voiceplay* (example VI-9). RCI Anthology of Canadian Music / Anthologie de la musique canadienne.

———. *Kuyas* (example VI-11). Centrediscs CMC 1183.

LeCaine, Hugh. *Dripsody* in *Electronic Music*. Folkways EM 33436.

Truax, Barry. *Sonic Landscapes* in *Sonic Landscapes. Electronic and Computer Music by Barry Truax*. Melbourne SMLP 4033.

Recordings of Other Works

Publicity recordings (excerpts only) available from CAPAC, 1240 Bay Street, Toronto, Ontario.

The RCI Anthology of Canadian Music / Anthologie de la musique canadienne contains works by the following composers:

John Weinzweig	Jean Coulthard
Serge Garant	Healey Willan
R. Murray Schafer	Gilles Tremblay
Jean Papineau-Couture	Norma Beecroft
Clermont Pepin	Otto Joachim
François Morel	Robert Turner
Harry Somers	Oscar Morawetz
Harry Freedman	Violet Archer
Bruce Mather	Micheline Coulombe-Saint-Marcoux

Canadian Music in the 20th Century. CBC 32 11 0046. Works by Morawetz, Anhalt, and Hétu.

Canadian String Quartet. Columbia MS 5764. Works by Pentland, Pepin, and Weinzweig.

Contemporary Canadian Music. Columbia ML 5685. Works by Somers, Papineau-Couture, and Adaskin.

Electronic Music by Canadian Composers. vol. 1. Melbourne SMLP 4024. Works by Southam, Archer, and Daignault.

Make We Joy. Polydor Stereo 2917.009. Choral music by Holman, Applebaum, Ridout, Paul, Mather, Freedman, Beecroft, and Charpentier.

Montreal Symphony Orchestra. RCA Victor LSC 2980. Works by Mercure, Prévost, and Somers.

Chapter VII

Reference

(Note: A complete list of the material published by the National Museum of Man can be obtained by writing directly to the Museum in Ottawa. Some of the publications are provided without charge.)

Bradley, Ian L. "Revised Bibliography of Indian Musical Culture in Canada," *Indian History* 10 (1977): 28–32.

Bradley, Ian L., and Patricia Bradley. *A Bibliography of Canadian Native Arts: Indian and Eskimo Arts, Crafts, Dance and Music.* Victoria: GLC Publishers, 1977.

Buller, Edward. *Indigenous Performing and Ceremonial Arts in Canada: a Bibliography.* Toronto: The Association for Native Development in the Performing and Visual Arts, 1981.

Maguire, Marsha, Pamela Feldman, and Joseph C. Hickerson. *American Indian and Eskimo Music: A Selected Bibliography Through 1981.* Washington: Archive of Folk Culture, Library of Congress, 1983.

Indians

Barbeau, Marius. *Chansons et danses indiennes*. Ottawa: Imprimeur du Roi, 1930.

Cloutier, David. *My Grandfather's House: Ilinglit Songs of Death and Sorrow*. Alamo, California: Holmgangers Press, 1980.

Crawford, David E. "The Jesuit Relations and Allied Documents: Early Sources for an Ethnography of Music among American Indians," *Ethnomusicology* 11 (1967): 199–206.

Densmore, Frances. *Music of the Indians of British Columbia*. Bureau of American Ethnology Anthropological Papers 27, 1943. Reprint. New York, 1972.

Foster, Michael K. *From the Earth to Beyond the Sky: An Ethnographic Approach to Four Longhouse Iroquois Speech Events*. National Museum of Man Mercury Series, Canadian Ethnology Service Paper no. 20. Ottawa: National Museums of Canada, 1974.

Garfield, Viola, Paul Wingert, and Marius Barbeau. *The Tsimshian: Their Arts and Music*. New York: Publications of the American Ethnological Society 18, ed. Marian W. Smith, n.d.

Goodman, Linda. *Music and Dance in Northwest Coast Indian Life*. Tsaile, Arizona: Navajo Community College Press, 1977.

Guédon, Marie-Françoise. "Canadian Indian Ethnomusicology: A Selected Bibliography and Discography," *Ethnomusicology* 16 (1972): 465–478.

Hauser, Michael. "Inuit Songs from Southwest Baffin Island in Cross-Cultural Context," *Etudes Inuit Studies* 2:1 (1978): 55–83 [part I]; 2:2 (1978): 71–105 [part II].

Hofman, Charles. *Drum Dance*. N. p., 1974.

Kolstee, Anton F. *Bella Coola Indian Music: A Study of the Interaction Between Northwest Coast Indian Structures and Their Functional Context*. National Museum of Man Mercury Series, Canadian Ethnology Service Paper no. 83. Ottawa: National Museums of Canada, 1982.

Kurath, Gertrude. *Dances and Song Rituals of Six Nations Reserve, Ontario*. National Museum of Canada Bulletin no. 220. Ottawa: 1968.

———. *Iroquois Music and Dance: Ceremonial Arts of Two Seneca Longhouses*. Washington, D.C.: U.S. Government Printing Office, 1964.

Massicotte, Jean-Paul, and Claude Lessard. "La danse chez les Indiens de la Nouvelle France aux XVIIe et XVIIIe siècles," *Revue d'ethnologie du Québec* 11 (1980): 49–61.

Nettl, Bruno. *North American Indian Musical Styles*. Memoirs of the American Folklore Society vol. 54. Philadelphia: American Folklore Society, 1954.

Stevenson, Robert. "Written Sources for Indian Music until 1882," *Ethnomusicology* 17 (1973): 1–40.

Vennum, Thomas, Jr. *The Ojibwa Dance Drum: Its History and Construction*. Smithsonian Folklife Studies no. 2. Washington, D.C.: Smithsonian Institute Press, 1982.

Witmer, Robert. *The Musical Life of the Blood Indians*. National Museum of Man Mercury Series, Canadian Ethnology Service Paper no. 86. Ottawa: National Museums of Canada, 1982.

Inuit

Beaudry, Nicole. "Le katajjaq, un jeu inuit traditionnel," *Études Inuit Studies* 2 (1978): 35–53.

Cavanagh, Beverley. "Annotated Bibliography: Eskimo Music," *Ethnomusicology* 16 (1972): 479–487.

──────. *Music of the Netsilik Eskimo: A Study of Stability and Change*. 2 vols. National Museum of Man Mercury Series, Canadian Ethnology Service Paper no. 82. Ottawa: National Museums of Canada, 1982.

──────. "Some Throat Games of Netsilik Eskimo Women," *Canadian Folk Music Journal* 4 (1976): 43–47.

d'Anglure, Bernard Saladin. "Entre cri et chant: les katajjait, un genre musical féminin," *Études Inuit Studies* 2 (1978): 85–94.

Eckert, Penelope, and Russell Newmark. "Central Eskimo Song Duels: a Contextual Analysis of Ritual Ambiguity," *Ethnology* 19 (1980): 191–211.

Johnston, Thomas F. *Eskimo Music by Region: a Circumpolar Study*. National Museum of Man Mercury Series, Canadian Ethnology Service Paper no. 32. Ottawa: National Museums of Canada, 1976.

──────. "Differential Cultural Persistence in Inuit Musical Behaviour, and its Geographical Distribution," *Études Inuit Studies* 1 (1977): 57–72.

──────. "Eskimo Music in Central and Eastern Canada," *Ethnologische Zeitschrift Zürich* 1 (1978 [1979]): 91–105.

Johnston, Thomas F., Matthew Nicolai, and Karen Nagozruk. "Illeagosiik!: Eskimo String-figure Games," *Music Educators Journal* 65 (1979): 54–61.

Lutz, Maija M. *Musical Traditions of the Labrador Coast Inuit*. National Museum of Man Mercury Series, Canadian Ethnology Service Paper no. 79. Ottawa: National Museums of Canada, 1982.

──────. *The Effects of Acculturation on Eskimo Music from Cumberland Peninsula*. National Museum of Man Mercury Series, Canadian Ethnology Service Paper no. 41. Ottawa: National Museums of Canada, 1978.

Nattiez, Jean-Jacques. "Comparisons Within a Culture: the Example of the Katajjaq of the Inuit," in *Cross-cultural Perspectives on Music,* eds. Robert Falck and Timothy Rice, pp. 130–140. Toronto: University of Toronto Press, 1982.

──────. "Some Aspects of Inuit Vocal Games," *Ethnomusicology* 27 (1983): 457–475.

O'Connell, Sheldon. "Music of the Inuit," *Beaver* 310 (1979): 12–17.

Pelinski, Ramón. *La musique des Inuit de Caribou: cinq perspectives méthodologiques*. Montreal: Les Presses de l'Université de Montréal, 1981.

Pelinski, Ramón, Luke Suluk, and Lucy Amarook. *Inuit Songs from Eskimo Point*. National Museum of Man Mercury Series, Canadian Ethnology Service Paper no. 60. Ottawa: National Museums of Canada, 1979.

Roberts, Helen H., and D. Jenness. *Eskimo Songs of the Copper Eskimos. Report of the Canadian Arctic Expedition 1913–18*. Vol. 14. Ottawa: F. A. Ackland, 1925.

Discographies

Lee, Dorothy Sara. *Native North American Music and Oral Data: a Catalogue of Sound Recordings, 1893–1976*. Bloomington: Indiana University Press, 1979.

Nattiez, Jean-Jacques. "Le disque de musique amérindienne: I: Le disque de tradition orale et ses problèmes," *Recherches amérindiennes au Québec* 8:4 (1979): 297–306.

──────. "Le disque de musique amérindienne: II: Introduction a l'écoute des disques de musique inuit," *Recherches amérindiennes au Québec* 10 (1980): 110–122.

──────. "Le disque de musique amérindienne: III: La musique indienne sur disque: cent ans d'ethnomusicologie." *Recherches amérindiennes au Québec* 11 (1981): 251–261.

Recordings of Works Discussed in the Text

Don't Leave Me (example VII-1) in *Songs and Dances of the Great Lakes Indians*. FE 4003.

Iroquoian Corn Dance (example VII-2) in *Songs and Dances of the Great Lakes Indians*. FE 4003.

Drum Dance Song (example VII-3) in *Songs and Dances of the Great Lakes Indians*. FE 4003.

Anthology: Recordings

Quesnel, Joseph. "Rions chantons" from *Colas et Colinette*. RCI CBC 234 Secect CC-15.001 and SSC-24-60.

Champagne, Claude. *Dance villageoise* in *The Hart House Orchestra*. Canadian Talent Library S 5030, and *Heritage*. Dominion LPS-21024.

Willan, Healey. *Introduction, Passacaglia and Fugue* in *Great Cathedral Organ Series: York Minster*. EMI Capitol CSD 1550, and RCI Anthology of Canadian Music / Anthologie de la musique canadienne.

————. *Rise up, My Love, My Fair One* in *Healey Willan at St. Mary Magdalene's*. SMM 0002; *The Choral Music of Dr. Healey Willan*. Capitol ST 6248; *Saint Simon's Sings*, Saint Simon's Church, Toronto. T 55653; *Music of the Church*. Hallmark ChS-3; *From Bach to Rock*. Capitol T 6071.

Papineau-Couture, Jean. "Prelude" from *Suite pour piano*. RCI Anthology of Canadian Music / Anthologie de la musique canadienne.

Tremblay, Gilles. "Phases" from *Suite pour piano* in *Contemporary Canadian Keyboard Music*. CBC SM 162.

Ridout, Godfrey. Etude no. II from *Two Etudes*. CAPAC QC 1185.

Weinzweig, John. Movement no. 1 from "Divertimento I." RCI Anthology of Canadian Music / Anthologie de la musique canadienne.

Schafer, R. Murray. Part V from *Requiems for the Party Girl*. Composers Recordings Inc. SD 245; Melbourne SMLP 4026; RCI Anthology of Canadian Music / Anthologie de la musique canadienne.

General Discography

Lists of Recordings

"Canada on Records," *Musicanada* 26 (1970); Supplements 1972 and 1974.

Great Canadian Music on Records. Available from Music Gallery Editions, 30 Patrick Steet, Toronto, Ont., M5T 1V1. A list of recordings featuring avant-garde and ethnic music.

Labbé, Gabriel. *Les pionniers du disque folklorique québecois 1920–1950*. Montreal: l'Aurore, 1977.

Mealing, F. Mark. *A Doukhobor Discography*. Castlegar, British Columbia: n.p. 1973.

Music Canada. Available from Radio Canada International, Box 6000, Montreal, P.Q., H3C 3A8. A list of recordings of Canadian music and commentary produced by Radio Canada International and CAPAC.

National Library of Canada. *Canadiana*. Ottawa: National Library of Canada, 1969–.

Taft, Michael. *A Regional Discography of Newfoundland and Labrador, 1904–1972.* St. John's: Memorial University of Newfoundland Folklore and Language Archive, 1975.

Recordings

General

Canadian Folk Songs. Columbia World Library of Folk and Primitive Music, Vol. 8. Edited by Marius Barbeau from the collections of the National Museum and the National Film Board, with contributions by Jean Gabus, Museum of Neuchâtel, and Ida Halpern. Columbia SL 211, 1954.

Far Canadian Fields: Companion to the Penguin Book of Canadian Folk Songs. Recorded by Edith Fowke. Leeder LEE 4057, 1975.

John Bartlett and Rika Ruebsaat: The Green Fields of Canada. Canadian Folk Workshop CFW 001. Folksongs in French and English. Available from 1537 Frances Street, Vancouver, British Columbia V5S 1Z2.

English-Canadian

Atlantic Fiddling. CBC LM 470, 1980. Notes by Jim Hornby and Paul Mills in English and French. Traditional fiddle tunes of the Maritime Provinces; various performers.

Authentic Canadian Folk Symbol: English and American Ballads, American Civil War / LaRena LeBarr Clark. Clark Records LCS 108.

Bunkhouse and Forecastle Songs of the Northwest. Folkways FG 3569, 1961. Notes by Stanley Triggs.

Canada at the Turn of the Sod: Lumbering, Railroading and Sea Ballads. LaRena LeBarr Clar. Clark Records LCS 110.

Folk Music from Nova Scotia. Folkways (P1006) FM 4006, 1956.

Folk Songs of Ontario. Folkways FM 4005, 1958. Recorded by Edith Fowke.

Folksongs of Saskatchewan. Folkways FE 4312, 1963. Edited by Barbara Cass-Beggs.

Foksongs of the Miramichi. Folkways FM 4053, 1962. Recorded at the Miramichi Folk Festival, Newcastle, New Brunswick.

Gaelic Folklore of Cape Breton Island. Rodeo RLP 60.

The Great Seal Hunt of Newfoundland. Rodeo RLP 80, 1959.

Irish and British Songs from the Ottawa Valley. Folkways FM 4051, 1961. Recorded by Edith Fowke.

LaRena Clark: Canadian Garland. Topic 12T140, 1965. Ontario Songs recorded by Edith Fowke.

Lumbering Songs from the Ontario Shanties. Folkways FM 4052, 1961. Collected and edited by Edith Fowke.

Marie Hare of Strathadam, New Brunswick. Folk Legacy FSC 9, 1962. Notes by Louise Manny and Edward D. Ives.

Maritime Folk Songs from the Collection of Helen Creighton. Folkways FE 4307, 1962.

The Music of Cape Breton. Vol. 1: *Gaelic Tradition in Cape Breton.* Topic 12TS353, 1978. Vol. 2: *Cape Breton Scottish Fiddle.* Topic 12TS354, 1978. Recorded by John Shaw and Rosemary Hutchison.

Nova Scotia Folk Music from Cape Breton. Electra EKL 23, 1955. Recorded by Diane Hamilton.

Ontario Ballads and Foksongs. Prestige / International INT 25014, 1962. Recorded by Edith Fowke.

Orain Cheap Breatain (Songs of Cape Breton). Celtic CX 38.

Salute to Cape Breton Island. Celtic CX 18. Fiddle tunes and mouth music.

Songs and Ballads of Northern Saskatchewan and Northern Manitoba. Folkways FW 8764, 1960. Compiled by Marvin Loewen and Shirley Davidson.

Songs from Cape Breton Island. Folkways FE 4450, 1955. Recorded by Sidney Robertson Cowell.
Songs from the Outports of Newfoundland. Folkways FE 4075, 1966. Recorded by MacEdward Leach.
Songs of an Ontario Family: British Ballads and Canadian Shanty Songs / LaRena Clark. QC 903.
Songs of the Great Lakes. Folkways FE 4018, 1964. Recorded and edited by Edith Fowke.
Tom Brandon of Peterborouth, Ontario. Folk-Legacy FSC 10, 1963. Recorded by Edith Fowke.
Triumph Street Pipe Band: the Bagpipe in Canada. Lyrichord LLST 7344, 1980. Notes by Allan Skalazub.
Where the Fraser River Flows—and Other Songs of the Pacific Northwest. Svookumchuk Records [no number], Vancouver.

French-Canadian

Acadie et Québec. RCA LCP 1020 / RCA CGP 139, 1959. Collected by Roger Matton.
C'est dans la Nouvelle France. Tamanoir TAMX 27005, 1979. Collected by Marc Gagné.
Jean-Marie Verret, fiddle, and Lise Verret, piano: French Canadian Dance Music. Folkways RF 120, 1983. Collected and annotated by Carmelle Bégin.
Musique traditionnelle du Québec. Le Tamanoir TAMX 32499. Seven records.
Songs and Dances of Quebec. Folkways FW 6951, 1956. Collected by Sam Gesser.
Songs of French Canada. Folkways FE 4482, 1957. Collected by Laura Boulton, Sam Gesser and Carmen Roy.
Sur la côte nord: musique folklorique du nord Québecois. Music Gallery Editions no. 17, 1978.

Ethnic

The Doukhobors of British Columbia. Folkways FR 8972, 1962. Recorded by Barbara Bachovzeff.
Ukraianian Christmas Songs. Folkways FW 6828, 1956. Choral groups recorded in Manitoba by Laura Boulton.

Native Peoples

An Anthology of North American Indian and Eskimo Music. Folkways FE 4541, 1973.
Blackfoot A-1 Singers. Canyon C 6132, 1975.
Canadian-Indian Folklore: An Autobiography / My Life in Recording. Folkways FG 3502, 1957. Recorded and edited by Marius Barbeau.
Cree Pow-wow Songs. Canyon C 6169, 1977.
Cree Tribal Songs. Canyon C 6163, 1977.
A Cry from the Earth: Music of the North American Indians. Folkways FC 7777, 1979. Edited by John Bierhorst.
Dance Songs. India House IH 4051-4052, 1972. Recorded by the Old Agency Singers of the Blood Reserve, Alberta.
The Drums of Poundmaker. Canyon C 6156-6157, 1977.
The Eskimos of Hudson Bay and Alaska. Folkways FE 4444, 1954. Recorded by Laura Boulten.
Fort Kipp Sioux Singers at Fort Qu'Appelle. Canyon C 6079, 1971.
Indian Music of the Canadian Plains. Folkways (P464) FE 4464, 1955. Recorded by Kenneth Peacock.
Indian Music of the Pacific Northwest Coast. Folkways FE 4523, 1967. Collected and recorded by Ida Halpern.

Innuit Throat and Harp Songs. Music Gallery Editions MGE 28, 1980.
The Inuit (Eskimos) of Greenland and Northern Canada. Vol. 1: Lyrichord 7379. Vol. 2: Lyrichord 7380.
Inuit Games and Songs / Chants et jeux des Inuit, Canada. Phillips 6586036, 1978.
Iroquois Social Dance Songs. Iroqrafts QC 727-729, 1969. Notes by William Guy Spittal.
Nootka: Indian Music of the Pacific Northwest Coast. Folkways FE 4524, 1974. Collected, recorded and annotated by Ida Halpern.
Pow-wow Songs. Canyon C 6134, 1975. Cree songs.
Pow-wow Songs. Canyon C 6135, 1975. Performed by the Sarcee Broken Knife Singers, Calgary.
Sioux Pow-wow Songs. Canyon C 6127, 1974.
Six Nations Singers Iroquois Social Music. Music Gallery Editions MGE 16, 1979.
Songs and Dances of the Great Lakes Indians. Folkways FE 4003, 1956.
Songs from the Battleford Pow-wow. Canyon C 6142, 1975.
Songs from the Blood Reserve. Canyon C 6133, 1975.
Songs from the Iroquois Longhouse. Library of Congress AFS L6. Recorded by William Fenton at Oshwekan, Ontario.
Songs of the Nootka and Quileute. Library of Congress AAFS L32, 1953. Edited by Frances Densmore.
Stoney Pow-wow Songs. Canyon C 6136, 1975. Assiniboin music.
World Library of Folk and Primitive Music. Vol 8. Columbia SL 211, 1953. Bella Bella and Kwakiutl songs recorded by Ida Halpern.

Films

Note: For addresses of independent film makers, see the annual catalogue of the National Film Board of Canada, 1 Lombard Street, Toronto, Ontario M5C 1J6.

Cattle Ranch. Contemporary Films, 1961. 16mm. Colour. 20 minutes.
Circle of the Sun. National Film Board of Canada, 1960. 35 mm. Colour. 29 minutes. Blood Indians.
The Crooked Beak of Heaven. 1975. 16mm. Colour. 52 minutes. Gitskan, Haida, Kwakiutl.
Dances of the Kwakiutl. Orbit Films, 1951.
In the Land of the War Canoes: Kwakiutl Indian Life on the Northwest Coast. University of Washington Press. 16mm. 47 minutes.
The Kwakiutl of British Columbia. University of Washington Press. 16mm. Black and white. 55 minutes.
Lake Man. National Film Board of Canada. 16mm. Black and white. 27 minutes.
The Living Stone. National Film Board of Canada, 1958. 16mm. Colour. 30 minutes.
Longhouse People. National Film Board of Canada, 1951. 16mm. Colour. 23 minutes.
Moontrap. National Film Board of Canada, 1963. 16 mm. Black and white. 84 minutes.
Okan Sundance of the Blackfoot. Calgary: Glenbow Foundation, 1966. 64 minutes.
Potlatch: A Strict Law Bids Us Dance. Pacific Cinematheque, 1975. 16mm.
Songs of Nova Scotia. National Film Board of Canada, 1958. 16mm. Black and white. 11 minutes.
This was the Time. National Film Board of Canada. 16 mm. 16 minutes. Haida.
Those Born at Masset: a Haida Stonemoving and Feast. University of Washington Press, 1976. 16mm. 70 minutes.
Totem Pole. University of California, Extension Media Center, 1963. 16 mm. 27 minutes.
Voyageurs. National Film Board of Canada, 1964. 16 mm. Colour. 20 minutes.

Index

Page references followed by an ''i'' indicate that an illustration is to found on that page; numbers followed by an ''m'' indicate that printed music is to be found on that page.

A la claire fontaine, 3–4m, 5, 6
Abel, Carl Friedrich, 33
Académie de musique de Québec, 73
Acadia, 19–20
Act of the Heart (Freedman), 126
Adaskin, Harry, 90
Adaskin, John, 112
Adaskin, Murray, 114, 124, 125
Adderley, Cannonball, 86
advertisements, 30–31, 33–34
Ah! vous dirai-je, maman, 42
Aitken, Robert, 111, 139
Alarie, Pierrette, 109
Alaska Inuit, 156, 161
Albani, Emma, 71i, 72, 80, 85
Alberta, 61, 106, 109
Algonkian Indians, 142, 144–45i–46, 148
All Smoke ceremony, 149
All the Bees and All the Keys (Beckwith), 128
Althus, Jacob, 30–31
Altitude (Champagne), 93m, 94m–95m
Ambrose, Robert, 80
Ančerl, Karl, 108
Anhalt, István, 114, 115, 116, 124, 129, 140
Anka, Paul, 110
Applebaum, Louis, 101, 139
Appleyard, Peter, 111
April Wine, 110
Archambault, E., 72
Archer, Violet, 92, 119, 121–22
Arctic Inuit, 156, 158–60, 161
aristocratic music and theatre, 9–12, 24
As You Like It, incidental music (Freedman), 126
ASCAP, 112
Association des Fils de la Liberté, L', 38
Asymetries No. 1. (Garant), 118
Atlantic Symphony, 108
Atwood, Margaret, 128, 138, 139
Auber, Daniel-François-Esprit, 52, 68
Aubert, Louis, 97
Auer, Leopold, 91
Auld Lang Syne, 86

Ave Maris Stella, 45
Avison, John, 108

Bach, Johann Christian, 33
Bach, Johann Sebastian, 66, 80
Bachman, Randy, 110
Baffinland Inuit, 156
bagpiping, 105
Baker, Carol, 110
Baker, Michael, 139
Balfe, Michael William, 68
ballad operas, 30, 37, 51–52, 67–68
ballads, 43, 48, 63–65
bands
   dance, 85–86
   military, 29, 31–33, 43, 50–51, 52, 69
Banff School of Fine Arts, 111
The Banks of Newfoundland, 23
Barbeau, Marius, 102, 105
barrel organ, 58–59
Bartók, Béla, 121
Battle, Rex, 86, 91
''Bay Psalm Book,'' 27m, 28
Beaumarks, 110
Beckwith, John, 101, 124, 128m–129m, 138
Bédard, Isadore, 56
Beecroft, Norma, 125, 139
Beethoven, Ludwig van, 41, 51, 54–55, 66, 67, 68, 78, 87
Bella Coola band, 152
''Belle rose blanche, La,'' 7
Bellini, Vincenzo, 52
Berger, Arthur, 138
Berliner, Emile, 84
Berliner Gram-o-Phone Company, 84
Bernardi, Mario, 108
Bertrand, Nicolas, 11
Beyond Me, 151m
Bickert, Ed, 111
big bands, 86
Billings, Wiliam, 34, 40
Bizet, Georges, 70
Blackfoot Indians, 149i, 150m

Blood Indians, 149i, 155–56
BMI, 112
Boccherini, Luigi, 31
Bold Wolfe, 21m–22m
Bords du St. Laurent, Les, 49
Bords du St. Lawrence, Les (Grobe), 45
Boss Band, 111
Boston Festival Orchestra, 78
Boucher, A. J., 72
Boucher, François, 72
Boucher-Belleville, Jean-Baptiste, 42
Boudreau, Walter, 139
Boulanger, Nadia, 116, 128, 129
Boulez, Pierre, 116, 117
Bouliane, Denys, 139
Bouton de rose, Le (Sabatier), 54
Boyd, Liona, 111
Brahms, Johannes, 70
Braman, Amasa, 41–42
Brassard, François, 92
Brault, Victor, 79
Braun, Victor, 109
Brébeuf (Schafer), 137
Brébeuf, Jean de, 12, 13
Brébeuf College, 116
Brideship, The (Turner), 114
British Columbia, 38, 61, 62, 106, 142, 151
British influence, 19–37, 40–41, 47–48, 91, 97, 116, 119
broadcasting, *see* radio; television
Brock, General Isaac, 38
Brooks, Shelton, 85
Broome, Edward, 80
Brott, Alexander, 108, 120
Brott, Boris, 108
Bruch, Max, 68
Buczynski, Walter, 139
Bull, Ole, 53
Bülow, Hans von, 70
Burr, Henry, 84
Bury Me Not in the Deep Sea, 47
Buxton, William, 139
Bytown Troubadors, 83

Cabot, John, 1
Cadwallader, E., 63–64m
Calgary Symphony, 87
calypso, 107
Cain (Contant), 79
Campbell, James, 111
Campra, André, 15
Canada
  geographic divisions, ix
  history
    native Indian, 141–42
    17th century, 1–2, 11, 19–20
    18th century, 20
    early 19th century, 38–39
    late 19th century, 61–62
    20th century, 82, 104–5, 106–7
  origin of name, ix
Canada Council, 102–12
Canada Dash—Canada Dot (Beckwith), 128
Canada Forever, Young Canada Was Here (Muir), 65
Canadian/a French Air, The, 45
Canadian Brass, 110
Canadian Broadcasting Corporation, *see* CBC
Canadian Church Psalmody, The (Clarke), 57
Canadian Electronic Ensemble, 110, 138
Canadian Federation of Music Teachers, 89
Canadian Grand Opera Association, 89
Canadian Institute of Music, 97
Canadian League of Composers, 115i, 124, 128
Canadian Marconi Company, 83
Canadian Music Centre, 102, 112, 113, 128
Canadian Music Council, 102
Canadian Opera Company, 89, 108–9
Canadian Patrol (Hughes), 84
Canadian Radio-Television and Telecommunications Commission, 110
Canadian Trio, 88
Canadien errant, Un, 44m–45
Cantata in Honour of the Prince of Wales (Sabatier), 54
Cape Breton, 19–20
Cardy, Patrick, 139
Caribou, 156, 158
Carnival Overture (Morawetz), 122
Cartier, Jacques, ix, 1
Caruso, Enrico, 84
Casavant, Joseph, 53, 72, 74
Casavant Frères, 72
CBC, 84, 89, 113
  National Radio Competition for Young Composers, 139
  Orchestra, 108
Centenary Choir, 83
centennial celebration, 113–14
Cercle philharmonique de Québec, 67
C'est dans la vill' de Bailtonne, 45–46m–47
Chalon, Jean de, 3
chamber music, 88, 109–10
  see also names of specific performing ensembles
Champagne, Claude, 79, 84, 88, 90, 91–93m–96, 173m–178m
  students of, 117, 118, 121, 124
Champlain, Samuel de, 1, 3, 8, 12
Chansons populaires du Canada (Gagnon), 44
Chantons noe, 15
Charpentier, Marc-Antoine, 15
Chateau Laurier Orchestra, 83
Châteauguay (Glackemeyer), 32
Cherney, Brian, 125, 139
Cherubini, Luigi, 50
Child, Francis James, 21
Children (Truax), 139
Children of Peace, 58–59

"Chopper's Song, The" (Clarke), 57
Chorégraphie I (Prévost), 119
"Chorus of Hunters," 57
church music, 15–18, 24–29, 34–35, 40–43,
50, 58–59, 65, 106
Cimaga, Gustav, 138
civic ceremonies, 29
Clarke, Douglas, 87
Clarke, Herbert L., 84
Clarke, James P., 51, 56–57i–58, 73, 166m–
167m
clergy, 11–15, 26
Clothilde, Charles, 78
CMC, 102, 112, 113, 128
Coastal Indians, 142, 152–54
Coates, Richard, 53, 58–59
Codman, Stephen, 50
coffee houses, music in, 24, 30
Cohen, Leonard, 110
Colas et Colinette (Quesnel), 36m–37, 120,
163m–165m
Columbia Graphophone Company, 84
Composers, Authors and Publishers Association of Canada (CAPAC), 102, 112
"Come to the Woods" (Clarke), 57
Comin' thro' the Rye, 76
composition
centennial commissions, 114, 132
educational purposes, 112, 131
within historical periods
early, 15, 16
18th century, 35
19th century, 64–65, 74, 81
20th century, 91, 114–16, 136–37
Indian, 144, 157
opera, 36–37
see also electronic music
concert life
early British, 23–24, 29–31
early French, 9–12
post-conquest Quebec, 31–33
early 19th century, 50–51
late 19th century, 68–72, 78–79, 80
20th century, 87–88
see also opera
concert programs, 29–30, 32, 69, 85, 88, 108,
110, 113, 115
Concerto for Harp and Orchestra (Weinzweig), 125
Confederation, 61, 81
Conservatoire de musique du Québec à
Montréal, 92
Conservatoire national de musique, 79
conservatories, 73, 89
see also music education
Contant, Alexis, 68, 79, 88, 97
Cook, Captain James, 38
Copland, Aaron, 127
Copper Inuit, 156, 161
Corbeil, Claude, 109

Corn Dance, 147m–148m
Coulombe-Saint-Marcoux, Micheline, 139
Coulter, John, 99
Coulthard, Jean, 88, 124
country dance, 23–24, 33, 49
country music, 110
Couture, Guillaume, 67, 68, 78i–79, 88, 90,
116
Creighton, Helen, 21, 105
Crépault, Napoléan, 80
Crew-Cuts, 110
Cross, Lowell, 132
Cummings, Burton, 110
Curtola, Bobby, 110
Czerny, Carl, 54

D'Albert, Charles, 48, 49, 168m
dance bands, 85–86
dance music, 7, 11, 23–24, 30, 33, 49, 50–
51, 105
Indian, 144, 145, 146–149, 151, 152, 155–
56, 158–61
Danse villageoise (Champagne), 93, 96m,
173m–78m
Daoust, Yves, 139
Darktown Strutters Ball (Brooks), 85
Daulé, Rev. Jean-Denis, 42
Daunais, Lionel, 88
Davidson, Alexander, 40, 41, 42
Davidson, Jimmy (Trump), 85–86, 110
Davidson, Teddy, 110
Davis, Andrew, 108
Début du coeur et du corps de Villon, Le
(Papineau-Couture), 117m
Decker, Franz-Paul, 108
Defauw, Désiré, 87, 108
Deirdre (Willan), 99–100m
Davidson, Jimmy (Trump), 85–86, 110
Davidson, Teddy, 110
Davis, Andrew, 108
Début du coeur et du corps de Villon, Le
(Papineau-Couture), 117m
Decker, Franz-Paul, 108
Defauw, Désiré, 87, 108
Deirdre (Willan), 99–100m
Dela, Maurice, 92, 124
del Vecchio, Rosita, 70, 74
Descarries, Auguste, 88
Deschesnes, Marcelle, 139
De Seve, Alfred, 72
Dessane, Antoine, 50, 56, 73, 80
Deux Âmes, Les (Contant), 79
Deux Poèmes (Mathieu), 97
Diamond Jubilee of Confederation, 83
Di Giovanna, Edoardo, 90
d'Indy, Vincent, 97
Disasters of the Sun (Pentland), 127
Divertimento No. 1 (Weinzweig), 125, 219m–
25m
Dolin, Samuel, 126, 139

Donizetti, Gaetano, 52
Donkey Riding, 47m
Don't Leave Me, 145–46m
Doukhobors, 106
Dripsody (LeCaine), 138
Drum Dance ceremony, 148m, 151, 160m–61
drums, 12, 145, 146, 148, 150, 151, 152, 158–61
Dubois, Théodore, 78, 79, 80
Dubois Quartette, 88
Duchow, Marvin, 92
Dumont, Henri, 15
Dutilleux, Henri, 119
Dutoit, Charles, 108
Dvořák, Antonin, 66, 68

Eaton Operatic Society, 89
Eckhardt-Gramaté, Sophie-Carmen, 124
Eckstein, Willie, 85
Edison Speaking Phonograph Company, 84
Edmonton, 87, 109
education, *see* music education
Edward Augustus, Prince, 31
Elastic Band Studies (Beckwith), 128
electronic music, 110, 114, 116, 129, 138–39
Elmer Iseler Singers, 108
"Emblem of Canada, The" (Clarke), 57
"Emigrants Bride, The" (Clarke), 57
"Emigrants Home Dream, The" (Clarke), 48, 57–58, 64, 166m–67m
"En roulant ma boule," 7
Encyclopedia of Music in Canada (Kallmann), x, 128
Enfants de Paris, Les, 62
English influence, 21, 22, 105
entrée royale, 9
Epitaph for Moonlight (Schafer), 137
Eskimos, 141, 158
Evans, Gil, 86

Faith, Percy, 85, 86, 91
Fall Fair (Ridout), 120m
Fantasmes (Prévost), 119
Fantasy on a Hebrew Theme (Morawetz), 122
Farnam, Lynwood, 72
fauxbourdon, 15
Feldbrill, Victor, 108
Ferguson, Maynard, 86
Ferries, A. D., 57
Festal Overture (Ridout), 119
Festival Singers of Canada, 108
Fétiche, Le (Vézina), 80
Field, Harry, 72
fiddles and violins, 15, 24, 27, 28, 52, 59
film music, 125, 126, 138
Fine, Irving, 138
Fisher, Edward, 73i, 80
Fleming, Robert, 101
flute, 15, 51, 59
    see also whistle flute
folk dances, Scottish, 24

folk music
    Anglo-Canadian, 21–23, 47–48, 86, 105–6
    French-Canadian, 2–8, 11, 43–47, 92, 105
    of other immigrant groups, 106–7
    late 19th century, 63
    20th century, 105–7
Folk Songs of Eastern Canada (Ridout), 119
Forrester, Maureen, 109
Forsyth, W. O., 65, 68, 80, 84
Fortier, Achille, 79
Foster, Stephen, 85
Four Iroquois Dances (McPhee), 102
Fowke, Edith, 21
Franck, César, 78
Freedman, Harry, 114, 124, 126–27
French influence, 1–18, 21, 24, 42–47, 75, 91, 116, 118
Fricker, Peter Racine, 136
From the Diary of Anne Frank (Morawetz), 122–23m–24
Frontenac, Comte Louis de, 11
fuging tunes, 34, 40

Gade, Niels, 78
Gagnier, J. J., 79
Gagnon, Ernest, 44, 45–46, 73, 75, 80, 105
Gallopade (Sauvageau), 54
Galloway, Jim, 111
Gandy Dancer, The (Faith), 91
Garant, Serge, 92, 118, 139
Garrard, Don, 109
Garrick, Steve, 86
Gas! (Beckwith), 128
Gauthier, Eva, 83
Gellman, Stephen, 139
George, Graham, 88
Gérin-Lajoie, Antoine, 45
Germania Singverein, 62–63
Gerster, Etelka, 74
Gigout, Eugène, 79
Gilbert and Sullivan, 68, 85
Gilbert Watson Orchestra, 86
GIML, 110
Girard, Jean, 18
Glackemeyer, Edouard, 53
Glackemeyer, Frédéric, 32–33, 50
Glick, Srul Irving, 114, 126
God Save the King, 52, 76
Godfrey, Mr., 26
gospel songs, 41
Gossec, François-Joseph, 33
Gottschalk, Louis Moreau, 53
Gould, Glenn, 111
Goulet, Joseph, 67
Goulet, Robert, 110
Goulet Orchestra, 67
Graduel romain, Le, 16, 42
Grand Trunk Waltzes (D'Albert), 48i, 49, 77, 168m
Grant, Warden of the Plains (Adaskin), 114

Grass Dance, 156
Gratton, Hector, 88, 90, 97
Greenland Inuit, 156, 161
Greenwich, 34m–35m
Greenwich, Sonny, 111
Grobe, Charles, 45
Guernica (Pépin), 119
Guilmant, Alexandre, 79

Halifax, 24–31, 49, 50, 52, 53, 66, 73, 87
Halifax Harmonic Society, 50
Ham, Albert, 69, 80
Hambourg Trio, 88
Hamilton, 53, 73
Hamilton Philharmonic, 108
Hand, Mark, 139
Handel, George Frideric, 41, 50, 51, 63, 66, 68, 80, 88, 115
Handful of Maple Leaves, A, 64–65
Hanson, Howard, 124
Hardy, Hagood, 110
Harnoy, Ofra, 111
harp music, 51
Harriss, Charles A. E., 80
Hart House String Quartet, 83, 88, 90
Hawkins, John, 139
Haydn, Franz Joseph, 31, 33, 50, 51, 66, 68, 88
Healey, Derek, 139
Heinrich, Max, 67
Heintzman and Company, Theodore, 72
Herbert, Victor, 70
Hercule et Omphale (Champagne), 95–96m
Heritage (Glick), 114
Hétu, Jacques, 108, 116, 139
Heydler, Charles, 76
Highland Laddie, 47
Highlevel Hornpipe, 86
Hindemith, Paul, 121, 122
Holman, Sallie, 68
Holman English Opera Troupe, 68
Holt, Patricia Blomfield, 101
Home Sweet Home, 72, 85
"Home Flowers" (Clarke), 57
Honegger, Arthur, 116, 118
Horn, Paul, 111
Horoscope, L' (Matton), 108
Hortulanae Musicae, 110
Hughes, Arthur Wellesley, 84
Huguenots, 12
Hultberg, Courtland, 139
Humbert, Stephen, 33–34, 40, 42
Humble, Irene, 84
Hund, Frederick, 53
Hunter, Tommy, 110
Huron Indians, 12–14
Hutterites, 106
hymnals, 24–25, 27–29, 34–35, 40–41, 42, 65
Hymns and Spiritual Songs, 24–25, 27, 28

I Know a Land (Cadwallader), 64m
Iglulik Inuit, 156
Images (Freedman), 126
Images du Canada français (Champagne), 92
immigrants, music of, 106–7, 116, 140
Improvisation (Somers), 131
In Memoriam, Hugh LeCaine (Keane), 138
In Search of Zoroaster (Schafer), 137
Indians, 12–14, 141–56
instrumental music groups, 50, 51, 66–67
  chamber music, 88, 109–10
  dance bands, 85–86
  orchestras, 87–88, 107–8
  see also military bands
Introduction, Passacaglia and Fugue (Willan), 99, 179m–98m
Inuit, 141, 156–61
Irish influence, 21, 23, 47m, 105
Iroquoian Indians, 142, 145, 146–49
Iseler, Elmer, 108
Israel (Weinzweig), 125

Jack Was Every Inch a Sailor, 105
Jacks, Terry, 110
Jacobs, Gordon, 124
Jarvis, Hannah, 33
jazz, 85–86, 110–11
Jean le Précurseur (Couture), 79
Jehin-Prume, Frantz, 70, 74, 79
Jenkins, George, 40
Jesous Ahatonhia, 13m–14, 43
Jesuits, 12, 14, 15
Jeune pucelle, Une, 13–14m, 43
Jeunesses musicales du Canada, Les, 102, 112
jigs, 49
Joachim, Otto, 139
Jobin, Raoul, 109
John Adaskin Project, 112, 131
Johnson, Edward, 85, 89–90i
Joies du foyer, Les (Crépault), 80
Jolliet, Louis, 16
Jones, Kelsey, 101, 114, 139
Joplin, Scott, 85
Journals of Susanna Moodie, The (Beckwith), 128
Jouve, Sieur, 31
Jugement de Salomon, Le (Lavallée), 74

Kallmann, Helmut, x
Kasemets, Udo, 139
Keane, David, 138–39
kelaudi, 159
Kelligrew's Soiree, The, 105
Kenins, Talivaldis, 124
Keyboard Practice (Beckwith), 129
Kingston, 53
kirk fiddle, 27, 28
Klein, Lothar, 139
Kodály, Zoltán, 129
Koenig, G. M., 139
Koffman, Moe, 111

Koprowski, Peter Paul, 139
Kotzwara, Franz, 20 n.3, 30
Krifft, W. B. de, 20 n.3
Kuyas (Somers), 135m
Kwakiutl rattle, 153i

Labrador Inuit, 156
Laliberté, Alfred, 88, 92, 97
Laparra, Raoul, 92
Laplante, André, 111
Laske, Otto, 139
Lauder, Henry, 84
Lauder, William, 72
Lauréat, Le (Vézina), 80
Laval, Bishop, 16
Lavallée, Augustin Pâquetdit, 74
Lavallée, Calixa, 54, 69, 74–75i–77, 79, 80,
    88, 169m–72m
Lavallée-Smith, Alphonse, 79
Lavigne, Arthur, 66, 72, 73, 80
Lavigueur and Hutchison, 72
Lays of the Maple Leaf (Clarke), 57i
Lebègue, Nicholas, 17
LeCaine, Hugh, 138
Le Flem, Paul, 102
Legundre, Napoléan, 76
Lehmann, Lilli, 67, 70
le Jeune, Fr. Paul, 14
Lescarbot, Marc, 2, 8, 9–10, 37
Letondal, Paul, 74, 88
Lightfoot, Gordon, 110
Lind, Jenny, 53
Linley, Thomas, 52
Livingstone, Bill, 105
Livre d'orgue de Montreal, 16–17m–18
Lombardo, Guy, 85, 86
Lorne, Marquis de, 76
Louie, Alexina, 139
Louis Riel (Somers), 109i, 114, 130, 132–
    33m–35m
Lou-Lou (Lavallée), 74
Love Me or Leave Me (Faith), 91
Lower Canada, ix, 11–16, 38, 45
    see also Quebec
Lucas, Clarence, 80–81, 84
Lucas et Cécile (Quesnel), 36
Lukey's Boat, 105
lumbering songs, 47–48
Lyon, James, 29
Lyre sainte (Molt), 55

McConnell, Robin, 111
MacDonough, Harry, 85
M'Farten, Reuben, 31
MacGeorge, Rev. R. I., 57
McGill Conservatorium, 80, 121
McGill University, 92, 129, 138
McKay, Cliff, 86
Mackenzie, Alexander, 38
McKenzie, Giselle, 110

MacKenzie, W. Roy, 21
Mackenzie, William Lyon, 38–39, 45, 59
Mackenzie Delta Inuit, 156, 158, 161
Mackenzie River Indians, 142, 150–51
McLaughlin, Murray, 110
McLuhan, Marshal, 136
MacMillan, Sir Ernest, 84, 87, 88, 91, 101–2,
    108, 124
McPhee, Colin, 97, 102
McQuhae, Allan, 83
Maid from Algoma, The, 85
Manitoba, 61, 106, 109
manuscripts, 15
Maple Leaf, The (Clarke), 57
Maple Leaf For Ever, The (Muir), 65, 75, 85
Maple Leaf Rag (Joplin), 85
Maritimes, ix, 20–24, 41, 47, 86
Markevitch, Igor, 108
Marr, Frances, 90
Marshall, Lois, 109
Martel, Oscar, 72
Martin, Fr. Charles-Amador, 16, 42
Martinez English Opera Company, 68
Mason and Risch, 72
Massey, Hart, 67
Massey (Music) Hall, 67, 91
Mather, Bruce, 126
Mathieu, André, 97
Mathieu, Rodolphe, 79, 88, 96–97
Matton, Roger, 92, 108
Mauro, Ermanno, 109
Mazurka caprice (Sabatier), 54
Mechtler, Mrs. 29–30
Mehta, Zubin, 108
Méhul, Etienne-Nicholas, 51
Melody Five, 85
Memorare, 78
Memorial to Martin Luther King, 122
Mendelssohn, Felix, 51, 88
Mendelssohn choirs, 66, 69
    in Toronto, 69–70, 102
Mennonite Children's Choir, 106, 108
Mennonites, 106
Mer à l'Aube, La (Piché), 139
Mercure, Pierre, 92, 139
Messer, Don, 86
Messiaen, Olivier, 116, 117, 118, 119
Metropolitan Choral Society, 51
Metropolitan Opera Company, 89, 90, 91
Metropolitan School of Music, 80
Meyerbeer, Giacomo, 52
Milhaud, Darius, 130
military bands and music-making, 12, 29, 31–
    33, 43, 50–51, 52, 69
Miller, Elma, 139
Miller and Drummond, 40
Mills, Frank, 110
minuet, 23–24, 33, 49
Miro, Henri, 88
Missae brevis (Willan), 98

missionaries, 12–15
Molt, Theodore F., 54–56, 75
Monk, Allan, 109
Montreal
    church music, 16–18
    composers, 79, 116
    concert life, 33, 52–53, 69, 79, 80, 87
    education, 73
    history, 38
    music societies, 66, 67, 89
    opera, 52, 68, 89, 107
    publishers, 49, 53, 72
    radio, 83, 86
Montreal Philharmonic Society, 67, 70, 78
Montreal Symphony Orchestra, 67, 87, 88,
    91, 107, 108
Moore, Mavor, 132
Morawetz, Oskar, 116, 119, 122–24
Morel, François, 92, 116
Morin, Jean-Baptiste, 15
Morin, Léo-Pol, 97
Morris, R. O., 124
Morton, Jelly Roll, 85
Moscheles, Ignaz, 54
Motet à la Sainte Vierge, 16m
Mouvement à la Pavane (Lavallée), 77,
    169m–70m
Mozart, Wolfgang Amadeus, 33, 41, 50, 51,
    68, 87
Mozetich, Marjan, 139
Much Ado About Nothing incidental music
    (Freedman), 126
Muir, Alexander, 65, 75
Murray, Anne, 110
Murray-Bay, 52
"Music and Musicians of Canada," 113
music business, 53, 72, 112–13
music education
    conservatories, 73, 89, 111
    individual instruction, 11, 30–31, 32–33,
        34, 51, 53, 54–55, 72–73
    opera, 108–9
    schools, 14–15, 58, 73, 89, 111, 112, 131
    singing schools, 41–42
    universities, 73–74, 89, 111
    youth groups, 111–12, 131
Music for a Young Prince (Ridout), 119, 120
music notation, 40, 42
music publishing, 48–49, 53, 72, 80
music societies, 33, 50, 51, 66, 112–13, 115
    Indian, 146, 149
musical instruments
    builders, 53, 72, 74
    of the early settlers, 7, 11, 18, 24, 59
    of the Indians, 142, 145i, 146, 149i, 150,
        151, 152, 153i, 159–61
    lessons, 30–31, 32–33, 51
    see also bagpiping, barrel organs, drums,
        fiddles, flute, harp music, kirk fiddle,
        military bands, organ, piano, rattles, vio-

lins, viols, whistle flute
Musique canadienne, 53–54
Mutations (Pentland), 127
Mystery Dance, 152

Nares, James, 20 n.3
National Arts Centre Orchestra, 108
national songs, *see* patriotic songs
National Youth Orchestra, 111
Nelson, Frank H., 77
Nelsova, Zara, 88, 91, 111
Netsilik Inuit, 156, 157, 158, 160m
New Brunswick, ix, 28, 33–34, 61, 105
New England settlers, 20–21, 41
New France, ix, 1–18
New Symphony Orchestra, 70, 87
Newark, 33, 38, 50–51
Newfoundland, ix, 52, 61, 105
    see also Saint John
Nexus, 110
Niagara, 33, 38, 50–51
Niagara, 41m
Niagara Temperance Society, 51
Nichols, Red, 86
Night Blooming Cereus (Beckwith), 128
Nimmons, Phil, 111i
Niska band, 152
No longer than Ten Minutes (Schafer), 137
Nordheimer Co., A. and S., 57, 72
North Country (Somers), 130m–31
Northern Lights (Somers), 130
Nouveau Recueil de cantiques, 42
Nova Scotia, ix, 19–24, 42, 61, 105
    see also Halifax

O Canada (Lavallée), 45, 54, 75i–76
O digne objet de mes chants, 42m–43
O Lord, Our Governour (Willan), 101
Offenbach, Jacques, 68
Office for Ste. Famille, 17m
"One Sweetly Solemn Thought" (Ambrose),
    80
Ontario, ix, 20–24, 38–39, 61, 69, 86, 105–6
    opera, 36–37, 51–52, 67–68, 88–89, 108–9
Opera Canada, 109
Opera Guild of Toronto, 89
operetta, 77
orchestras, 87–88, 107–8
    see also names of specific orchestras
Orchestre quadrille, 53
Orchestre symphonique de Québec, 67, 87,
    91, 108
Orchestre symphonique de Montréal, *see* Mon-
    treal Symphony Orchestra
Order of Good Cheer (Ordre de bon temps), 8
Orford Quartet, 109
organ
    builders, 53, 72
    music, 16–18, 26–27, 29, 59
Original Canadian Quadrilles, 49

Orme and Son, J. L., 72
Orpheus Club, 66
Ottawa, 45, 72, 80, 83, 87
Owl Dance, 149, 156
Oxford, 25m–26m, 27m, 28m
Ozawa, Seiji, 108

Pacific Coast Indians, 142, 152–153i–154
Paderewski, Ignaz, 70
Pale Horse, Pale Rider (Freedman), 126
Pan, 126
Papillon, Le (Lavallée), 76m
Papineau, Louis Joseph, 38–39, 45
Papineau-Couture, Jean, 114, 115, 116–17m,
    119, 202m
Par derrièr' chez ma tante, 44m–45
Par derrièr' chez mon père, 5–6m, 45
parlor songs, 63–65
Parlow, Kathleen, 90–91
Parlow String Quartet, 88, 91
Parochial Choral Society, 50
Parry, Sir Hubert, 80
part-songs, 50
Passacaglia and Fugue (Somers), 108
patriotic songs, 45, 55–56, 57–58, 63–64m–
    65, 75–76, 84, 113
Peacock, Kenneth, 21
Pellegrini, Maria, 109
Pellerin, Hector, 85
Pelletier, R. O., 79
Pelletier, Wilfrid, 79, 87, 91
Pennycook, Bruce, 139
Pentland, Barbara, 90, 114, 115i, 124, 127m
Pépin, Clermont, 92, 118–19
Peterson, Oscar, 86, 111
Philharmonic Society
    see entry under specific city
phonograph, 83–85
piano
    builders, 53, 72
    music, 48–49
Pianos Lesages, Les, 72
Picasso Suite (Somers), 130
Piché, Jean, 139
Pièces pour piano (Tremblay), 117–18,
    203m–5m
Placide, Brother, 85
Plains Indians, 142, 149i–50, 155–56
Plainsongs (Archer), 122
Plateau Indians, 142, 151–52
Playford, John, 25, 28
popular music, 43–49, 63–65, 85–86, 110–11
Porter, Quincy, 116
Potlatch, 152m, 154m
Pousseur, Henri, 117
Poutrincourt, Baron de, 9
Powwow, 155–56
Prelude and Allegro (Archer), 121–22
Prévost, André, 115, 116, 118, 119
Prince d'Orange, Le, 3m, 5, 6

Prince Edward Island, ix, 61, 105
PRO Canada, 112
Processional romain, Le, 42
psalms, 25–28, 31, 40, 41–43
Psalms of David, The (Miller and Drummond),
    40
publishing, *see* music publishing
Purcell String Quartet, 109–10

Quadrille Band, 51
Quadrille sur cinq airs canadiens (Dessane),
    56
quadrilles, 49
Quasars (Pépin), 119
Quebec
    composers, 79–80
    concert life, 31–33, 50, 52–53
    education, 14, 73
    folk music, 44, 105
    history, ix, 19–20, 38, 61
    Inuit, 156
    military bands, 31, 69
    music societies, 66–67, 87, 117, 118
    national song, 45
    opera, 52, 68
    publishers, 49, 53, 72
    sacred music, 12–18, 42
    social life, 11–12, 23
Quebec Harmonic Society, 33, 50, 56
Quebec Symphony Orchestra, *see* Orchestre
    symphonique de Québec
Québécoise, La (Dessane), 56
Queen's College, 129
Queen's University Electronic Music Studio,
    138
Quesnel, Joseph, 35–36m–37, 120, 163m–
    65m
Quilico, Gino, 109
Quilico, Louis, 109

Ra (Schafer), 137i
Rabbit Dance, 151
radio, 83–84, 87, 88, 89, 110, 113, 128
ragtime, 85
Rajah, Le (Vézina), 80
rattles, 145, 146, 150, 151, 152, 153i
Ravenscroft, Thomas, 25, 28
RCA Victor, 84, 113
Rea, John, 139
Read, Daniel, 34m–35m, 40
Reaney, James, 128
réception, 9, 10, 37
*Réception de Monseigneur le Vicomte
    d'Argensen, La,* 10
Recollects, 12–13
recording, 83–85, 87
Recueil de cantiques des missions, 42
Red Ear of Corn, The (Weinzweig), 125
Red Roses, 64–65
reels, 49

reggae, 107
Regina, 87
Registered Music Teachers, 89
Remenyi, Eduard, 70
Requiems for the Party Girl (Schafer), 137, 226m–27m
Rêverie (Couture), 78
Rhys, Horton, 52
Ridout, Godfrey, 37 n.33, 101, 115, 119–21, 206m–18m
"Rions chantons" (Quesnel), 36, 163m–65m
Rippling Water Jig, 86
Rise Up, My Love, My Fair One (Willan), 100–101, 199m–201m
Robbins, Dave, 86
Rogers, Bernard, 124
Romances sans paroles (Jehin-Prume), 70
Romanelli, Luigi, 91
Rose Latulippe (Freedman), 114
Rossini, Gioachino, 50, 51, 52
Round Dance, 151
Routhier, Judge A. B., 75
Rover Boys, 110
Royal Conservatory of Music, 73, 90, 108
Royal Fusiliers, 31
Rubinstein, Anton, 70
Ruche harmonieuse, La (Crépeault), 80
Rush, 110

Sabatier, Charles, 54, 74
Sacred Harmonic Choir, 51
Sacred Harmony (Davidson), 40, 41, 42
sacred music, *see* church music; tribal rituals
Sagard-Théodat, Rev. Gabriel, 12
Saint John, 33–34, 42, 50, 52, 53, 66
St. John Oratorio Society, 66
St. Joseph, Mother Marie de, 14–15
St. Luke, John, 50
St. Paul's Singing Society, 50
St.-Jean Baptiste Society, 4
Saint-Saëns, Camille, 78
salon music, 48–49, 54, 64, 77
Sam Slick (Jones), 114
Saskatchewan, 61, 106
Sauvageau, Charles, 53–54
Savoyards, 89
Scalero, Rosario, 118
Schafer, R. Murray, 115, 120, 124, 126, 136–37i, 139, 226m–27m
Schoenberg, Arnold, 108
schools, *see* music education
Schumann, Robert, 78,
Schumann-Heink, Ernestine, 84
Scottish influence, 21, 23, 24, 27, 47m, 105
Seitz, Ernest, 65
Selection from the Psalms of David, A (Jenkins), 40
Serial Sound Structure Generator, 138
Sentenne, Léon, 78 n.18
Septuor Haydn, 66–67

Sewell, Jonathan, 53
Shand, Patricia, 112
shape-note format, 40
Shantyman's Life, The, 47m–48
Shapero, Harold, 138
Sharon Fragments (Beckwith), 128
Sharon Silver Band, 59
Sharon Temple, 58–59, 128
sheet music, 48–49, 72
Shivaree, The (Beckwith), 128m–29m
Si tu te mets anguille, 44, 45
Siege of Quebec, The (Kotzwara), 20 n.3
Silver, Harvey, 111
Simcoe, Elizabeth, 23, 31
Simon Fraser University, 109–10, 136, 139
Simoneau, Léopold, 109
singing schools, 41–42
"Single I Will Never Be" (Lavallée), 77, 171m–72m
Sioux Dance, 156
Slavey Indians, 151
Smith, Leo, 90, 102
Snow, Hank, 110
Société canadienne d'opérette, La, 89
Société de musique contemporaine du Québec (SMCQ), 117, 118
Société des concerts symphoniques de Montréal, 87
Société des festivals de Montréal, 89
Société Sainte-Cécile, 67
Société symphonique de Québec, 67, 87
social occasions, 49, 105
    Anglo-Canadian, 24, 33, 50
    French-Canadian, 7–8, 11
    Indian, 144, 146, 155–56, 158
Sol canadien, terre chérie (Molt), 55m–56m, 75
Solipsism while Dying (Ciamaga), 138
Some of These Days (Brooks), 85
Somers, Harry, 108, 109i, 114, 115, 124, 126, 130–36, 139
Son of Heldenleben (Schafer), 137
Song for healing sickness, 157m
Sonic Landscape No. 3 (Truax), 139
Souvenir d'Amérique (Jehin-Prume), 70
Spanier, Herbie, 111
Spanish Ladies, 105
Speeches for Dr. Frankenstein (Pennycook), 139
Spud Island Breakdown, 86
square notation, 42
Squid-Jiggin' Ground, The, 23
Stamitz, Johann Wenzel Anton, 31, 33
Stampeders, 110
Staryk, Steven, 111
Sternhold and Hopkins, 25
Stock, Frederick, 70
Stratas, Teresa, 109
Strathcona, Lord, 90
Strathy, George W., 73

Stravinsky, Igor, 108, 116
Suckling and Sons, I., 72
Suite canadienne (Champagne), 92
Suite pour Piano (Papineau-Couture), 116, 202m
Sukis, Lilian, 109
Sulak, Alice, 158i
Sulak, Donald, 158i
Sun Dance, 149, 150, 155
support organizations, 112–13, 115
Susskind, Walter, 108
Swan, Timothy, 40, 59
swing bands, 85
Symonds, Norman, 108
Symphonie gaspésienne (Champagne), 92
Symphonie pour voix humaines (Mathieu), 97
Symphony for Ten Parts (Pentland), 127m

Tafelmusik, 110
Talon, John, 2, 11
Tanguay, Georges-Emile, 97
Tape Music Composition (Keane), 139
Tapes from Gilgamesh (Truax), 139
Tea Dance, 151
television, 84, 110, 113
Thalberg, Sigismond, 53
Thanksgiving Anthem for the taking Montreal, A (Nares), 20 n.3
Théâtre de Neptune, 9–10, 37
Théâtre du Société, 36
theatre productions, 9–12, 30, 50
see also opera
Théberge, Paul, 139
Theme for Variations (Somers), 131
Thompson, S., 57
Thomson, Heather, 109
Three Preludes on Scottish Tunes (Ridout), 119
Tiq (Lavallée), 74
Toronto
concert life, 51, 52, 53, 68, 69–70
education, 73
history, 38–39, 51
music societies, 66, 67, 87, 88
opera, 68, 89
publishers, 49, 53, 72
see also University of Toronto
Toronto College of Music, 73i, 80
Toronto Conservatory of Music, 73i, 80, 90, 91, 97, 101, 124
Toronto Conservatory String Quartet, 88
Toronto Consort, 110
Toronto Mendelssohn Choir, 69–70, 85
Toronto Philharmonic Society, 51, 56, 67
Toronto Symphony Orchestra, 70, 84, 87, 101–2, 107, 108
Toronto Symphony Youth Orchestra, 111–12
Torrington, F. H., 67, 68, 73i
Tourangelle, La (Anhalt), 129, 139
Toward My Friend, 151

Tremblay, Amadée, 79
Tremblay, Giles, 92, 116, 117–18, 203m–5m
tribal rituals, 141, 144, 155–56
Algonkian, 145
Inuit, 156–61
Iroquoian, 146–49
Plains, 149, 155–56
Mackenzie River, 151
Pacific Coast, 152
Trinity College, 73
Trio con Alea (Pentland), 127
Truax, Barry, 138, 139
Tsimshian rattle, 153i
Tudor Singers, 108
Turgeon, Bernard, 109
Turner, Robert, 92, 114, 124, 139
Twinkle, twinkle, little star, 42
Two Etudes (Ridout), 120–21m, 206m–18m
Two-Part Inventions (Ciamaga), 138
Tyson, Sylvia and Ian, 110

Union Harmony (Humbert), 34–35, 40
Union musicale, 66
United Empire (Hughes), 84
United States influence, 40, 41
University of Alberta, 122
University of British Columbia, 138
University of Montreal, 116
University of Toronto, 73, 90, 109
Electronic Music Studio, 138
faculty, 56, 97, 101, 119, 124, 128
Upper Canada, ix, 20–24, 33, 38–39, 45, 50
Upper Canada College, 90
Urania, 29
Ursulines, 12, 14, 15–16, 129

Valse de Ménéstrel (Sauvageau), 54
Vancouver, 63, 86, 109
Vancouver Chamber Choir, 108
Vancouver Symphony, 87, 108
Varèse, Edgard, 102, 116, 117
Venez mon Dieu, 15
Verdi, Giuseppe, 52, 68
Vermandere, Joseph, see Placide, Brother
Veronica (Contant), 79
Vespéral romain, Le, 42
Vézina, Joseph, 67, 76, 79–80, 87
Vickers, Jon, 109
Victor Talking Machine Company, 84
Victoria, 62–63, 66
Victoria Philharmonic Society, 62–63
Victoria Theatre, 62
Vieuxtemps, Henri, 53, 70
Villon, François, 117
violin makers, 72, 74
violins and fiddles, 15, 24, 27, 28, 52, 59
viols, 11, 15, 59
Vive la canadienne, 5–6m, 45–46, 76
Vivier, Claude, 139

vocal music groups, 50, 66, 88, 106, 108
  see also opera
Vogt, A. S., 69, 97
Voiceplay (Somers), 131m–32m
Von Kunits, Luigi, 70, 87, 90, 102
Voyageurs, 6–7, 63

waltz, 49
Wagner, Richard, 78
Wall, Mr., 51
Walter, Arnold, 118, 124
War Dance, 156
Warner, Viere, 26–27
Waren, Samuel Prowse, 53, 72
Watanabe, Butch, 86
Watts, Isaac, 24–25, 27
Watts, Thomas, 51
We'll Rant and We'll Roar Like True New-foundlanders, 105
We're from Canada (Humble), 84
Weber, Carl Maria, Freiherr von, 68
Webern, Anton, 118
Weinzweig, John, 90, 101, 108, 114, 115i,
  120, 124–26, 219m–25m
  students of, 130, 136, 138
Weir, Stanley, 76
Welsman, Frank, 87, 91
Whaley, Royce and Company, 72

What a Friend We Have in Jesus, 41
whistle flute, 145i, 146, 150, 151, 152
Whitehead, Alfred, 102
Whole Book of Psalms, The, 25
Widor, Charles-Marie, 79
Widow, The (Lavallée), 74, 77, 171m–72m
Wieniawski, Henri, 70
Wild Stream Leaps, The (Clarke), 57
Willan, Healey, 90, 91–92, 97–98i–101, 119,
  124, 179m–210m
Williams, Will and Walker, 85
Willis and Company, 72
Willson, David, 58
Wine of Peace (Weinzweig), 108
Winnipeg, 63, 87
Winnipeg Symphony, 108
World Is Waiting for the Sunrise, The (Seitz),
  65
World Soundscape Project, 136–37, 139

Ye Gentlemen of England, 22
Ye Maidens of Ontario, 22
York, 38–51
  see also Toronto
Ysaÿe, Eugène, 70
Yukon Indians, 142, 151, 156

Zen, Yeats and Emily Dickinson (Somers), 130

605-3